I

A CHAPLET FOR CHARLOTTE YONGE

This is rather a scruffy copy (ex. library),
but it's a lovely & rare book and I felt you'd
enjoy it. I'm not writing inside it in case you
have it already, in which case I'll have it back!
It comes with lots of love for Christmas
to you and Gervase & best wishes for all your
1994 activities.

Ann

A Chaplet for
CHARLOTTE YONGE

Papers by

GEORGINA BATTISCOMBE   KATHARINE BRIGGS
LETTICE COOPER   ALICE FAIRFAX-LUCY
ANNIS GILLIE   RUTH HARRIS
ELIZABETH JENKINS   MARGARET KENNEDY
MARGHANITA LASKI   VIOLET POWELL
CATHERINE STORR   KATHLEEN TILLOTSON
RACHEL TOWNSEND

Together with
GENEALOGICAL TABLES & BIBLIOGRAPHY

Also some little-known pieces by
CHARLOTTE YONGE
LAST HEARTSEASE LEAVES, AUTHORSHIP, etc.

Edited for the Charlotte Yonge Society by
GEORGINA BATTISCOMBE AND MARGHANITA LASKI

PUBLISHED IN LONDON BY
THE CRESSET PRESS

Published in Great Britain by
The Cresset Press, 11 Fitzroy Square, London, W. 1.
First published in 1965

ISBN. X 22530631 X 06

236961

Printed in Great Britain by
The Camelot Press Ltd.
London and Southampton

Foreword

BY GEORGINA BATTISCOMBE

Whatever may be said of the Charlotte Mary Yonge Society nobody can deny that it has been a source of unalloyed pleasure to all its members. We hope that through this little book we may be able to share that pleasure with a wider circle.

Thanks are due to Catherine Storr who, with Marghanita Laski, worked through innumerable volumes of *The Monthly Packet*, the magazine edited by Miss Yonge, and extracted from them much buried treasure; to Violet Powell for her fascinating and, we hope, accurate series of genealogical tables; to Kathleen Tillotson for her diligent work on the bibliography, and for providing the title for the book; and also to Mr. John Howard, of the Cresset Press, who has made publication possible.

Contents

Contents

Part Three: Pieces by Miss Yonge

Part Four: Tables and Bibliography

PART ONE

Introduction

Charlotte Yonge as a Novelist

By Elizabeth Jenkins

The charm of Charlotte Yonge's novels is unique and impossible to convey to those who have not read them; only the novels themselves can do that. She has, it is true, certain drawbacks. Extraordinarily talented only, not a genius, she sometimes allowed her *idée fixe*, the necessity of obedience to the Church and to parents, to impose a distorting influence on story and character. Since this idea is at present totally exploded, it is the more remarkable that she should now be the object of an enthusiastic and expanding cult; her renaissance of popularity shows that she possessed the power, by no means universal among greater writers, of establishing an immediate *rapport* with the reader that acts like magic and defies explanation.

Her circumstances shaped her work, as every novelist's must. She lived all her life in a quiet Hampshire parish and the durability and intensity of her impressions were combined with the energetic liveliness of her mind. Two men deeply influenced her; one was John Keble, the initiator of the Oxford Movement, who gave her strong religious feeling, her love of history and her instinct for submission, the direction of a devotion to the Anglican Church. The other was her father, a severe, handsome man, a distinguished soldier who had given up the army for his wife's sake. His career established the pattern in his daughter's novels, that it is right to relinquish professional and worldly success for a useful life in quiet surroundings. The classic instance of this occurs in *The Daisy Chain*, where the gifted medical student Dick May has taken a country practice and becomes Charlotte's famous and beloved Dr. May, while his contemporary has become Sir Matthew Fleet, the eminent London consultant, to the great loss of his humane and spiritual qualities.

Charlotte Yonge's high-strung notion of filial obligation pervades all her books; obedience to parents is binding, to

3

parents admittedly silly, selfish or even disreputable. Her own filial duties were made light by an intense liking as well as an intense love for both her parents, and this side of the situation she treats particularly well. The child's happiness in having the parent with it has never been better shown than in the May children's delight in Dr. May's society; the vehement affection of her six small sons for the young widow Lady Temple is the most attractive part of *The Clever Woman of this Family*; the demanding but protective affection of Nuttie for her beautiful young mother in *Nuttie's Father*, the gay, exhilarating relationship of Mrs. Brownlow with her younger daughter Babie in *Magnum Bonum*, are instances of the family situation at its best, where the child's only complaint against the parent is the not having enough of his or her society.

In dealing with romantic love, she is less successful; the most vivid emotion in her books is not that between lovers but between relations. The affection between Harry and Mary May in *The Daisy Chain*, and Felix and Geraldine Underwood in *Pillars of the House*, of Lucilla Sandbrook in *Hopes and Fears* for the father from whose loss when she was six years old she has never recovered, are much more convincing in their intensity than the emotions she tries to depict between pairs of lovers of whom she approves; here the conversations are apt to be wooden and improbable; but it is, none the less, surprising with what realism she describes a courtship or a marriage when she disapproves of either or of both the parties.

The most life-like pair of lovers, as lovers, whom she ever produced, are Arthur and Violet Martindale in *Heartsease*. Arthur, the thoughtless, selfish but affectionate young Guards' officer, marries on her sixteenth birthday an extremely beautiful girl, the daughter of a country solicitor. He keeps the wedding a secret from his aristocratic parents, then launches his child-wife on his formidable family without giving her proper support. The early years of this marriage, with Arthur's alternating fits of selfish impatience and engrossing fondness, and Violet's fright and misery and artless happiness, are extraordinarily well done, and the reader, without one word of direct statement, fully believes in the sexual connection. One wonders how Charlotte Yonge knew so much about *le jeune homme moyen sensuel* whose likeness she does not produce again.

4

Another marriage of which she is severely critical, and therefore realistic in her treatment, is that in *The Daisy Chain* between George Rivers and Flora May. The beautiful, well-meaning, self-opinionated Flora, 'so quiet, reasonable and determined', accepts George Rivers from worldly motives but thereafter does her duty unremittingly by a heavy, stupid though loving husband. In the crisis of her baby's death, the misery of having to support this husband, entailed on a girl whom events have pushed to the verge of nervous collapse, is described with the most acute insight.

It is a matter of opinion whether Guy and Amy, the radiant young couple of *The Heir of Redclyffe*, exist in the reader's mind as real people or merely as the hero and heroine of a highly successful novel, but no one will deny the reality of the other pair, Guy's cousin Philip Morville and Amy's sister, the beautiful, harassed Laura. These two commit the sin, in Miss Yonge's eyes, of having, not an engagement even, but an understanding with each other, unknown to Laura's parents. The power of the novel is shown, in that, though the reader scouts Charlotte Yonge's opinion of the moral issue, this does not impair the strength of the situation. Philip, clever and high minded but lacking in humility, allows himself, partly through unrecognized envy, to become unfairly and uncharitably critical of the warm-hearted, impetuous Guy. Entrenched in this position of superiority, he cannot admit that he himself could ever deserve reproach. Nevertheless, driven by circumstances, he does what, in his own impartial judgement he would consider wrong, and urges a secret understanding on a girl who, but for him, would think it wrong herself. The psychological condition of the pair in their suppressed and restless misery is so well drawn, it makes irrelevant the, to our eyes, inadequate nature of the wrongdoing.

The Heir of Redclyffe, Charlotte Yonge's first important novel, published in 1853 when she was thirty, brought her immediately to the ranks of best-selling novelists who enjoy also a *succès d'estime*. Characteristic of her as it is, the book is *sui generis* among her works. None of her other novels, coming in its place, would have hit the reading world with such impact. The blazing success of *The Heir* established her so firmly that she had a public already eager for the quieter, more mundane works that followed it.

Unlike her other novels, the book has not only a small

cast but a taut, effective plot. Philip Morville begins by nursing a hostile attitude towards his cousin the wealthy, ingenuous Sir Guy; the latter, on his honeymoon with Amy in the Alps, comes to the rescue of Philip who is ill of a fever contracted through his obstinate neglect of advice. Philip recovers in their care, but Guy takes the fever and dies of it. Philip is driven nearly out of his mind by remorse for his injustice and unkindness, and by horror at the fact that, since Guy's posthumous child proves to be a girl, the property he once envied Guy is now his own. The sinister implication of the book's title is sometimes overlooked; it applies, on the face of it, to Guy himself, but, when the story opens, Guy is already the reigning baronet. The heir of Redclyffe is Philip.

The marriage of Guy and Amy lasts only three months, and Amy is then left to live out the rest of her life under the inspiration of her young husband's memory. Charlotte Yonge's great gift for developing character is perhaps never more strikingly shown than in the scene at Guy's burial. To the dismay of everyone, Philip has left his bed and appears, wild and ghastly, among the party at the graveside. Mr. and Mrs. Edmonstone have not the presence of mind to deal with him. It is the heretofore childish, timid Amy who takes charge of him and leads him away. Guy had said to her before he died: 'You must take care of Philip'. The originality of the book lies in the fact that it translates the struggles and adventures of chivalric romance into a moral sphere and a domestic décor. With a poetic felicity that she did not repeat in any later book Charlotte Yonge showed the bright, comfortable, enclosed home of the Edmonstones where most of the action takes place, against the background of Guy's home, far away on the cliffs of Cumberland, a mansion of crumbling red sandstone built round a courtyard 'of thunderous echoes' with the sound and movement and the living light of the sea beyond it, just as she showed the gay, companionable, sweet-natured young man struggling with and mastering the inherited curse of a temper that can turn murderous. It was said at the time that part of the book's tremendous appeal was that it made goodness exciting.

Charlotte Yonge produced many successful novels of a self-contained kind, though none of them repeated the success of *The Heir of Redclyffe*, but most of her admirers feel that her unique achievement, surpassing even *The Heir*, consists in those extended family chronicles of Mohuns, Merrifields, Mays and Underwoods. Though capable of warm friendships she was shy, and did not attract to herself that sort of social life which, while it acts as a temporary check on creative work, when kept within bounds, imposes also a useful discipline on it. Her teeming energy combined with her lack of distraction accounted for a tremendous literary output, not only in a variety of works but in the length of many of the novels. As a child she took ecstatic delight in visiting her cousins, the Yonges of Puslinch; at home, though happy she was solitary, and amused herself by inventing large families of children who lived in the summer house. This biographical detail is of especial interest to those whose favourite novels are *The Daisy Chain* and *Pillars of the House*.

These works, dealing with the Mays and Underwoods respectively and appearing, the first in 1856, the second in 1873, are the great props of her family structure, but the Mohuns and Merrifields had made their appearance as early as 1847 in *Scenes and Characters* when Charlotte was twenty-four. First shown as children, the boys and girls grow up and reappear in later books. Her grip on a vast number of characters, all of whom develop with faultless consistency, linking with each other through a series of novels, is amazing. She both astonishes and convinces us by the fidelity with which her children foreshadow their personalities as adults. A brilliant example is that of Kate Caergwent, shown as a little girl in *Countess Kate* of 1862, who, by 1873, has developed into a complete grown-up likeness of herself in *Pillars of the House*. One of the longest stretches of time over which Charlotte Yonge keeps characters in mind, to produce them convincingly in advanced middle age, is the period from 1847 to 1888, at the end of which Jane and Adela Mohun, created in *Scenes and Characters*, come out again in *Beechcroft at Rockstone*. They appear even again, in 1895, in *The Long Vacation*. It is the utter fascination of these reappearances that accounts for much of the charm of such very late books as *The Long Vacation* and *Modern Broods*.

Of the two great family novels, some will say that *Pillars of the House* is the *chef d'œuvre*, but on the whole, popular feeling judges *The Daisy Chain* to be Charlotte Yonge's work at its very summit. For one thing it contains both of her most beloved characters, Dr. May and his daughter Ethel. Dr. May (and this is admirably conveyed) is not only a sympathetic but an extremely clever doctor; he is warm-hearted and impetuous, and not seldom ill-judged in his treatment of his family. The elder children can see this but it does not diminish their respect, still less their affection for their father. Only a reading of the book will give the true brilliance of this portrait of the lively, impatient, humorous, tender-hearted doctor, who lives for his patients and his children, and has never forgiven himself for the carriage accident that caused his wife's death and the spinal injury to their eldest daughter Margaret.

Ethel, unlike her good-looking sisters, favours her father, but whereas Dr. May's thinness, sallowness and long nose do not make him unattractive, in Ethel they amount to positive ugliness, and in her, her father's impetuosity has become clumsiness. Her keen intellect, her longing to help, which in the end achieves her childhood's ambition, to found a church in the desolate, neglected region of Cocksmoor, her energy and goodwill, unrebuffed by the reproaches her awkwardness bring upon her, her utter disinterestedness and her love for her whole family make her unforgettable. Her likeableness is extraordinary. The novel succeeds not so much by the separate adventures of the characters as by their action upon the rest; the love, anxiety, irritation, pride and intense concern that occupy the family for each other create an overpowering sense of home, so perfectly realized that the book seems bathed in a transparent golden glow. All the members are thoroughly convincing, but Dr. May and Ethel are immortal. They seem to exist with an independent life of their own.

Charlotte Yonge often introduced adventures by land and sea, crimes and injuries at home, but seldom with complete conviction. Her best passages are entirely domestic, and here much of her success lies in her lively receptive attitude to the texture of daily life, as it was lived by the comfortably off but well-ordered and disciplined middle class. Any notion that the Victorians must have been bored for lack of our amusements is contradicted by the sense of pleasurable occupation that fills her pages. One remembers the zest with which Guy and Amy gardened and read and played and sang, the scene of the May children blowing bubbles, in which the details of the process are described with a wonderful accuracy, Lucilla Sandbrook's photography, and her making flies for fishing, 'manipulating the gorgeous silk and feathers', among tables and ottomans piled 'with a wild confusion of books, prints, periodicals and caricatures', and discussing engagements at the rate of five a day, and the eager botanizing of Nuttie Egremont who organized an expedition by train to capture a specimen of water-soldier from a mere in the local park. At the end of Miss Yonge's life, when she had already said she was too old to understand the young, she still shows her sympathy with youthful crazes. In *Modern Broods*, 1900, she invests bicycling with a rapturous delight, and speaks of 'the sparkle of bicycles' seen outside the hedge, as if the machines had a fairy quality.

Charlotte Yonge wrote so well for children (*The Little Duke* must be one of the best children's books ever written), it is not surprising that her ideas about teaching children should have been highly intelligent. *The Stokesley Secret* has a remarkably good instance of this, where the young governess Christabel Fosbrook teaches the five-year-old David to teach himself addition and subtraction, and there is another in *Magnum Bonum* when the eight-year-old Armine, asked if he knows the meaning of a Latin sentence, delights the schoolmaster by saying:

'Isn't it when the geese cackled?'

'What do you know about the geese?'

'We played at it on the stairs. Jock and I were the Romans and Mother Carey and Babie were the geese.' Carey Brownlow had a most modern-sounding method of education. The children's desks stood all about the drawing-room, and her stimulation of their intellectual curiosity was such that they recognized no division between amusement and work.

Associated with the impressions of daily life are the visual descriptions at which Charlotte Yonge excels. The celebrated one of the Edmondstones' drawing-room, the centre of the family life, with its glowing fire and stands of fragrant plants, is matched by that of the schoolroom in *The Daisy Chain*, solid, spacious, shabby, painted green and blue; there are dozens more, not only interiors of fascinating period interest to us, but all instinct with the personalities of the people who inhabit them.

Dr. Annis Gillie explains the scope and accuracy of Charlotte Yonge's clinical observation; here it is only possible to comment on her gift for describing physical appearance, and making the reader see a pretty or a beautiful girl. Sometimes she creates the image by minute detail, as when she says

Lucilla Sandbrook's eyes were 'of that deep blue upon that limpid white' that is like old porcelain, and that her gold eyelashes were so long and glossy they caught the light. More telling, perhaps, is the impression of Laura Edmondstone's beauty, of which hardly any detail is given, except that she had pink cheeks and chestnut curls. Guy points her out in the ballroom as 'the young lady with the wreath and the beautiful hair'; otherwise her beauty is apprehended as if it were light. It is created by such a simple sentence as: 'Laura raised her beautiful face to his', at a particularly poignant moment in a scene between Laura and Philip.

It is not possible to tell the reader everything that he will enjoy in Charlotte Yonge's novels. Let him find out for himself. Let him look at the first page of *The Daisy Chain*, where the schoolroom is filling with boys and girls for the beginning of the day's work, Miss Winter is being maddening and Ethel's frock has already been torn out of the gathers; or at the first page of *Pillars of the House* where nine children are collected on the stairs in varying states of excitement over the arrival of their eldest brother's birthday money which they know will mean a treat for themselves. Or let him open one of the novels at random, become engaged in a scene, a couple of characters, and go backwards to find out their past as one does in real life, and the spell will begin to work.

Mrs. Battiscombe has put the matter in a nutshell in a remark supposed to be made by someone who is told sternly, to Miss Yonge's disadvantage, that *Little Women* is a work of art. The reply of this person, given with a whimper, is: 'I don't want works of art. I want Ethel and Dr. May.'

The Charlotte M. Yonge Society

By Marghanita Laski

The Charlotte M. Yonge Society erupted into life on 28
November 1961. For a little while before this, a few friends
had been saying that it would be nice to meet occasionally
and talk about Miss Yonge's works. Then suddenly, as it
seemed, friends suggested friends, we all met together, and
the Society was formed in almost the shape in which it exists
today.

This shape is somewhat unusual, being carefully devised
to meet our specific purposes, and as it has worked well and
may meet similar purposes for other people, it is worth
describing.

Principally we wanted to ensure that the Society should
confine itself to its original purpose which was to talk about
the works of Miss Yonge. None of us was seeking a social life
inside it (though this it did, incidentally and pleasantly,
provide at our meetings), and all of us had known societies
which themselves quickly became more important than their
original purposes, so that the main aim became to preserve
and enhance the standing of the society, and the original
purpose soon no more than a means to that end.

So we tried from the start to build-in the impossibility of
institutionalization. We decided to confine ourselves to
fifteen members, as the largest number which could enjoy
face-to-face discussion without organization. We decided to
have no officers, no subscriptions, no premises, no headed
writing paper or any other possessions. It was then a question
of seeing how this worked out in practice.

It soon became apparent that we could if we wished have
a huge society, interest in Miss Yonge's work being astonish-
ingly widespread. With some regrets for those who would
like to come, we still decided to stick to our original number.
We allow guests to the speaker and organizer at each meeting,
and the rest of us may bring a guest only if members cannot

11

come. But we did, in response to demand, hold one big meeting when guests almost without restriction were brought by everyone.

At first we thought we should need two organizers to deal with each quarterly meeting, a London member who would arrange luncheon and a country member who would cope with the secretarial work. It soon became clear that country members had no difficulty in arranging meetings in London, and that the secretarial work was small. So now each of us in more or less alphabetical turn arranges a meeting, coping with the correspondence involved, and asking another of us who conveniently can to give the paper.

Our financial arrangements are simple. We each pay our hostess for the time being a sum towards our meal; this started at 3*s*. 6*d*. and is now 10*s*. The hostess-organizer bears the cost of the meal over and above this, and pays for the postage, etc. involved in organizing the meeting.

We own—a generous gift—an almost complete set of *The Monthly Packet*; this is housed by a London member. Our other possessions live in an imitation-leather briefcase, handed from organizer to organizer. They consist of an exercise book of minimal minutes, some letters, signatures and photographs of Miss Yonge (also a gift), and typescripts of the papers so far given.

Formality at meetings is kept to a useful minimum. The organizer acts as chairman, deals with such small business matters as may arise—perhaps an announcement of books for sale by a member, rarely the choice of a new member. We have lost four members, two by death and two by resignation, and so far have chosen our new members by general agreement. The paper is then read and discussed. There are no formal thanks.

The form of the Society has proved suited to our needs and we have enjoyed four happy years of quarterly meetings.

Last December, when all the founder members who remained had given their papers, the purists among us suggested that the Society be closed. This was partly due to a wish to go out on a crest rather than face possible decay, partly due to pride: the closure of societies is rare, and we felt that to close ours would finally prove our successful avoidance of institutionalization. It was felt too that, devoted as we were to Miss Yonge's works, we could not pretend that these provided indefinite subjects for discussion.

But a larger number felt that there was still more to be said, and, also, that pleasure should not be nipped for the sake of purism. So we are going on, with fewer meetings, but sometimes with more guests. Our only regret—though this was accidental, not decided—is that we have no men members.

At the time of writing, our membership is as follows:

> Betty Askwith
> *Georgina Battiscombe
> *Katharine Briggs
> *Lettice Cooper
> Elizabeth Eccleshare
> *Alice Fairfax-Lucy
> *Annis Gillie
> *Ruth Harris
> Margaret Kennedy
> *Elizabeth Jenkins
> *Marghanita Laski
> *Violet Powell
> *Catherine Storr
> *Kathleen Tillotson
> *Rachel Townsend

* indicates a founder member.

PART TWO

The Papers

The Linked Stories

The following papers make it clear that, apart from a few admirable novels such as *The Heir of Redclyffe, The Clever Woman of the Family, Heartsease,* the Society's interest is principally concentrated on what we call the linked novels and stories, those in which, either centrally or glancingly, Charlotte Yonge refers to a single created world of people and places. These novels and stories are listed below, with the names of the more important people and, where link-forming, the places that appear in each.

Titles in italics are of stories peripheral to the main stream; people are generally named only if they appear in more than two stories, though sometimes their reappearances may be a matter of no more than a reference.

Newcomers are advised to start by reading *The Daisy Chain,* to go on to *The Trial,* its immediate sequel, and thence to *The Pillars of the House.*

1847 SCENES AND CHARACTERS
Mohun, Rotherwood

1854 THE CASTLE BUILDERS
Berners, Somerville, Willoughby

1855 *The Lances of Lynwood*
De la Poer (ancestors)

1856 THE DAISY CHAIN
Anderson, Bramshaw, Ernescliffe, May, Rivers.

1857 *Dynevor Terrace*
Conway, Omersfield

1861 THE STOKESLEY SECRET
Merrifield

1862 COUNTESS KATE
Caergwent, De la Poer

17

1862 *Hopes and Fears*
Charlecote, Fulmort, Whittingtonia (St. Matthew's and St. Wulfstan's)

1864 THE TRIAL
Anderson, Bramshaw, Ernescliffe, May, Rivers, Ward

1871 A LINK BETWEEN THE CASTLE BUILDERS AND THE PILLARS OF THE HOUSE
Berners, Somerville, Willoughby

1873 THE PILLARS OF THE HOUSE
Anderson, Audley, Berners, Caergwent, Charlecote, De la Poer, Ernescliffe, Fulmort, Harewood, Lamb, Lightfoot, Knevett (Tanneguy), May, Somerville, Travis, Vanderkist, Ward, Whittingtonia.

1876 *The Three Brides*
Bowater, Rollo

1879 *Magnum Bonum*
Brownlow, Grinstead (Underwood), St. Wulfstan's

1885 THE TWO SIDES OF THE SHIELD
Conway, Hackett, Merrifield, May, Mohun, Rotherwood, Vincent, Ward

1885 *Nuttie's Father*
Brownlow, St. Wulfstan's, Underwood

1888 BEECHCROFT AT ROCKSTONE
Bowater, Flight, Hackett, Harewood, Henderson, Liddesdale (Berners), May, Merrifield, Mohun, Ormersfield, Rollo, Rotherwood, Somerville, Travis, Underwood, Vanderkist, Vincent, White

1889 COME TO HER KINGDOM (reprinted 1890 in *More Bywords*)
Arthuret, Merrifield

1890 *Mrs. Batseyes* (in *More Bywords*)
Brownlow

1892 *The Cross Roads*
Mohun

1893 THE STROLLING PLAYERS (with Christabel Coleridge)
Armytage, Merrifield, Mohun, Ormersfield, Rotherwood
(This book also derives from *Jack O'Lantern* by C. Coleridge)

1895 THE LONG VACATION
Anderson, Armytage, Audley, Brownlow, Caergwent, Ernescliffe, Flight, Fulmort, Hackett, Harewood, Henderson,

Lamb, Lightfoot, May, Merrifield, Mohun, Rivers, Rotherwood, Somerville, Tanneguy, Travis, Vanderkist, Vincent,
Ward, White

1900 MODERN BROODS

Armytage, Arthuret, Audley, Brownlow, Flight, Fulmort,
Harewood, Henderson, Lamb, Lightfoot, May, Merrifield,
Mohun, Rotherwood, Somerville, Tanneguy, Travis, Under-
wood, Vanderkist, White

Charlotte Yonge's Ethics:
Some Unfashionable Virtues

By Katharine Briggs

No one can deny that Charlotte Yonge had an exceptionally vivid and delicate discrimination on all ethical questions, a sensitivity of palate which makes our modern gropings seem crude and coarse. We are not to blame for this; in our generation we have lived through so many moral shocks that we have developed callosities and have lost our natural reactions; we have to make our way as best we can by the rather dubious light of reason. It is therefore perhaps worth considering whether there may not be something to be said for the unfashionable virtues that Charlotte Yonge sometimes advocates and something against the failings she condemns, which we now think of as venial.

Charlotte Yonge was of course conditioned by the narrow and ingrowing circle in which she lived and by the strictly private method of her education. We see her limitations most clearly in books in which her imagination was not engaged; *Womankind* is an example. She says a good many shrewd and interesting things in the course of this book, but the whole presses in on one with a sense of claustrophobia, and one cannot help being disappointed that her wisdom and understanding are less than one would suppose them to be. Her failure in that book is really a measure of her success as a creative artist. When her imagination stirs, she knows more than she knows that she knows. We recall Chesterton's anecdote of the lady who said to him, talking of Philip's mother-in-law, 'Thackeray didn't know it, but she *drank*'. And indeed every creative artist reveals to us more than he knows himself.

I think that we should all agree here that the thing which makes Charlotte Yonge constantly readable in spite of some unhappiness in style is her power of creating characters in the round. All her best characters, and there are a great many of them, can be looked at from all sides. They are individual, and yet they grow out of their heredity and environment. The particular power that she had, which is rather rare among novelists, was to create people of delightful goodness. It is often said that the good people in books are dull, and the villains are much more interesting. People like Long John Silver and Redgauntlet fascinated us all when we were young. But this is not so in real life. Most of us have been lucky enough to know a few people who were shiningly good, the best company in the world, with whom one was at once at ease because they were without malice. You do not meet them in many novels, but there are numbers of them in Charlotte M. Yonge, and all different just as they are in real life: Felix, honest and sturdy and modest and affectionate, Lance, sensitive, but full of merriment and charity, little Stella Eudora, a kind of poem of youth and unconscious goodness, Ethel and Dr. May, Louis Dynevor, full of wayward charm, and yet with an unerring moral instinct, honest Phil in *Scenes and Characters* and comical, good-natured, earnest Frank in *The Castle Builders*—a kind of richness such as you might find in Heaven. They are all different, yet the individuality is obtained without caricature, by a method almost as temperate as Jane Austen's. We can spend happy hours gossiping about her characters, agreeing and disagreeing about them as heartily as about our personal acquaintances. Indeed, it is the passionate desire to gossip about Charlotte Yonge's people that has called this Society into being.

In the course of our conversations a good many people have expressed some impatience at the virtues which Charlotte Yonge advocated, most of them, as it happens, very unfashionable today. Of these, I am choosing to talk about chastity, humility, resignation and filial piety. The very names of these virtues seem ridiculous to some people today, and yet I think we could very well do with more of them than we have. One of the Oxford dons was telling me a short time ago that she was working on Milton's *Comus* with one of her students and found that the girl did not recognize chastity as a virtue at all. She quite saw that one ought not to have an illicit love affair if it hurt anyone else; she probably admitted that one ought not to lie about it, but she regarded the notion of chastity for its own sake as a fetish. She was probably like many others of her generation who have only two cardinal virtues, Truth and Kindness, and I must say many of them live up to them splendidly.

21

For the younger generation Charlotte Yonge further handi-
capped herself by establishing decorum as a guard for chastity.
One of the difficulties about decorum at that time was that
the marriage code was then half-way between the arranged
marriage of earlier times and the romantic marriage for love
which had made its first appearance in the modern world at
the Renaissance. A nineteenth-century girl was in an awkward
position. In the first place modesty forbade her to set her heart
on anyone who had not first made clear his preference, but
in the second place it was considered mercenary of her to
marry for anything but love; and yet if she saw enough of
the young man to find out if she loved him or not, she was
probably regarded as having encouraged his advances. Fanny
in *Mansfield Park* pointed out the dilemma very clearly, but
a lot of other girls must have suffered from it after her time.
The girl was supposed to be innocent and ignorant of the
whole business until the young man proposed, or his attentions
at least became marked, and after that she must leap to it,
and do some very decisive thinking indeed. In *Magnum
Bonum* poor Esther got into great disgrace for only saying
'If——', and in the same book we find, 'The mothers would
hardly have liked the subject of the maidens' talk in their
bower' about a very innocuous discussion between Babie and
Sydney; but in *The Young Stepmother* Lucy was allowed to
marry Algernon Dusautoy, of whom both her father and
stepmother entirely disapproved, because she had gone so
far in meeting him that she could hardly withdraw with
honour. Parents were often rather disingenuous in their
attempts to shield their daughters, especially such foolish
parents as Mrs. Robert Brownlow, who really disapproved
of Esther's marriage with Bobus because they were first
cousins, but put it on the grounds of a breach of maidenly
decorum, so that poor Esther was thoroughly muddled, and
very much feared that she would be blamed when she was
proposed to by an unexceptionable young man who was a
brilliant match besides. In *The Young Stepmother* Albinia
shied away from a discussion with Sophy which would
have made things easier between them later. 'Dear Sophy,'
she said, 'these are not things good to think upon. There
is quite enough to occupy a Christian woman's heart and
soul without that—no need for her feelings to shrivel up
for want of exercise. No; I don't believe in the passion
once in the life being a fate, and pray don't you, my Sophy,

or you may make yourself very silly, or very unhappy, or both.'

With Sophy's introverted nature this snub might easily have done more damage than it did; and it was a fortunate thing that she and Albinia were able to understand each other after Albinia had managed to infect Sophy with her belief that Ulick O'More was in love with her. Thanks to this good understanding Sophy was able to overcome her morbid tendencies and to treat her disappointment with magnanimous common sense.

Ethel May in *The Daisy Chain* noticed herself falling in love, resisted the temptation to mock-maidenliness, and stopped before she had gone too far. Some of the other hero-ines were capable of a clear-sighted scrutiny of their own feelings and a gentle but firm determination to be married to the man they chose. Phoebe Fulmort in *Hopes and Fears* was one of these and perhaps owed it to Miss Fennimore's clear incisiveness and the rational outlook she inculcated.

A good many of the accidentals of decorum in the books seem to us very ridiculous now, like, for instance, the notion in *Hopes and Fears* that there was grave impropriety in Lucilla and Horatia Sandbrook going to Ireland together without a chaperone; but basically the ground that Honor took was rational, that no woman can transgress the code of her own age without paying a price for it. Honor was perhaps a little outdated in her own period, but so was Robert Fulmort. Lucilla had to pay the price, but I think she subconsciously wanted to pay it. She had been brought up in childhood to be the darling of a male household, and she needed the company of men, but the shattering blow of separation from her father had killed all power of equal love in her, and she could only be happy with a father-figure, someone who represented her short idyllic time of childhood. She wanted power over Robin but she did not want to marry him.

Humility is the crown of Christian graces, and those who are fortunate enough to be born with natural humility are not only a long step towards holiness but they are well equipped to taste happiness as well. Those of us who are cursed with a natural pride know that it is not only the greatest of the spiritual sins but also the heaviest piece of baggage a man can carry through the world. One or two of the most delightful of Charlotte Yonge's characters were born with a natural humility. Louis of *Dynevor Terrace* seems to have inherited his from his mother, who had few other virtues, Lance Underwood of *The Pillars of the House* has it and Phil Mohun of *Scenes and Characters*, and Guy of Redclyffe, and Frank, the delightful schoolboy in *The Castle Builders*; in fact most of those whom I mentioned in my earlier list. Two good people who are full of pride are Philip Morville of *The Heir* and Flora May, Ethel's sister. These two have hard measure meted to them because they are worth it. Their pride and their hearts are broken together, but they rise to great nobility. Only their pride has taken its toll. They are never capable— broken or unbroken they never were capable—of the joy and delight that Guy and Louis and Lance could feel. It was humility that bore Dr. May through the remorse that a less good man would have suffered for his wife's death and Margaret's injury, and turned it to repentance. Ethel was capable of pride, though never very liable to it; and her unselfconscious and objective mind saved her from the torments which it gave to her brother Norman.

Probably the reason why resignation is so unfashionable today is that it rests upon the belief in a personal Providence who orders our lives in every particular and presents us each day with opportunities and tests. This is very foreign to the temper of the modern world, and to many people resignation seems mere flaccidity of mind. I think most of us are impatient of the resignation of our friends—great friends, whose sufferings are real pain to us. At least we are impatient of it if we notice it; if it is imperceptible and takes the form of cheerfulness in trouble we are very glad of it.

I myself cannot help being a bit impatient of Guy's resignation. I think he fell into the mistake of anticipating the will of God—guessing beforehand what it would be and running to meet it. This is always the chief danger about resignation, that one can start resigning oneself too soon. It is as well to remember the homely proverb:

> *For every evil under the Sun*
> *There is a remedy or there is none;*
> *If there is one, try and find it,*
> *If there is none, never mind it.*

Even that leaves unsolved the problem of when to stop trying to find the remedy for the evil and when to start never-minding it. Still, it opens a possibility which Guy might have explored. . . .

The real, full-length study of resignation is in *Heartsease*. Violet, though she was delicate, sensitive and shy, was a person of a good deal of energy and force of character. Action came more natural to her than inaction. John Martindale, on the other hand, was of a passive disposition; he readily learnt resignation, but he had no natural spring of energy. He taught Violet how to endure, and how to wait till the right time to act, and he learnt from her that he had allowed his ill-health and his disappointed love to make him unnecessarily passive, so that he neglected the duties that lay close to his hand. All this sounds rather drab when it is put down in a summary, but it grows naturally out of their characters and is developed with great delicacy and variety of incident in the particularly well articulated plot.

There are so many deaths, so many illnesses and accidents in Charlotte Yonge's books that the theme of resignation is always recurring. We think of Amy losing Guy, of Margaret May losing Alan, of dear Caroline Brownlow's failure in *Magnum Bonum* to resign herself to her husband's death, and the restless years that followed it, until she finally made her way through to acceptance. Surely grief was never more subtly painted, so that our hearts ache for her, and for the loss of that young delight that was never to come back.

Very early in the writings, in *Henrietta's Wish*, we have Henrietta's complete failure in resignation, which costs her the benefit she could have got from her mother's last weeks. In the book, which is less wise and less skilfully handled than the later ones, Henrietta seems hardly dealt with and unfairly judged in comparison with her cousin Bee, who is much more blameworthy; but I think the intention is to show not so much want of filial duty as wilfulness, a kind of clamouring for things instead of taking them as they come, an essential lack of resignation. For this, I think, we must remember, that for Charlotte Yonge resignation is not merely a passive acceptance of ill-fortune, but an active attempt to co-operate in God's Kingdom in the course of every day.

You may very well say that I have proved no merit or advantage in this virtue; but there is a great deal to be said for the readiness to take things as they come, for sitting lightly to the things of this world, and for practising a kind of spiritual ju-jitsu, in which by falling with the misfortune you overcome it.

In this age, when we cultivate clamorous desires and

measure our wealth rather by our wants than our sufficiency, every tenth person seems either to be having or to have had a nervous breakdown. I can only remember one real nervous breakdown in all Charlotte Yonge—Bertha Fulmort's, in *Hopes and Fears*—and she, poor child, was entirely unfortified by a Christian background. A great many of the women, of course, suffered from hysteria, which perhaps gave them a safety-valve, but Charlotte Yonge rightly treats that as mainly physical, and it was probably largely due to tight lacing.

I have kept my most difficult and unpopular virtue to the last—Filial Piety. Charlotte Yonge is rather a fanatic here, almost unbalanced on the subject. One after another of her characters is ruthlessly sacrificed to filial duty. Ethel May nipped her love affair in the bud so as to devote herself to her father. That, however, was a rather special case; Margaret was an invalid, Flora was married, none of the others was old enough and Ethel and her father were particularly congenial to each other. Besides, Dr. May was well worth the sacrifice. There were other cases much more extreme. Helen Fotheringham was allowed, even encouraged, by John to work herself to death over the care of a doting grandfather. It was a difficult case; nursing help was not so easy to get then as it has become since, mental homes and old people's homes could hardly be said to exist; but it seems that common sense might have found at least a partial solution of the problem. In *Nuttie's Father* it is still more doubtful whether it could be considered Nuttie's duty to devote herself to the care of a prodigal father, who was only partially redeemed at the cost of two innocent lives, his wife's and his little son's. Of course the little son was a complication; Nuttie had to look after him, and it would have been impossible to take him away from his father. But the most extreme case of all is perhaps Mary Ponsonby of *Dynevor Terrace*, who broke off the engagement sanctioned by her mother and went to Lima to submit herself to the father who had hastily married a Limenian girl straight from a convent.

There is something in all these cases which trespasses against common sense and a reasonable balance of duties; but perhaps if we look at them within the broader framework of Charlotte Yonge's ethics we shall see the general sanction of her position. I think her attitude to filial piety is very much connected with her attitude to resignation. It depends directly on the belief that our circumstances are planned for us by

God for the training of our souls or for some other unguessed good, and are part of a general and interlocked plan for the whole world. This does not necessarily mean that people must sit passively exactly where they were born—energy and the full use of their given powers is their contribution to the pattern of life—but it does mean that they must be very sure that they have fulfilled all the duties within their circle before they step out of it to look for others.

A key book on this is again *Heartsease*. We have two examples here of the temptation to move away from direct family authority and to give paramount influence to a friend. Emma Brandon made a silly choice of confidante and set Sara Theresa Marsden up as a kind of female pope. Sara Theresa was flattered by Emma's confidence, and placed herself as a barrier between her and her mother. Being a fool, she naturally led Emma disastrously astray. Theodora, who owed a great many of her troubles to a disastrous friendship in the first place, finally set up a much wiser mentor in Violet; but Violet, although she was lonely and desperately in need of Theodora's help, refused to take the place of her family, and sent her back to her kind, weak father and her foolish mother, overshadowed by Mrs. Nesbit, the evil genius of the family. Both Violet and Theodora had dreary paths to tread after that, but they came out into happiness in the end.

So strongly did Charlotte Yonge feel the duty of keeping within the limits of the family and of natural obligations that in *Hopes and Fears* she blames Honor Charlecote for adopting the little Sandbrooks, when she might very justly have felt that Honor had had a leading of Providence in that direction. All the healthy friendships made in her books bring the friend into the orbit of the family. Meta Rivers is a friend not only of Flora May but of Margaret and Ethel; she soon becomes Flora's sister-in-law and finally marries Norman. Bill Harewood in *The Pillars of the House* is early drawn into the Underwood family, and becomes part of it by marrying Robina. Claude in *Scenes and Characters* is suspicious of the warm friendship which Lilias feels for Alethea, but Alethea is already half-way to being engaged to William, though Lily does not know it. Gertrude May falls into an enthusiasm for Cherry Underwood, but finally keeps it in the family by marrying Cherry's brother, Lance. The Brownlows and Evelyns of *Magnum Bonum* were so bound and cross-bound by links of friendship that they became practically one family even before the double marriage with the Robert Brownlows sealed the connexion. Sometimes close propinquity was allowed to count as a ground for friendship, as in *My Young Alcides*, but on the whole there seems to have been a strong feeling among the Yonges that young women's friendships outside the family circle are generally unwholesome, sentimental and fraught with danger. And Charlotte, shy, and pretty tightly confined within her family, dutifully concurred.

How poor most of our lives would be, what a lot of help and delight we should have missed, if our generation had been rigidly tied by that notion! But we must remember that we have the opportunity to work with our friends, and that most of the friendships that would have been open to girls of Charlotte Yonge's generation would have been mere love-in-idleness, without the discipline of working for a common cause or of being tired together. That discipline belonged then to the family circle.

Another consideration about Charlotte Yonge's treatment of filial piety is that as a rule family duty is presented by her from the child's side, but she leaves us in no doubt that the parent has a duty as well. Only a few of her protagonists happen to be parents, but in *Heartsease* Violet has the perpetual problem of balancing her duty to her husband with her duty to her children; her husband, Arthur, though not much given to introspection, yet knows that he has failed lamentably as a parent. Caroline Brownlow of *Magnum Bonum*, a delightful and devoted mother, comes to learn where she had made mistakes; in *The Heir* Mr. Edmonstone's folly is plain to everyone; even Dr. May has his parental errors, which recoil chiefly on his sons Richard and Tom. In *The Castle Builders* we are left in no doubt that Lady Willoughby is a broken reed as a mother, and poor Frank is put into a tragic situation by his father's peremptoriness and insistence that he shall not only submit to having all his hopes for his future broken but shall enjoy and be grateful for their ruin. In *Hopes and Fears* Lucilla Sandbrook owed her difficult temperament to her father's fond follies, and the young Fulmorts had to struggle as best they could out of the godlessness of their father's house. It is a curious thing that in the children's books of this present century all the parents have to be wise, kind and understanding (which is why they always have to go away at the beginning of the book, so that things can happen); but in the moralistic books of the eighteenth century and in Charlotte Yonge's books parents were allowed to be frankly bad sometimes, and very often faulty.

There seems to be an inescapable dilemma about filial duty. I am sure you will all have noticed that if a girl is giving up her life to looking after her parents we feel it to be a shame; she can only be young once, we say, her opportunities are going, what will she do when they die? If, on the other hand, all the younger generation go off to their own work or pleasures, and the mother who looked after them in their childhood is left ill and under increasing disabilities to fend for herself in loneliness we cry out against their selfishness, particularly of course if the mother is a friend of ours, or if she is an attractive old lady. No doubt, where there is common sense and charity and imagination on both sides things can be arranged, but often these fail or wear out on one side or another, and then we have to make do as best we can without them. The vexed question of the care of old Mrs. Meadows in *The Young Stepmother* is a case in point. There was no ideal solution, but they had to do the best they could.

We might spread ourselves for quite a while in discussing the personal reasons for the importance of these four virtues to Charlotte Yonge. The time and circle in which she lived and her own psychological bias had their part in determining them, and particularly their part wherever we find over-emphasis; but do not let us yield too readily to the pleasures of psychological probing, almost an addiction at the present period. Beyond the personal is the impersonal and the super-personal.

In the course of discussion, Marghanita Laski once very truly and acutely said that the main theme of Charlotte Yonge's writings is the Kingdom of God. Every one of these virtues falls into its place in a theocentric universe directed by a personal God, to whom each individual soul has direct access, and for whom each individual destiny is of importance. If you take this background away these virtues have no sanction and are mostly mere nonsense. And yet it seems that it is for want of these virtues that our whole civilization is sick. Because so few of our young people understand why they should be chaste, our sex life is falling back into savagery; pride has hurried us into two world wars and still makes us greedy for status symbols and for more goods than we can use or enjoy. People break their hearts with discontent, and wreck their nervous systems by ineffectual attempts to transcend inevitable limitations, and for want of family piety homes are broken up all around us.

Charlotte Yonge owed her grasp of character to an imaginaation as sympathetic as it was lively, fostered no doubt by her quiet, restricted life. But she owed the kind of people she created and the kind of theme on which she worked to her faith, which, restricted though it might be to Anglicanism, and to one fashion of that, was yet strong enough to put her in touch with the whole of Christendom. We do not read Charlotte Yonge's books only to escape into a less complicated world than ours, nor even for the pleasure of meeting good and delightful people. The world she introduced us to is in many ways a restricted one, sheltered perhaps morally, though not from misfortune or death, but it is a world that is overshadowed by higher truths and in touch with greater realities than we are introduced to even by the gigantic sweep of modern Science.

Charlotte Mary Yonge, Dramatic Novelist

By Lettice Cooper

Now and then it happens that a writer almost disappears
for a time from the general reader behind an image which
seems to have been created out of a misunderstanding or
exaggeration of part of his work. Kipling was one of these.
The portrait is now steadily being cleaned. I think that
Charlotte Mary Yonge is another. I believe that for most of the
people who have not read her, or who vaguely remember
reading one of her books when they were young, her image
is that of a mild, unexciting, domestic novelist entirely
preoccupied with the day-to-day affairs of the Victorian
nursery, schoolroom and drawing room.

To people like ourselves in this Society nothing could be
farther from the truth. We know Charlotte Yonge as an
outstanding last-century story-teller. This means that she
did not feel any obligation to confine herself in her novels to
her visible experience. The sensitive young man who writes
a rather good novel about a sensitive young man and then,
not being interested in anything else, writes another not
quite so good novel about a sensitive young man, would not
have been a novelist at all to Charlotte Yonge or to her
contemporaries. They lost sight of themselves in their
created world. I would never say that Charlotte Yonge had
a dull life—I do not think that any writer has a dull life.
But apart from her writing she had as quiet and sheltered and
undramatic a life as any woman could have. Yet her range
extends far outside the home, and she is in two important
ways a superbly dramatic novelist.

First in the more obvious way. There is hardly a novel of
hers in which the story is not precipitated by a violent
explosion of circumstances outside the ordinary run of
domestic life. In her first important novel, *The Heir of Redclyffe*, there is the shipwreck on the Shag rock and the rescue,
a fine piece of dramatic writing, and most necessary, not only

31

because it predisposes Mr. Edmonstone to go and meet his ward on his twenty-first birthday, but because it shows us Guy as a resolute man of action, and not just as a charming undergraduate playing with girls in a summer garden.

In *The Pillars of the House*, Fernando Travis, who fills such an important rôle in the Underwood chronicle, is brought into their home by the terrible fire in the Fortinbras Arms, in which Fernando's faithful negro servant saves his life by jumping with him from an upper window and protecting him with his body in the fall.

It is interesting that both these two dramatic scenes gain in excitement by being presented indirectly, at one remove. We do not go out to the Shag rock with Guy in the boat. We are on the shore with the agonizingly anxious Markham and the sympathetic Mr. Ashcroft, watching for a glimpse of the boat as it rises for a minute on the crest of a wave, trying to see through the glasses if it is Sir Guy who is crawling with the rope along the sea-washed rock. And I do not think we are any the less aware of the terror of the Fortinbras Arms fire in the middle of that crowded industrial town because we do not rush out into the street with Felix and Lance, but crouch trembling on the end of the bed with Wilmet and Cherry, hearing the distant sounds and seeing the red glare in the sky.

Of course like all good novelists Charlotte Yonge varies her technique. We are actually there on the spot when another great fire destroys the house of Martindale in *Heartsease*, and so puts an end to the influence of that baleful *eminence grise* of the Martindales, Mrs. Nesbit, and leaves the rôle empty, to be filled by the gentle but equally potent Violet. The fire also reveals the sadistic terms of Mrs. Nesbit's will. I have always felt a great sympathy with Arthur on that occasion in his moments of natural impatience with that sickening little Johnnie.

In *The Daisy Chain* there is the joyful return of Harry May after another shipwreck in which he was believed to have died. Drama here has its full scope because the letters from the Antipodes announcing that Harry is alive have not reached the May family before he does. Charlotte Yonge was so delighted with this effect that she repeated it with Flora in London. 'Mary's letters are apt to bear keeping, you know', and kept they are, until Flora *sees* Harry. It is a rule of the game that no letters from the Antipodes are ever received in

England before the arrival that they announce; little Dick walks in unheralded in *The Trial*, and so does Dolores Mohun's father just as she is going into the Law Courts in *Two Sides of the Shield*. *The Trial* is an intensely dramatic novel; there are the murder, the court scenes, the sentence, the petition that saves Leonard's life, but condemns him to perpetual imprisonment, and Tom May's startling discovery in a Paris hospital of the piece of evidence that clears Leonard.

Magnum Bonum is another very dramatic novel. Here are the sudden sweeping away of the two who have been almost parents to Caroline as well as husband and mother-in-law; the little boys' adventure in the boat; Alan's stilt accident that leads to the exotic little cousin, Elvira; the unexpected inheritance; the terrible adventure of Jock and Armine on the mountainside, and John Brownlow's dramatic run after the Fordham party that really saved his cousin's life; Janet's startling marriage and the discovery of the later will; the sudden change in the Brownlow fortunes; Elvira's return, as usual unheralded by any letters; her account of her meeting with Janet; the yellow fever episode.

How did the idea ever grow up that Charlotte Mary Yonge was a mild domestic writer only? In *Dynevor Terrace* Louis is wounded on the Paris barricades, and there is the supreme drama of Oliver's return with the announcement that has been the dream of his life: 'Mother, Cheveleigh is yours.' And, as so often in life and also in Charlotte Mary Yonge, the drama is followed by irony: the dreary restoration to a completely ruined Cheveleigh. 'Take what you want, said God, and pay for it,' is one of the leitmotifs of Charlotte's novels, whether she knew the proverb or not, and one of her most fruitful sources of drama.

Other characters of hers find themselves in the Law Courts besides Leonard Ward: Dolores Mohun for her half-understood misappropriation of a cheque; Rachel Curtis in *The Clever Woman*, although even the Law Court scene is hardly as dramatic as that moment in Ermine Williams' sitting-room when the Indian ink slowly peels off the faked woodcut, and the honest, innocent, blundering Rachel begins to see for the first time that she has placed her trust in a scoundrelly charlatan at the cost of great suffering to the children she meant to help. Poor Rachel, how severely she was punished for the sin of 'trying to be clever'—such a frequent source of reproach in our youth—but I do not think that children get into trouble for it nowadays; perhaps their parents are too anxious about the eleven plus and the G.C.E.

I could go on for ever with these instances of strongly dramatic events in Charlotte Yonge's novels, but I want if I may to remind you also of the other, and I think more important way in which she is a very dramatic writer. This way that I have been talking of, the inclusion of unusual and unexpected events to give a turn to the story, belongs as well to the film, the T.V. play, the detective novel. I think that Charlotte Yonge also excelled in the true novelist's drama, the impact of character on character, and the situations that develop out of these encounters. This kind of drama can occur when two characters are out for a quiet walk together or when one of them is alone in a room thinking. It depends first of all on the author's power of seeing into the heart of the situation, and also on his power of telling it in a way that sustains tension. 'The first thing that matters about a novel,' said Henry James, 'is that it should be interesting.' Tension is one of the first things that make it interesting, and tension is the essence of drama. The dire moment for any novelist when he is writing is the moment when tension goes, when what should be taut and vibrant and moving steadily forward towards a climax suddenly becomes a limp sagging rope, only to be retrieved by pulling harder or thinking more deeply or going back to readjust some earlier mistake in direction—or even by taking a day or two off. I should think that Charlotte Mary Yonge, a born story-teller with an unflagging narrative gift, experienced fewer of these moments than most of us!

I should like to clarify what I mean by taking a trivial lightweight character from the novels and showing how much dramatic tension Charlotte extracted from her. I am thinking of Alice Knevett in *The Pillars of the House*, which, to me, in the complexity of the web and the skill with which it is woven, is the most remarkable of all the novels. The introduction to this figure of fate is almost casual; the thread is so gently slipped into the pattern that we hardly notice it. Wilmet reports that the Misses Pearsons' seventeen-year-old niece, Alice Knevett, who can't get on with her young step-mother at home, is coming to Bexley to live with her aunts for a time while she helps in the school and learns to teach.

'Rather a nice looking little thing,' Wilmet reports. She adds with her infallible instinct for seeing 'what it may lead

to': 'I don't know whether we shall get on well together.'
There are more casual reports. Alice is stiff and cold, and
won't make friends with anybody. The Misses Pearsons are
worried about her; they think she cries alone in her room
and have begged Wilmet to try and thaw her out.

Then, still at one remove, comes the first scene in which
Alice appears, described by the excited Angela, and by Wilmet
when they come home at the end of the day. We see the
bullying older girls turning over the little trifles in Alice's
workbox and laughing at them and asking what they cost.
Alice who, like many trouble-makers, is always a passive
figure, has neither the sense nor the spirit to shut down the
workbox lid. She just cries, until Wilmet comes to the rescue
and tells the girls that Alice doesn't like it. They slink away
and there is a scene of tears and temper in which Alice pours
out how much she hates her stepmother, and how she can't
bear the idea of being a teacher—'It's the horridest thing in
the world'—and finally there is a burst of adoration for Wilmet,
her only friend.

Then after what had really been a very gradual skilful
preparation comes the first actual appearance of this new
figure on the stage. Wilmet brings Alice home and leads into
the room the 'little sparkling diamond beetle' in a cloud of
fresh lilac muslin. At first Alice puts on airs—'visiting shop
people' is how it seems to her—but she is soon natural, and
Felix comes from the shop spruced up for his sister's guest,
and so the train is fired which is to half-kill Felix and push
Edgar over the edge into ruin.

There are three incursions from the outside world into the
enclosed family circle of the young Underwoods—I do not
count Marilda, who is family—Fernando Travis, Bill Harewood and Alice Knevett. And how brilliantly they are all
used, how skilfully the three different strands are woven into
the Underwood tapestry, how they cross and re-cross one
another, adding enormously to the richness of the texture!
Fernando Travis was perhaps the most unexpected. Who of
us would have thought of Fernando, a figure so remote from
Bexley or Vale Leston? But I think that perhaps the pattern
made by Alice Knevett is the most brilliant of all.

Of course poor overburdened Felix falls in love with her,
and knows he cannot admit the idea of ever marrying anybody with all these brothers and sisters on his back, and
believes that nobody is aware of his feelings. And of course

he hasn't a chance when Edgar turns up in his Tyrolese hat, green knickerbockers, belt, knapsack, loose velvet coat, and fair moustache and guitar and all. How much it enhances the dramatic intensity of Charlotte's novels that she is so very good at bringing to life the physical presences of her characters! I do not think that any girl in any book, not even Dora Copperfield, or Beatrix Esmond, or Hetty Sorrel in *Adam Bede*, has ever sounded to me as pretty as Violet in *Heartsease*, and Edgar's physical charm is so vividly presented that he cannot appear without the pages lightening.

In a novel of this size and scope the author's angle of vision is constantly shifting. We see a great deal through Cherry's eyes, through Wilmet's, through Felix's. We never see Alice from inside, only from outside as the other characters see her, and I think I am right in saying that we never see from inside Edgar; so that we are given just two glimpses to show the developing relationship between Alice and Edgar: the play, whose most successful scene is the one in which the poet, Master Ratton, complete with velvet coat and guitar, is mesmerizing the Princess Fiordespina, looking particularly pretty; and the game of verses describing people, in which Edgar calls Alice 'Caressing, purring, traitor kit, Fatal to Master Ratton'. Edgar already knows far more about Alice than Felix does. He goes in with his eyes open.

The party splits up. Edgar goes back to London to his undisciplined attempt to be an artist, and when Robina and Angela go to the new school at Brompton, Alice goes too, to teach while she perfects her accomplishments.

Now we leave this thread in the tapestry and take up another. How this constant change in the weave refreshes the reader, and with what skill Charlotte keeps all her large cast in play! Nobody, except perhaps Fulbert when he goes to Australia, is ever lost sight of. We are startled by the announcement of Alda's engagement to Fernando Travis, at a time when everybody is expecting to hear that he is engaged to Marilda. Felix is summoned to London to deal with this delicate situation, and we are so entirely preoccupied with it that we hardly notice that he snatches an hour from the love affairs of the grown-up people to go and see the two schoolgirl sisters in Brompton.

Then, sharply, Felix's own drama cuts across the affairs of Alda and Marilda and Fernando. In the chilly deserted school garden, from the lips of the sober, honest Robina, Felix learns that Edgar and Alice are engaged and have been carrying on a secret correspondence, first trying to use Robina as a go-between, then, when she refused, Angela. Edgar laughs at Felix for taking the whole thing too seriously, but does not deny the engagement, which comes as a terrible blow to Felix, so it is Alice who first reopens the Vale Leston theme, since the decline in health which follows this shock sends Felix to Ewemouth and so to the visit to old Fulbert and the beginning of the restoration.

Meanwhile, a few weeks after the scene in the school garden, a curt note from the headmistress and a distressed letter from Robina announce that the secret is out. Edgar declares that he stands by the engagement. Robina and Angela are just not expelled. Alice is carried off by her indignant father to Jersey, and appears to vanish from the scene. Not so very long afterwards the Underwoods hear, through the Misses Pearson, that Alice is married to a Monsieur Achille Tanneguy, a Frenchman who works in a wine agency in Pau. Edgar laughs off the news and it is only afterwards we learn that it was from that time that his carelessness about money became recklessness and that he gave up any serious attempt to work at his painting.

Now we seem to have lost Alice forever. We are absorbed in other strands in the weave and forget all about Madame Tanneguy, married to her wine merchant in Pau. We forget her partly because we are so truly absorbed. The tension is hardly ever slackened: Alda's wedding, Lance's musical aspirations and dissatisfactions, Cherry's pictures in the Royal Academy, and then the whole drama of Edgar's forgery and flight; the situation, which might have been saved if he had been able to confess to Marilda, completely lost by that one dramatic glimpse of Spooner in a cab. Charlotte uses the dull respectable old clerk in this moment of heightened tension knowing perfectly well that the most undramatic and unlikely people can suddenly play a part as the unconscious instruments of drama. Fernando goes after him. And then comes the shattering news of John Harewood's possibly fatal accident, and the sober, prudent Wilmet not only goes off to him with his father, but marries him out of hand so as to be able to stay with him. In spite of Wilmet's governessy ways with her brothers and sisters it is impossible, or I find it impossible, not to like anyone so absolutely sound-hearted.

And now comes Robina's scarlet fever, a drama in itself

when the poor girl is working herself to a frazzle for the Senior Cambridge. Did she ever sit for the exam? I do not think that she can have done so, unless she sat for it at Biarritz or did the papers by post. Anyhow, she joins the Harewoods and I wonder how many readers are alerted when they come to Pau for one night on their journey? I certainly was not when I first read this book. I was surprised when Robina said that Madame Tanneguy lived in Pau and that the Misses Pearson had heard nothing from her and wanted to know if she was all right.

This seems now to be Wilmet's crisis. She has been boss of the young Underwoods for so long; her husband has been so much an invalid, she has not yet had to accept that she is not his boss and that she promised in the marriage service to obey him. There she is, alone in the room after John and Robina have gone out, fighting out the conflict that is probably going to decide the whole trend of her married life. It is one of those vivid dramas that can take place when one person is alone, and we are too much caught up in it to be wondering what the news of Alice will be. Then come the footsteps on the stairs, the opening door, John Harewood flushed and panting, Robina, the healthy, solid Robina, nearly fainting, and as John measures the stimulant for Robina panting on the couch he answers Wilmet's frantic inquiries in a few words: 'A duel. The husband was killed but it was hardly Edgar's fault.'

It is again Robina, the character in the book perhaps the least like Alice, who tells her story. Again the scene loses nothing in drama, rather gains, from being told at second-hand. We hear the concierge say *Au quatrième*—not what we expected for the wife of a prosperous wine merchant; we climb the steep, dirty stairs, and we ring the bell and hear the child's trotting feet inside the door; then, as the door opens, we see Alice in her widow's weeds rising from the chair with the baby in her arms, and hear her scream and Robina's.

We learn of how Edgar, on the stage in the theatre, saw Alice in the audience and broke down—Edgar was always an incurable amateur. We hear of Alice's betrayal of her feelings and the duel which her husband forced on Edgar, and of Tanneguy's death from his wounds. It is a beautifully ironical close to all this drama, a Greek-play ending to the day when at last Wilmet, with an effort that nearly cracks her in two, forces herself to admit to her husband that she had been wrong not to go and look for Alice when he asked her to, and he murmurs something about Jeanne D'Albret and 'goes to sleep in her face'. And then follows the sequel to Alice's adventures, her return to Bexley and her little attempts to enslave Felix again, and how from being a sacred obligation to him because she was widowed by his brother, she becomes a bore and marries the good meek Ernest Lamb. All this is the perfect ironical end to the drama. Could Charlotte have extracted more riches from one flimsy young woman? Can anyone doubt that this is a master novelist?

But of course dramatic tension in any novel springs in the first place from the choice of a dramatic theme; I mean the theme as distinct from the plot, which is the working out, the embodiment of the theme. When we examine Charlotte Mary Yonge's novels closely it becomes clear that she nearly always chose one of two themes—the fulfilment of a task or a reconciliation. *The Pillars of the House* is the fulfilment of a task, Felix's task to bring up in the faith and fear of God the family of eleven brothers and sisters entrusted to him by his dying father. *The Daisy Chain* is the fulfilment of a task, to provide and endow a church for Cocksmoor. *Magnum Bonum* is the fulfilment of a task, to rear a son fitted in brains and character to carry on the father's discovery. The reconciliation theme occurs in other books: *The Heir of Redclyffe* is the story of Philip's reconciliation with Guy; the first and most interesting half of *Heartsease* is the reconciliation of Theodora with Violet, and as the sub-title is *The Brother's Wife*, Charlotte Yonge evidently felt that to be the main line of the book. *Beechcroft at Rockstone* is the reconciliation of Gillian with Aunt Jane. In *Two Sides of the Shield* Dolores Mohun is reconciled at the end with Aunt Lily and Mysie. I would even say that the real theme of *The Trial* was the reconciliation of Tom May with his father and his father's values, and that *Dynevor Terrace* was the reconciliation of Louis with his father, when he came home with the very bride his father would have chosen for him—and, oh dear, what a dull girl! These two themes are the spinal cords and central nervous systems of the novels. Because of them they are far more dramatic than if they were just family chronicles.

Is there in the second choice of theme an indication of one reason why Charlotte Mary Yonge, although such a very good novelist, is not, I think we should all admit, a great one; why, although her narrative gift is equal to George Eliot's or Emily Brontë's, we cannot count her their equal? The first reason, of course, lies in what she was born with. She was endowed with feeling and intelligence rather than with intellect or passion. But I believe that, much as she was, she could have been even more, and that the explanation lies partly in this theme of reconciliation. I believe that, at some time too early in her life for her to remember it, she went through a period of mute rebellion against her mother. It is interesting to notice that all these reconciliations in her books are between people of the same sex. I think that love and duty made the small child Charlotte Mary repress these rebellious feelings for ever, so as to return to that love and harmony with her mother whose even partial loss she had not been able to bear. So she accepted for life in the emotional core of her heart the rôle of the good little girl, she opted for submission, for an unawakened sexual life and for a refusal to question even for a minute the standards in which she was brought up. This inevitably narrowed her work. It was not a question of what she refused to experience; it was the question of what she refused to imagine that limited her. The marvel to us and to those like us who admire her heartily is what she did achieve in spite of her limitations.

Harriett Mozley: A Forerunner of Charlotte Yonge

By Margaret Kennedy

Harriett Mozley was Cardinal Newman's sister. Her husband, Tom Mozley, was a parson, a fellow of Oriel, and a keen, though erratic, supporter of the Tractarian Movement. Her books made a considerable stir in the early 1840s. *The Fairy Bower*, published anonymously, deals with a group of children between the ages of ten and thirteen. It was promptly followed by a sequel, *The Lost Brooch*, in which the same characters appear after an interval of about seven years. Both these books have obvious links with the work of Charlotte Yonge. A third, *Louisa*, is more of a typical contemporary novel, and less worth our scrutiny.

Charlotte admired Harriett. In an article on children's literature in *Macmillan's Magazine*, September 1869, she says:

'Just as the *Tracts for the Times* were moving the thinking world, there appeared a little book called *The Fairy Bower*, ostensibly a mere child's story, but written with a peculiar suggestiveness of portraiture that rendered it a somewhat puzzling study to heads of families.'

She goes on to describe the stories and characters in other books as though, after twenty-eight years, they were already somewhat forgotten and out of date. She ends by saying:

'Altogether these two are memorable books, and though nowhere inculcating any distinctively High Church doctrines, yet there can be no doubt that they did their part towards the Church movement by manifesting the unloveliness and unsatisfactoriness of this particular phase of surburban Evangelicalism. Another work done by them was the creation of the class of literature now termed "books for the young", standing between the child's story and the full-grown novel. We do not mean that there were no such books before, but

41

as a school they seemed to rise up either in imitation of, or almost in rivalry to, *The Fairy Bower* and *The Lost Brooch*. Most people who had any power of writing felt that though anything so curiously clever and covertly satirical as these was impossible, yet something more distinctly improving could be produced upon the same field.'

She evidently thought so herself. In a preface to a late edition of *Scenes and Characters* she mentions 'the impulse to literature for young people given by the example of that memorable book, *The Fairy Bower . . .*' and concludes: 'On that wave of opinion my little craft floated out into the great sea of the public.'

In December 1899 she wrote an article on Harriett Mozley in the *Guardian*, beginning:

'Half a century has passed since a story, ostensibly for children, came forth anonymously, and it may be wondered at that we revive the remembrance of it, for it was not one to take the fancy of the very young so as to become a nursery classic. The distinctions of right and wrong, the cases of conscience and the character-drawing are a great deal too subtle for the childish mind.'

Charlotte Yonge admired Harriett's talent but did not entirely approve of her as a guide for young people. This is understandable, since Harriett's own attitude, in the Tractarian controversy, is somewhat obscure. She satirized Evangelicals, but did she endorse High Anglican principles? We know that she was horrified when her brother went over to Rome and in 1843 she had a scare lest her husband should do likewise. He met some amiable priests on a holiday abroad and took such a fancy to them that he threatened to 'Romanize'. Newman, however, advised him to think it over for a year. Since Tom Mozley does not seem to have thought anything over for more than five minutes his enthusiasm waned, and Harriett's panic subsided.

Her main target, in both books, is a large family called Duff, living at Winterton in south London. The parents are nonentities. The household is ruled by Miss Newmarsh, a terrifying governess who has entire charge of the four elder girls. Of these, Constance is the prize exhibit, a museum piece of pious arrogance, yet, as a character, perfectly convincing. When I first read these books, nearly sixty years ago, I longed to see Constance taken down a peg or two, and I still give the same response whenever I think of her. As Charlotte

Yonge says: 'She and her sisters will always be realities to us.'

Fanny, her twin, pretty, silly and romantic, writes verses which they all regard as proofs of genius. Mary Anne, the eldest, is neither good, clever, nor attractive, but manages to exploit the family reputation for virtue, talent and beauty. Charlotte, the youngest and the most amiable of the four, is despised as totally ungifted. They are all obliged to keep daily diaries, recording their spiritual experiences; these are inspected by their governess on Saturdays.

There is, besides, a schoolboy, Campbell, and a herd of unimportant small fry in the charge of a forbidding Nanny.

Mrs. Duff's sister, Mrs. Ward, has married into a somewhat higher social circle. She is gay and worldly and packs her girls off to boarding school as soon as possible. She also has a schoolboy son, George, and the small fry is consigned to an easy-going Nanny.

The young cousins meet frequently since the Wards live at Fulham. The Duffs deplore the unspirituality of the Wards but are a trifle subdued by the fact that Mr. Ward's brother is Lord Musgrove and lives in Grosvenor Square. Professedly unworldly, they are terrific snobs. The Wards laugh at the Duffs and put up with them, as cousins were so often obliged to do in the Victorian Era.

The catalyst in this tribal brew is Grace Leslie, an only child, who lives a secluded life with a widowed mother. In each book she encounters the Duffs for a month. On each occasion she capsizes their claim to moral superiority—not from any personal antagonism or ill will, but simply by being herself. She also modifies the hilarious inertia of the Wards, who have laughed at the Duffs for so long that they are immune from shock. She triggers off some active resistance to Duff arrogance.

The period of *The Fairy Bower* is Regency—a fact which readers are liable to forget. The whole landscape suggests a later date and it is something of a shock when Grace's mother talks of the Prince Regent and of her young days when 'our good King was in health'. In my edition of the book, published in 1866, we are told that Grace's father, dead four years when the story opens, had fallen 'in one of the first engagements in the dreadful Nepaul War'. This puts his death in 1814 and the story in 1818. Charlotte Yonge, in her *Guardian* article, says that he fell in the Burmese War and comments that 'in

those days it was hard to find a recent war in which to
dispose of a soldier'. No such dilemma attends the year 1818.
It is unlike Charlotte to be careless on such a point, and I
wonder if there are not discrepancies in the facts recorded
in different editions. Harriett may have had her own reasons,
after 1841, for pushing the story back to a period when the
leading Tractarians were still schoolboys or undergraduates,
and their controversy far in the future, thus clearing herself
from any accusation of sympathy for Romanizers.

Grace, aged ten, goes with her mother to spend some days
with the Wards and there she meets the Duffs. They are all
preparing for a grand Twelfth Night party. Grace suggests
to Mary Anne Duff that it might be amusing to decorate a
small ante-room with festoons of paper flowers and concealed
lights, thus making it into a fairy bower for a pet parrot.
Mary Anne, in Grace's absence, appropriates this idea and
announces it to the others as her own. The Wards are astonished at such unwonted evidence of taste and originality in
a Duff. This shabby little trick shocks Grace, when she
discovers it, but she does not think it important enough for
protest. She lets Mary Anne take credit for the scheme
although she is obliged to accept the burden of its execution,
since she knows how to make paper flowers and can teach
the others; Mary Anne had never seen or heard of them
before.

Emily, the eldest Ward girl, soon guesses the truth and
taxes Grace with it, only holding her tongue at Grace's earnest
entreaty. The importance of the bower is inflated by the
degree of praise which it wins from the adult guests at the
great party. Mary Anne, 'the fair architect', is ceremoniously
crowned queen of the evening. The Duffs exult in this new
family triumph. Lord and Lady Musgrove invite pretty Fanny
to stay with their young daughter, a gratification which the
Duffs describe as 'an opportunity to do good in Grosvenor
Square'. Grace is appalled at the deception but feels that she
should have protested at once or not at all.

She does not even confide in her mother, a reticence for
which she gets no approval from Charlotte Yonge. It creates
a situation which might, no doubt, become a somewhat
puzzling study to heads of families.

The truth, however, does burst out some days later, thanks
to the indignant candour of Emily Ward. When questioned
directly by Grace's godfather, who has also smelt a rat, she

tells what she knows to be true. The effect of this exposure on the Duffs is revealingly described in a letter from their governess to Mrs. Ward:

'Mrs. Duff is very much depressed. Mr. Duff is unexpectedly angry and in favour of some severe punishment for Mary Anne. Miss Newmarsh has with difficulty persuaded him that kindness, not severity, is more likely to touch the heart of her dear though fallen pupil. For three months the culprit is to lie in bed of a morning a quarter of an hour later than her sisters, and to sit up later at night. These privileges will give her leisure to reflect upon her sin. Fanny fears unfavourable repercussions in Grosvenor Square. Charlotte has, sad to say, made no reference to this hullabaloo in her spiritual diary; she has a bad cold, poor child, and has never shown the acute feelings of her sisters. Constance's notices of Mary Anne's unhappy fall are truly edifying; she has made public reference to it in their Scripture Realization lesson, for which she had prepared a few remarks, very striking and touching.'

The Lost Brooch renews the attack. Tom Mozley wrote of it in 1841, that he expected it to beat *The Fairy Bower* in popularity. 'I think it the completest shew up of certain things that the world has yet seen.'

They are all in their later teens. George Ward and Campbell Duff are at Oxford. Miss Newmarsh has departed and Constance has taken her place as family dictator. Grace and her mother again pay a visit. They join a Duff–Ward holiday at Hastings, taking with them, as a temporary maid, a young girl called Jessie Baines.

The Duffs have contrived entirely to expunge all memory of the Fairy Bower from their minds; Campbell, who had gone back to school when the truth burst out, has never been told of it. They hope to do good to poor Grace Leslie, since she is probably worldly and unspiritual. Good is also to be done to the maid Jessie but she antagonizes Constance by obstinately going to church rather than to chapel. When the Hastings holiday ends Grace is invited to spend a few days alone with the Duffs at Winterton, and a permanent situation is found in that neighbourhood for Jessie.

Constance Duff has founded a model penitentiary, which she means to run personally if only she can find inmates for it. At Hastings she had lost a coral brooch and there had been a slight scare of burglars one night. Soon after the return to Winterton she publicly accuses Jessie of stealing the brooch and of having conspired to admit the burglars. She confronts the terrified girl with a choice between immediate arrest and prosecution or full confession and three years' incarceration in the model penitentiary.

Grace defends Jessie with skill and tact; as a guest at Winterton she is in a difficult position. The parents are inert. The protests of Campbell and Charlotte are ignored. The Wards, however, when enlisted by Grace, come to Jessie's rescue. George Ward reveals that he himself had made the mysterious noises in the night which gave rise to the burglary scare. Emily locates the brooch. Constance herself had absent-mindedly locked it up in her work box, not her dressing case. When compelled by Emily to search the work box, in the presence of the whole household, she is obliged to remember this fact, and there is the brooch.

George insists that she shall write, clearing Jessie Baines, to all the people amongst whom she has spread this slander. 'Constance was grand,' he says later, when describing the tussle to Grace and his sisters. 'We had a squabble over every line . . . and I felt satisfied when I had got the letters safe in my pocket; for Mary Anne has such slippery ways, and Constance is in so ticklish a state of morals, that I could not be sure of what might befall them, in the way of erasures, or postcripts, or re-writing, if I had not taken them out of harm's way. So after this . . . I asked Constance whether she did not think she had made a great goose of herself. She said, no, and that if it came over again, she should do exactly the same. . . . Then I said that she, who was such a lover of truth and candour, could not have any scruple in confessing as a matter of justice . . . that Jessie was raised in her opinion, and not the unprincipled girl she had taken her for. She replied, not a bit raised: she thought of Jessie Baines exactly as she had done all along . . . that if a person was unspiritual, it did not matter whether he were a murderer, or a thief, or simply unspiritual, for that all were in the same condition; and that if *she* thought, much more pronounced, a person unspiritual, he or she *was* unspiritual; and that further, she did pronounce Jessie Baines unspiritual; therefore Jessie Baines was so, and it was impossible for her to injure Jessie by any thing of any kind she could say against her; therefore, she had not injured the said Jessie, and she did not think better or worse of her than she had done before. Q.E.D. . . . I asked her what she said to the ninth commandment. She replied, that I talked of what I did not understand, for that we were no longer under the law.'

Tom Mozley's 'shew up' is in fact an indictment of the moral chaos which attends any claim to personal infallibility. The young Duffs recognize no authority. They range from chapel to chapel, 'sitting under' those preachers of whom they patronizingly approve. Harriett depends, for her effect, upon the exasperation which such people can evoke. It seethed in the bosoms of many Tractarian supporters, though not, perhaps, supporters of the first order. The great leaders were more concerned with the shortcomings and the inertia of the Anglican church.

Duff types were doubtless pretty common in 1841, but it can be asked whether they are fair samples of suburban Evangelicalism. Winterton is clearly Clapham, and the Duff circle a lampoon on the Clapham Sect; nowhere in this land-scape can we find room for a Wilberforce. That the Duffs might not have been personally acquainted with such a neighbour is probable but it is improbable that they would fail to brag of him. If the year 1833 saw the beginning of the Oxford Movement, it also witnessed a signal triumph for the Evangelicals, the abolition of slavery in all British Dominions.

A shew up which ignores all that is genuinely exalted and disinterested, all service to humanity, on the other side, has but a limited value. It is the weakest form of attack upon any religious community to point out that some odious and unscrupulous people profess adherence to it. The same can be said of all religious communities.

Charlotte Yonge clearly disliked the remorseless, full-scale attack upon Constance and says that 'she is a really sincere and religious person, and we wish we had been allowed to go on with her history, when her youth was outgrown'. This is typical of Charlotte's humanity. A young writer who greatly admires her, once said to me that she could show how people mature, and that this is a rare feat in a novelist. She does so in the stories of Albinia Kendall of *The Young Stepmother* and Rachel Curtis of *The Clever Woman of the Family*. They do not alter; having outgrown their youth they do not become perfectly different characters. But, if anything genuine is there, time and experience ripen it. Gifts of a substantial kind are needed for such a theme.

Clement Underwood of *The Pillars of the House* is her masterpiece in this line. He too is sincere and religious, but is also a self-satisfied prig until he has the good luck to get drunk and to incur humiliating ridicule. For a time he regards this as a cosmic catastrophe. He has not merely made a fool of himself; he has brought his ideals and principles into disrepute. His brother Felix eventually persuades him not to make such heavy weather of it. He grows up and becomes an admirable person, though he is never rewarded with the love and praise showered upon his glamorous brothers. Stiff and shy, devoid of personal charm, he plods on, sticking to his principles, and his family continues to call him Tina. He is never jealous of Felix. A warmth towards him steals upon the reader as the book closes, and a sympathy which we might never have felt had we met him in real life at Vale Leston. It is possible that Constance, in Charlotte's charitable hands, might have followed some such path when she had outgrown her youth.

As a novelist concerned with young people and their problems Harriett spans a gulf between Jane Austen and Charlotte Yonge. She has affinities with both. In her world, as in Jane's world, the young get little guidance from their elders. Parents are either inadequate or off stage. In Charlotte's world the elders are firmly in the saddle, even though they are dead and buried, like saintly Mr. Underwood. The young are never left to their own devices for long. Some mature mentor, some Miss Charlecote, turns up to furnish the necessary guidance.

Harriett's best passages of satiric comedy almost bear comparison with Jane. In *The Lost Brooch*, for instance, Mary Anne Duff has been informing the neighbourhood that, Mr. Taylor, a hitherto favoured preacher, is 'fast declining into formality and self-righteousness; it would be an act of Christian charity for anyone to give him a solemn warning'. This is reported to him. When next he dines with the Duffs he immediately accosts Mary Anne and asks her, in friendly tones, to tell him how he has erred. Mary Anne, disconcerted, can only falter: 'I said you did not preach the Gospel.'

'I know that, my dear Miss Mary Anne, I know that,' returned her pastor. 'But I am anxious to know in what respect you conceive I do not preach the Gospel. You are aware that the Anabaptists, Fifth Monarchy men, Antinomians, Hutchensonians, Dunkers, Jumpers, Ranters, and Brothertonians, have all cried out that we do not preach the Gospel.'

Upon which Mary Anne goes into hysterics. He tries to

calm her but 'the more he talked the more others spoke and sympathized in Mary Anne's distress. All had different pieces of advice for poor Mary Anne: Salts—hartshorn—burnt feathers—a little water—lie flat—walk about—sit still—go into the air—be fanned—go out of the room—do not stir. . . .' In the height of Mary Anne's ecstasy of distress, just as a move was being made for conveying her to a sofa, Mr. and Mrs. Baron were announced, and Mrs. Duff stepped forward to receive her guests with three pocket handkerchiefs, steeped in vinegar, eau de Cologne and hartshorn, hanging upon her arm. 'You come into a distressing scene,' said she; 'Here is poor Mary Anne in one of her fits; her feelings are too much for her, and quite overcome her, poor thing.'

This scene typifies both the gulf and the bridge. The wit and the style recall Jane Austen: the subject matter, never. Concerning religion Jane observed which might be termed a Shakespearean reticence.

For Harriett and Charlotte religion was a major theme, and their strongest technical link is, perhaps, the framework of a huge Victorian family. The Wards and the Duffs prepare the way for the Underwoods, the Mays, the Merrifields and the De la Poers. They are more like little nations than families. However much these siblings may vary amongst themselves they bear a tribal stamp; they could belong to no other clan. The Wards, on one occasion discuss this point: Emily comments:

'We say that is so like the Duffs. I should have known that for the Duffs anywhere. And yet, when I examine, it is neither like Mary Anne, nor Constance, nor Campbell, nor anyone in particular.'

This framework is less common today. Families are smaller. Girls are seldom herded with their sisters in a home schoolroom, and their friendships are less regimented. In the last century many women, especially those who did not marry, never took a peep beyond this tribal frontier; they had no means of crossing it. Seventy years ago, at Cheltenham Ladies' College under Miss Beale, two day-girls were not allowed to walk to and from school together unless permission from both sets of parents had been given, so strong was the prejudice against day-schools as likely to foster 'unsuitable' friendships.

Harriet's admirers often express surprise that so original and witty a writer should now be completely forgotten when

49

others of her period, far less gifted, have partially survived. Susan Ferrier, for instance, is installed in Dent's *Everyman* edition; Harriett does not figure in the *Oxford Companion to English Literature*, nor in the *Dictionary of National Biography* save as a wife and a sister.

A possible answer might be that, in spite of her gifts, she was a poor artist. Her material was original but she handled it in a clumsy amateurish way. She could not even manage straight narrative. Her stories take two steps forward and one back. She will begin a chapter with: 'We have forestalled some of the events of the next week, and must now continue them', and returns to earlier episodes which might just as well have been narrated in their time sequence.

Her worst fault she shares with Susan Ferrier. She could not perceive the limits which must be set upon satire in a book where sympathetic characters are to take the central place. If the satire is too uninhibited, characters fall into two groups, apparently made of different material, and communication between them becomes strained. Jane Austen early perceived this pitfall, and modified her satire, but it could be said that Mr. Collins and Lady Catherine de Burgh are slightly over-done. Elizabeth Bennet loses some of her reality in her scenes with them and her dialogue becomes a little stilted. I believe that in a later book they would have been quite as funny but not such figures of fun.

Charlotte escaped this pitfall, since she had little turn for satire, and she shows her technical superiority in her sense of perspective and middle distance when minor characters are involved. The reader is never in doubt as to which people, in a huge cast, are of prime importance and which are only occasional protagonists. Harriett had no notion of this. Everybody, when on stage, is presented with as much emphasis, as much in the round, as everybody else. Some stranger will crop up, in one chapter, and cut such a figure that we expect him to play a vital part in the ensuing drama, but then he vanishes for ever.

Nor could she manage dialogue. She simply reports every-thing that was said, with all its digressions, interruptions, ambiguities and repetitions. It is very natural dialogue, too natural for 'Nature is the enemy of Art'. In Charlotte's dialogue we get the impression of knowing all that passed; actually she gives only the essence of it, as do all good novelists.

As for plot, Harriett does not seem to have been aware that any such shaping is necessary. Charlotte says some very good things about plot in her preface to *Scenes and Characters*. She calls it 'all a matter of arrangement': the shaping of the material, by alterations of tempo and varying emphasis, so that it leads up to some peripeteia affecting the fates of the principal characters. It must please the reader by surprising him yet strike him as credible and compatible with facts which he has known all along. The skill of a Jane Austen, Charlotte says, is required to produce a perfect plot without doing violence to the ordinary events of everyday life; whereas 'another can do nothing with half a dozen murders and an explosion; and of arranging my materials, so as to build up a story, I was quite incapable. It is still my great deficiency; but in those days I did not even understand that such an attempt was desirable.'

I would suggest that Charlotte's plots are at their best in her shorter stories and that she offers a perfect one in *Countess Kate*. Cumulative catastrophes plunge the poor child into chronic disgrace although the reader is throughout aware of her intrinsic integrity, generosity and intelligence. Then suddenly, by dint of these very virtues, she takes a somersault. Her uncle Giles comes home from India. Talking to Lord De la Poer he forgets that Kate is in the room and discusses Lady Barbara's evident dislike of the child. Kate rushes forward, explains that it is all her fault, confesses that she ran away, and in five minutes secures a home in which she can grow up happily. A place in her uncle's heart might not have been easy to win. He might, for the rest of his life, have pitied the girl and tried to do his duty by her, without ever growing fond of her or coming to know her well.

Harriett blows up a crisis and then allows it to deflate. The story meanders on at unquickened pace, touching upon minor themes, until it stops for no particular reason. After the dramatic discovery of the lost brooch we have another hundred pages dealing mostly with a comic sub-plot.

An adventurer calling himself Osmond Guppy has scraped acquaintance with the Duffs at Hastings and won their good graces by posing as a converted character. His real name is Obadiah Boodle, but neither name suits the style of the novel; they are too farcical and an instance of Harriett's carelessness. He makes sheep's eyes at Constance and Mary Anne, and a dead set at poor, silly Fanny who has expectations of a legacy from a rich old lady. Then more promising quarry turns up and his attentions cease. Constance believes that he is in love with Mary Anne and that the only obstacle must be some debts which he had run up before he was converted, and to which he has confessed, probably as the first step towards a touch. She writes to him suggesting ways in which the money can be raised which will set him free to marry her dear sister. No Duff money need be sacrificed. An appeal to the Truly Spiritually Minded can be published in a religious newspaper on behalf of a newly-converted character in financial straits. Also she means to keep for sale in the Duff drawing room, and in the drawing rooms of their friends, 'a standing basket of the shell and sugar plum figures, as well as the raisin chimney sweeps, which have this year so happily taken the taste of the religious public'.

Exposure of frauds upon the wealthy pious is no doubt part of the shew up. The episode also illustrates a point made by Charlotte in her *Guardian* article; she gives Harriett credit for showing that 'the want of the sense of the absurd is really a serious want of character, injuring the sense of right and wrong'. It also throws light upon the tolerant attitude of the Wards to the Duffs. The absurd can make us laugh so much that we are blinded to some underlying menace. The Wards and Grace are convulsed when they hear of the raisin chimney sweeps; they would have been more shocked had Constance devised less ridiculous means for rooking her pious neighbours on behalf of a scapegrace brother-in-law.

The whole episode is very funny since Mr. Boodle supposes that the dear sister involved must be Fanny and, in his adroit reply, suggests that, had he been free to marry any of them he would have aspired to Constance herself. This establishes him for ever in her good opinion. But it comes too late in the book and is an anticlimax.

Such technical faults do an author little harm when types and social background are contemporary and the target of satire is easily recognized. They can account for his prompt disappearance when times change. Harriett was, however, far more gifted, witty and original than the majority of novelists who have never found it necessary to master their craft. It is something of a curiosity in literature to find such genuine creative power combined with such immunity from an artist's discipline. Pundit after pundit has emphasized the discipline which governed all Jane Austen's work. We have only to compare Harriett Mozley with Charlotte Yonge to perceive the frontier which divides the professional from the amateur. Charlotte had certain deficiencies but she knew what they were and strove to make up for them. For Harriett carelessness was permissible so long as the shew up was driven home.

She had much to attack but little, apparently, to defend. Her admirable characters go to church. We hear nothing of what they think or feel when they do so, or of the influence of the church upon their lives. There is, in consequence, a kind of uncertainty in her manner of presenting Grace, the heroine of both books. Grace must be shown as more religious than the Duffs. Since their worst vice is arrogance she must be excessively humble and always ready to believe that others are better and wiser than herself. This humility is piled on a little too thick. As Charlotte complains, we are called upon to admire her rather too often. Nor is it easy to believe that anyone so quick-witted, sensitive and perceptive, could have spent three weeks at Hastings with the Duffs, or have gone with them to Winterton, still believing them all to be wonderfully good and clever. That she might have been impressed by Constance is credible, since Constance has a genius for blowing her own trumpet, but Mary Anne's conceit and inferiority are exposed in everything that she says and does throughout both books. It is asking too much to suggest that Grace submitted to Mary Anne's patronage and counsel, although it is true that people in their late teens will put up with a good deal from a contemporary if they are very much interested in the subject under discussion.

'Are you not used to search narrowly into your motives?' asks Mary Anne on one occasion. 'I know it is a hard task to the carnal mind, but renewed natures rejoice in the work of self-examination; they rejoice whether they are abased or exalted because they know where to cast all their burdens. Do you keep a diary?'

Grace, we are told, always considered that any person who talked on serious subjects was serious and religious, and meant to do good; she therefore was pleased at Mary Anne's talking on such subjects, although she felt grieved and pained that she could not respond in the same strain.

'I mean a journal of your experiences,' said Mary Anne. 'If you are a Christian, you must have experiences. Why do you not keep a diary?'

'I am afraid to do so,' said Grace.

'Ah, there it is,' cried Mary Anne. 'The half-hearted are afraid, they are afraid to see their own weakness and deformity.'

'That is not exactly what I mean,' said Grace. 'I am afraid of saying what is not true; besides, I really do not know what I could say.'

'The humble Christian can never be at a loss there,' said Mary Anne. 'I have kept a journal from my earliest youth, and know the value of it. You cannot deny that self-examination is a Christian exercise, and how can you examine yourself if you do not keep a journal? My belief is that no person can be a Christian who does not keep a journal. . . . It seems the easiest thing in the world to me . . . you know you must be in some sort of frame every minute; and you must have passed a day profitably or unprofitably, or heard conversations, or sermons, or prayers, edifying or unedifying. Nothing is easier than to put these down, and record a notice, thankful or humble, as may be. Then there are all the opportunities of doing good which occur, and which should be mentioned.'

'But I am so different from all of you,' said Grace. 'I never do good to anyone. I cannot.'

'Of course, the same is not expected from babes as from established Christians,' replied Mary Anne. 'But you might try.'

Over theology Grace may not have felt herself qualified to hold her own in such a discussion, but where matters of taste are concerned she is equally meek. At the dinner party, when Mary Anne had hysterics, the young ladies are called upon for music. Grace, who is a fine performer, is frequently asked to play and 'the Misses Duff thought themselves bound to return her kindness each time by a piece of their own. They played nothing but duets, generally Mozart's overtures, or pieces by Rossini; but by some ill fortune they always got very long pieces of the latter composer, which they played very slow, and Grace, among many others, could not recognize any cadence as one she had ever heard before.' Grace does not however, conclude that their performance is deplorable and she is distressed that other guests should ask her to play so often because 'both Mary Anne and Constance, especially the former, were accustomed to make remarks upon her execution, which led her to fancy it was of a sort they particularly disliked; she had therefore more than once played only a simple melody, such as she thought could displease no one.'

54

This abnormal humility puts Harriett into something of a dilemma since Grace must never, never figure as a prig. She is therefore obliged to laugh a great deal too often. 'Said Grace, laughing', frequently accompanies the poor girl's gravest remarks. This incessant tinkle of girlish laughter is out of character. One believes in Grace and one likes her but one feels that her author is not doing her justice. Far too often she is presented as a contrast to the Duffs rather than a person in her own right.

I do not believe that any such uneasiness assailed Jane Austen when presenting Fanny Price. Readers might call Fanny a prig. Some readers do, but that possible catastrophe never troubled her creator. Jane held her tongue about religion but she knew where she stood.

The same might be said about a host of charming girls minted by Charlotte, of whom the flower of the flock is, to my mind, Phoebe Fulmort. Charlotte, safely ensconced under Keble's wing, knew where she stood, and what she defended. She feared neither Rome nor Dissent. In her view he had established a durable fence protecting the Anglican Church on either side.

Having scanned the shew up, no reader can be sure where Harriett stood, or whether she ever made up her own mind about it. To compare these three writers is to endorse the critical maxim that, in art, affirmations are more important, more valuable, and more permanent than denials.

Charlotte Yonge as a Critic of Literature

By Kathleen Tillotson

Charlotte Yonge might have been surprised at being called a critic of literature. But I believe there is much common ground between her and the great critics; reading her criticism, I have been reminded sometimes of Dr. Johnson, and also of Matthew Arnold, her exact contemporary. In her more modest way and her more restricted sphere she too is concerned with 'the best that has been known and thought in the world', and with 'high seriousness', with 'poetry as a criticism of life'; and especially with literature as an instrument of culture —right down to Standard I in the National Schools.

'Good poetry is formative: it has, too, the precious power of acting by itself in a way managed by nature, not through the instrumentality of that somewhat terrible character, the scientific educator.' That is Matthew Arnold.

'Turning over the Fairy Queen at will, not being noticed or directed; that is the way to be saturated with the characters and descriptions, to have the poetry not so much admired as felt.' And that is Charlotte Yonge.

The first rule that Arnold laid down for contemporary criticism was *disinterestedness*, the 'free play of mind', the 'independence of sects and parties'; and in this respect we may sometimes find her deficient. But she is far less restricted by her religious doctrines and her moral standards than one might expect. 'Paradise Lost ought to be known thoroughly; not for the doctrine, for that is heretical, but the glorious elevation of the descriptions, the sound and cadence of the verse. . . .' Many Anglicans in her time looked askance at the Calvinistic doctrine of the *Pilgrim's Progress*; but she says: 'surely the wondrous allegory is true of the whole life of man, and should be read and known by heart in early uncritical youth'. Trust the expert; she had known 'the Pilgrim' intimately, as she goes on to say, since she was six years old.

My quotations so far have been from an article called

56

'Great Old Books' written two years before her death, for the magazine *Mothers in Council*. For Charlotte Yonge was a critic of literature in the explicit and formal sense—writing articles, reviews, commentaries, prefaces, and editing texts and anthologies with notes and introduction. Even if we leave out of account the regular 'Hints on Reading' and 'Conversations on Books' in *The Monthly Packet*, there remain enough critical essays to make a couple of sizeable volumes. But this is only a part of the relevant material. Critical dicta are to be found everywhere—in her unfinished autobiography, in her (too few) surviving letters, in reminiscences such as 'A Real Childhood' and 'My Reading',[1] in *Womankind* and *An Old Woman's Outlook*; and, of course, in many of her novels and tales. For one of the ways in which her characters are lifelike is that they read, and talk about what they read: unlike the characters in novels of our own time who may be guaranteed by their authors to be highly cultured, but whom we cannot imagine holding such discussions as the Edmonstones and Guy on Malory, Manzoni, and Byron. These cannot be simply set aside as 'dramatic'. Her own views are as easy to infer in this field as in the contiguous fields of manners and morals, and can often be confirmed from explicit statements outside the novels. No one could mistake the direction of the two discussions of Byron in *The Heir of Redclyffe* (although Guy and Philip *seem* to change sides), or of the 'set look of pain with which Robert heard passionate verses of Shelley and Byron fall from [the] dying lips' of Edna Murrell in *Hopes and Fears*: we hardly need the confirmatory evidence of Charlotte Yonge's comments on the Palm Sunday song in *Musings on the Christian Year*, written, she says, when 'Byron was exercising a perilous fascination over the contemporary youth; and that Mr. Keble was greatly moved with the force, fire, and musicalness of the latter, may be heard in the ring of more than one of his own poems. It seems as though it were under the burning sense of grief and sorrowful indignation at the glorious powers wasted and abused by men like Byron and Shelley, that the quiet Oxford scholar burst forth into the zealous protest. . . .'

And there is the interesting negative evidence that in all the hundreds of chapter mottoes I have looked at, representing quotations from some sixty or seventy English poets, I have not found one from either Byron or Shelley. With regard to

[1] *Mothers in Council*, 1892, 1893.

Byron, the embargo is not quite complete: the historic interest of the famous eight stanzas on the eve of Waterloo from *Childe Harold* procures their admission to one of her anthologies, *Historical Ballads*, Part III (1882), designed for 'children of the highest standards' in the elementary schools. All her quotations and literary references, sympathetic and otherwise, are based on first-hand reading: she did not herself use books of extracts, or speak on hearsay evidence. The novels provide the best evidence of the extraordinarily wide range of that reading and of a catholicity of taste in poetry and fiction at times surprising, as well as of strong personal preferences and, indeed, reasoned critical principles. Criticism is sometimes expressed through the writings of her characters —'The Waif of the Moorland', 'The Chapel in the Valley', and Lily Mohun's imitation of Scott. In certain novels, literature is part of the central theme. Its power to mislead is seen in a relatively crude form in the case of Dolores in *Two Sides of a Shield* reading books about persecuting aunts, but sometimes much more subtly: in her presentation of both Charlotte ('the lady of Eschalott') and Isabel Conway in *Dynevor Terrace* the author clearly discriminates, through character and action as well as discussion, between the true and the false in literary romance. Two novels in particular are steeped in literary reference: *Scenes and Characters* is almost *too* full of Scott; and in *The Heir of Redclyffe* Sintram almost ranks among the *dramatis personae*. Charlotte Yonge has given Guy many of her own literary affections—for Malory's *Morte d'Arthur*, very little known in the 1850's ('Sir How much?' said Charles when Guy referred to Sir Galahad) and priggishly patronized by Philip; for Southey's *Thalaba*;[1] for Manzoni—*The Betrothed* was 'king of all novels'[2] for her. Without these, Guy's character would be less clearly defined.

But I must turn now to her directly critical work, and except for incidental allusion leave the novels aside, at least until the end. In Charlotte Yonge's criticism, the range of reference is somewhat more confined, for here, her explicit concern is with literature *for the young*; and her most solid and comprehensive critical work, the series of three articles (twenty-six double-column pages) in *Macmillan's Magazine*,[3] has the general title 'Children's Literature of the Last

---

[1] Cf. letter of 1850 (Christabel Coleridge, *Charlotte Mary Yonge*, 1903, p. 161).
[2] *Monthly Packet*, 1881.   [3] Vol. XX, July–September 1869.

Century'. Here she is writing for a wider and more sophisti-
cated public than the readers of *The Monthly Packet* and
Mothers in Council, and is attempting a full and discriminating
survey; and the detail, the weight, the authority with which
she sets in historical perspective such writers as Mrs. Trimmer
(of the *Fabulous Histories*), Thomas Day (of *Sandford and
Merton* and the less-known *Little Jack*—'a charming tissue of
enterprise and adventure'), Maria Edgeworth, Mrs. Sherwood
('first in the field of pious slaughter'), and Mary Lamb's *Mrs.
Leicester's School*—all this marks her as one of the first serious
critics of children's books. (She has not had enough suc-
cessors.) Perhaps these articles stimulated the interest in
eighteenth- and early nineteenth-century children's stories
such as she collected a year later with a delightful introduction,
in her *Storehouse of Stories*. I wish these articles had also led
to reprints of the author whose work she examines in detail
as marking the most important new development in her own
time, 'the creation of the class of literature now termed
"books for the young", standing between the child's story and
the full-grown novel'—Harriett Mozley, who wrote *The
Fairy Bower* and *The Lost Brooch*; Charlotte Yonge speaks
elsewhere of the 'wonderful cleverness and irony' of her books,
'such as none but a Newman could write',[1] and her own
sense of indebtedness to them is clear in her Preface to
Scenes and Characters.

Her field is less confined than might appear for she comes
to what she calls the 'somewhat Irish conclusion' that books
written expressly for children should be 'used as little as
possible': 'Bring children as soon as possible to stretch up to
books above them, provided those books are noble and
good. . . .' 'A good book *is* a good book to whosoever can
understand it, and there is often a power of grasping a part
of the meaning when there is no power of explanation.'[2]

In short, she believed (like Matthew Arnold) that only the
best was good enough for the young; elsewhere she makes it
clear where the best was to be found. Her conviction perhaps
originated in personal experience, in a childhood nourished
on Shakespeare and Scott, of having Shakespeare read aloud
to her by her father, starting with *Midsummer Night's Dream*
at the age of seven, and being turned loose on Bowdler's

---

[1] Letter of 1896 (Coleridge, 339–41), and *The Guardian*, 20 December 1899.
(See the earlier paper on Harriett Mozley by Margaret Kennedy.)
[2] *Macmillan's*, pp. 456, 450.

Family Shakespeare at twelve ('not *well* Bowdlered' she notes in retrospect); of hearing an episode from *Anne of Geierstein* read aloud at six and herself reading *The Talisman* at ten. That was the beginning of a life-long love-affair: 'My prime literary affection must ever be for Sir Walter';[1] and it included the poetry as well as the novels (she quotes it more frequently even than Shakespeare, Wordsworth, and Keble), and included the man as well as the works—'the most noble-hearted and loveable of men, in spite of errors and mistakes'.[2] She uses a love of Scott as a touchstone for her characters, contrasting Mysie's enthusiasm over *The Talisman* with the inferior taste of Dolores and her citation of Maude Sefton's brother who found it 'all rot and bosh'; 'Countess Kate' draws Sylvia into playing 'The Lady of the Lake' on the sands, despite her objection—'Oh! I've learnt that in my extracts; but I never did my poetry task out of doors!'; Elizabeth in *Abbeychurch* tells how she learnt from *Ivanhoe* to like history; and Louis Fitzjocelyn's devotion to the novels makes him an even more attractive hero.

At the same time the reading of any novel was treated as a luxury to be rationed; she read *The Talisman* at ten 'as a special treat after a carriage accident', her allowance when in normal health being a chapter a day interspersed with straight history; Lily Mohun has to be curbed when she reads three-and-a-half Waverley novels in about a week, and the mother in *Magnum Bonum* who reads *Woodstock* aloud to her children on a Sunday is obviously asking for trouble. And with contemporary novels, especially in serial form, there is always a suggestion that these are indulgences appropriate to the disabled, the convalescent, and the railway traveller.

But it is noticeable that in bringing children to 'stretch up to books above them, provided those books are noble and good' she made few concessions to those who would expurgate such books to avoid bringing a blush to the cheek of the young person. She was firm, and courageous for her time, in her view that 'no child was ever contaminated by the Fairie Queene, Don Quixote, The Vicar of Wakefield, or the Arabian Nights'; 'coarse allusions . . . are not half perceived by young readers, and do not do anything like the amount of harm equal to the benefit of the great book itself to the mind and character';[3] 'Such coarse jests as may be found in Shakespeare,

---

[1] Coleridge, p. 113. [2] *Mothers in Council*, 1899.
[3] *Mothers in Council*, 1899.

or the allusions that now and then occur in Scott, are nothing compared to the harm in many a book that can be read aloud without an immediate blush'.[1]

She had a strong sense of the disinfecting power of great literature; and also in practice she makes a distinction, which I am sure is valid, between the ancient and the contemporary: 'The real romance does not do the harm that the baby novel does . . . the undesirable passages are far less perceived than they are later in life;' 'a real good novel about grown-up persons, above all a historical romance, is far safer reading than the many representations of interesting little girls of ten or twelve, who become the lady-loves either of grown-up men, or of boys of their own age. . . .'[2]

In recommending a 'free run' of Shakespeare, Spenser, and Scott, she perceived one safeguard in the child's lack of sympathy with the sentiment of love as distinct from romance: 'the tender feelings of the hero and heroine are utterly uninteresting, but the adventures and disasters they undergo, their bravery and constancy, are delightful, and raise the whole tone of the mind.'[3] Or, in Mysie's version of the same view: 'grown-up books are the nicest! at least when they don't begin being stupid and marrying too soon. They must do it at last to get out of the story, and it's nicer than dying, but they can have all sorts of nice adventures first.'

'It's nicer than dying'; but Charlotte Yonge would never protect children from the tragic. The death of Fergus McIvor in *Waverley* had for her an 'inevitability' that justified it; and it was far better that a girl should 'weep for Lucy Ashton' (in *The Bride of Lammermoor*) than 'turn over the good little book where a child like herself flirts with her brotherly first cousin, and marries him at last.'[4] She is an astringent critic, particularly severe on the pietistic pathos of what she calls, in *Womankind*, 'the *weak* religious tale', 'the little child who goes about asking people whether they are Christians . . . the equally unnatural one who is always talking about its white robes. Both alike die young, and are equally unreal and unpractical.'

As well as the ennobling effect of genuine romance, she looks for the 'real and practical'. These unnaturally pious children (who, incidentally, transgressed the Tractarian code of reticence on religious subjects) are obviously 'unreal'; they

[1] *Mothers in Council*, 1894.　　[2] *Womankind; Monthly Packet*, 1865.
[3] *Macmillan's*, p. 450.　　[4] *Macmillan's*, p. 450.

are also unpractical even in the intended moral effect, since the inevitable conclusion for young readers is simply that 'it is very dangerous to be good'.[1] There were other tales of virtuous intention which she found positively unmoral: *The Wide, Wide World* and *Queechy* had 'the very grave and injurious effect of teaching little girls to expect a lover in any one who is good-natured to them. Nothing ought to be more rigidly avoided, for it fills the child with foolish expectations and dreams, which poison her simplicity of mind and her present enjoyment.' 'Though boys seldom are influenced by story-books, yet girls are, and theirs being the passive side, unable to take the initiative, is exactly that which it is most cruel to impress with vain aspirations.'[2] In *The Monthly Packet* too she had warned little girls 'that they themselves are particularly uninteresting in the eyes of both boys and men . . . at that time of life; and that the surest way to be discontented and ridiculous is to think themselves likely to be the objects of such devotion as was Fleda in *Queechy*'.[3]

But in any case it was in her view 'a fatal thing' for a story to be 'overdone with moral. To force events, even imaginary, to illustrate some maxim, is ruinous.' She objected to many modern so-called fairy-tales, full of 'poor little sprites loaded with priggishness', and advocates a return to the 'genuine— we had almost said authentic—fairy tale', such as Grimm and the traditional Irish and Norse tales. 'The trumpery, arbitrary, moral fairy [is] . . . an absolute injury to both taste and to antiquarianism'. In the category of fairy-tale the only 'modern inventions' that she found to praise were *Undine, Sintram*, and 'the best of Andersen'; and also, using the term fairy tale in a broader sense, two very recent publications that were 'really original'—*The Water Babies* and *Alice in Wonderland*. (It is an instance of her perception; she could not know in 1869 that they would become classics.)[4] The 'latent though not consistent meanings' in *The Water Babies* made it more attractive to her than 'even the exquisite bits of fun in Alice'. 'Fun and playfulness' she approved—'we do not believe there can be sparkle where there is not depth'[5]—but not buffoonery or burlesque; it is not always an easy distinction to apply, but I think it is clear that she looked for a certain delicacy in

[1] *Monthly Packet*, 1852.   [2] *Macmillan's*, p. 309.   [3] *Monthly Packet*, 1865.
[4] *The Water Babies*, cf. *Magnum Bonum*; *Alice*, cf. *What Books to Lend and What to Give* (1887).
[5] *Macmillan's*, pp. 306–7, 452–3.

her 'fun', and was particularly suspicious of exaggeration, caricature and slang.

These she found too common in books for boys 'of the whole Mayne Reid school', with their 'series of adventures not absolutely impossible individually, but monstrously improbable in rapid succession', feeding the love of sensation. As for boys' school stories, they are in any case 'more read by mothers, sisters, and little boys longing to be at school than by the boys themselves'—a shrewd comment, and perhaps still true? Those she commends include *The Crofton Boys* and (rather unexpectedly) *Tom Brown's Schooldays*, unapproached by any of its imitators, least of all by *Eric*, that 'morbid dismal tale, which we hope no mother or boy ever reads, since it really can answer no purpose but to make them unhappy and suspicious, besides that it enforces by numerous telling examples that the sure reward of virtue is a fatal accident.'[1] In short, and here again is her favourite theme: boys should be 'wholesomely fed on the real sound romance': 'We have little liking for "books for boys". If boys have healthy, intelligent minds, they would be doing much better if they were reading books for men'[2]—such as history, travels, exploration. And these should be read if possible in their original form ('some *real* books, not an abridgment or a compilation').[3] She is severe on the 'tons of babyish "Stories from Froissart" &c . . . all the raciness taken away, and foolish explanations weakening the point'.[4] Her one complaint of Mrs. Charles's *Chronicles of the Schönberg-Cotta Family* is that it presents 'a lady's Luther, without his force or coarseness'.[5]

Her demand for the 'real' took other forms; imaginative illusion for her, as for many but not all readers, was destroyed by minor factual errors as well as gross improbability. She found many examples of the Edgeworths' ignorance in the *Parent's Assistant*—'Did they really suppose that . . . bees amiably allowed their mistress to come with a spoon, and help herself to a slice of their comb without more ado?'[6] She had no patience with a modern novel whose heroine travels from London to Somerset by way of Exeter, or a poem which represented the evening star as rising in the west, 'going up

---

[1] All quotations from *Macmillan's*, pp. 453–4. Cf. *Monthly Packet*, January 1859, where *Eric* is reviewed: 'it enters upon schoolboy trials of which our girl-readers had better not hear'.
[2] *Macmillan's*, p. 453.   [3] *Womankind.*
[4] *Macmillan's*, p. 456.   [5] *Monthly Packet*, 1865.
[6] *Macmillan's*, p. 303.

backward';[1] the close of the *Mill on the Floss* was weakened for her by the 'sacrifice of probabilities'—'the cool Tom Tulliver would certainly have made Maggie loose her fatal clasp and have tried to drag her to the bank'. Her knowledge of history gave her a keen eye for anachronism: 'it is a great mistake to hang a tale of the Early Church upon a modern love story. The Christian maiden, if destined for a wife, was given away too early to have a real choice.'[2]

But in her introduction to the third volume of *Historical Ballads*, which includes scenes from Shakespeare's history plays, Gray's 'Bard', and Scott's poems, she makes an important distinction. The facts in these poetical versions of history are 'not *in all cases* borne out by research into contemporary documents, and the characters appear in different lights'. It is still possible that both may be true, but at any rate, 'the poetical point of view has been that of almost all past literature, and the knowledge of it is quite as essential to cultivation of mind as is that of the demonstrable fact.' As she says elsewhere 'there is a truth in romance . . . too venerable to be interfered with.'[3]

Her strong sense of the respect due to a traditional story may be seen in her liberal view of the morality of mythology and fairy tale. There is a pleasant instance in *Aunt Charlotte's Evenings at Home with the Poets* (1881), where poems chosen by herself and the children are framed in conversational comments. After 'The Bear and the Goblin' has been read, there follows this dialogue:

> *Grace* The man said what was not true.
> *Aunt Charlotte* That can't be helped, my dear; the story is an old one, and came down from ancient heathen times, when truth was not esteemed the same way.
> *Edmund* Besides it was only a goblin.
> *Alice* I suppose truth is truth, whether concerned with a goblin or not.

In this volume we may see in practice her principle of stretching children's minds. It is a very gentle process, taking advantage of their natural childish interests, so that, for example, an evening is devoted to fairy lore. They get Shakespeare's Queen Mab and 'Ye spotted snakes with double tongue', part of Drayton's *Nimphidia*, and Bishop Corbet's farewell to the fairies (Alice's comment is 'Well done, Bishop!').

[1] *Two Sides of the Shield.*   [2] *Womankind.*   [3] *Monthly Packet,* 1864.

Grouped together on one evening under 'Cats' they have Gray's Ode, Cowper's 'Colubriad', and Wordsworth's 'Kitten and Falling Leaves', with comments that unobtrusively link these three poets with literary history. They were among her own favourites, especially Wordsworth. Like Honor Charlecote of *Hopes and Fears*, she 'had grown up among those who fed on Scott, Wordsworth, and Fouqué'. But her tastes, unlike Honor's, grew with those of the new generation, 'that of Kingsley, Tennyson, and Ruskin'. To these she might have added, from her own reading, both the Brownings; but frequency of quotation shows that Tennyson was the living poet who appealed to her most, and it is good to know that the admiration was reciprocated. She appears to have read his volumes as they came out: Emmeline and Kate in *The Castle Builders* discuss *The Princess*, 'which so embodied an ancient vision of their own that it perfectly enchanted them'; 'Ulysses', 'The May Queen', 'The Talking Oak', 'Locksley Hall', and *In Memoriam* are all quoted several times—in 'The May Queen' it is the 'wonderful exactness to the details of Nature' that she praises, 'the oat-grass and the sword-grass and the bulrush in the pool',[1] but more frequent (allowing for date) are quotations from the *Idylls of the King*, and these had a special attraction for her, for they brought out the 'undercurrent of spiritual meanings'[2] in the Arthurian legends that she knew so well. She was quick to read Arnold's 'Tristam and Iseult' too, and quotes it appropriately in *Heartsease*; and almost all the modern rehandlings of Arthurian story which followed Tennyson and Arnold are noticed in *The Monthly Packet* of the 1860s. The notes in her *Tom Thumb* (1855), and much in the *History of Christian Names* (1863), show her to have been well ahead of her time in Arthurian scholarship.

From the poetry of her own century there are a few noticeable omissions besides Shelley and Byron; I have not come across any quotations from Keats, Morris, Swinburne or Rossetti. Keats's poetry was little known until the 1850s, thirty years after his death; the other silences, if they are so, must be otherwise explained. She could separate the man and his work, but she preferred not to have to; her only extensive commentary on the works of a poet is *Musings on the Christian Year and Lyra Innocentium*, an expression of personal admiration and of piety (in the true sense) rather than literary criticism. As 'Aunt Charlotte', she lets Alice read aloud a

---

[1] *An Old Woman's Outlook.*   [2] *Monthly Packet*, 1858.

translation from Goethe, and to the child's question 'Was he not a great poet?' her answer is 'He was the greatest and most original poet that Germany has ever had; but I do not think he was either a great or good man'. To her as to Dr. Johnson there were 'laws of higher authority than those of criticism'.

I could end here. But there is still the question of her views on the great Victorian novelists; and on this the evidence is not very decisive, so I have thrown it into the form of a kind of appendix—a selection of references which do little more than indicate her familiarity with their works, and here and there some criticism; but all this is particularly wide open to correction and supplementation.

It covers Dickens, Mrs. Gaskell, Trollope, and George Eliot; on Charlotte Brontë and Thackeray there are mere indications that she had read them; and though all Hardy's novels had appeared before her death, all I have found is a single warning reference to *Tess*.

For Dickens we have, for example, in *Abbeychurch*, a reference to 'Miss Squeers in the agonies of death' (*Nicholas Nickleby*); in the *Castle Builders*, Herbert quotes the same heroine's 'I hate everybody, and wish everybody was dead'; in the *Heir of Redclyffe*, Amy crying over little Paul Dombey's death, and Charley's quotation of 'the great Mr. Toots'; in *The Daisy Chain*, Ethel's 'horrid old lady in some book' ('Rose-coloured curtains for the doctor') is of course Mrs. Skewton; in *Dynevor Terrace*, Louis has read *David Copperfield* and quotes 'Barkis is willing'; one of Jem's boys has his ears boxed for reading *Pickwick* in school; in *Two Sides of the Shield* Bessie says Miss Fosbrook taught her to be 'as jolly as Mark Tapley among the rattlesnakes' (*Martin Chuzzlewit*); in *Womankind* there is a reference to Gradgrind (*Hard Times*); *An Old Woman's Outlook* cites 'Joe Gargerry' [*sic*] in *Great Expectations* and his song of 'Old Clem' as a survival of St. Clement, patron saint of blacksmiths. Ten references to seven different novels (not always named) does not sound like disapproval. But in *Womankind*, recommending a 'free run' of 'Scott, Shakespeare, Spenser', she adds that she does not include 'the Dickens school', and in the *Monthly Packet* (1851) she explains her objections to Dickens as reading for the young: 'The finding amusement in slang and caricature does not promote good taste, refinement, or well chosen language; and though some of the scenes and persons who

66

figure in them are described with much pathos and beauty, the general tone is exaggerated, and likely to give false views. There is a graver objection, which will be best expressed in the language of an old review by Sir Walter Scott, whom all will acknowledge as a master in all that is really excellent in the writing of fiction. "As a writer, it must still be considered a blemish, in the eyes at least of those who think differently, that virtue should be studiously inculcated with scarcely any reference to what they regard as the mainspring of it; that vice should be traced to every source except the want of religious principle . . ." Here is the principle that, more than all the talent, the power, the pathos of Scott, makes his books, in the main, wholesome as well as delightful reading, and the want of which, more than vulgarity and extravagance, renders those of Mr. Dickens untruthful and undesirable.'

But she went on reading him herself: and what was read by Amy and Ethel and Louis Fitzjocelyn is by implication not wholly disapproved. She is surely with Charles in mocking at Philip for giving Laura his gracious permission to read *Dombey* 'when she has a cold or toothache' and withholding it from Guy.

To Charlotte Brontë I have found only a few very general references (one in the letter of 1857, which also mentions Jane Austen and Trollope),[1] and only a few to Thackeray: there are several references to *Vanity Fair*[2] and to *The Newcomes*, which both Ermine and Rachel in *Clever Woman of the Family* have read: ' "A simple-hearted old soldier always means a very foolish old man." "Witness the Newcomes" [said Ermine] with her usual amusement in tracing Rachel's dicta to their source.'

Mrs. Gaskell gets a number of affectionate references—with a few reservations; for example, Violet is 'delighted' with *Mary Barton*, recommended by John 'on his system of diversion for her mind', and in *What Books to Lend and What to Give* it is described as 'an unrivalled tale of joys and sorrows in Manchester forty years ago. Full of beauty and pathos; never to be forgotten.' In the 1886 Preface to *Scenes and Characters* she refers to Mrs. Gaskell's enviable skill in making 'a perfect little plot out of a sick lad and a canary bird' ('Libbie Marsh's Three Eras'). In *The Monthly Packet Cranford* is commended as 'the best . . . of all the sketches of uneventful town life', 'an excellent lesson in the respect that

---

[1] Coleridge, p. 213.　　　　　　　[2] Coleridge, p. 22.

may be united with a full sense of the ridiculous' (an acute comment); *North and South* was a 'striking story', though its 'latitudinarianism' was inevitably objected to.[1] In *Womankind* there are references to Mrs. Dobson (in *Sylvia's Lovers*) and to 'poor Clare's abhorrence, a bread and cheese supper' (*Wives and Daughters*); Clare's treatment of Molly also supplies her with an instance in her article on 'Stepmothers' in *Mothers in Council* (1895). In the *Macmillan's* article 'Libbie Marsh' and several other short stories are highly praised; but the publishers are criticized for putting them in the same volume as 'a terrible ghost story' (probably 'The Old Nurse's Story') and 'Lizzie Leigh', 'a piteous tale of the sin we most carefully keep from children's knowledge'.[2]

To Trollope her attitude, on the slight evidence I have, seems rather cautious. Her conversation with the Lord Lieutenant shows she had read *Barchester Towers* in the year of its appearance.[3] In the *Clever Woman of the Family* Mr. Clare has *Framley Parsonage* read aloud to him by Rachel, rather than his curate whom 'it would not edify'; but it is clearly part of Rachel's re-education. In *Womankind*, in the chapter on 'Courtship', Emily Hotspur dying of love for her good-for-nothing cousin is 'an insult to womanhood'. And in 1881 in a notice of the current magazines in *The Monthly Packet* she was rather 'alarmed' by two of his serials, *John Caldigate* and *Dr. Wortle's School*.

For George Eliot we have not only casual references like Alick Keith's picking up *Silas Marner* at a railway station, but some explicit criticism. The long review of Cross's *Life* in *The Monthly Packet* of 1885, where the views of herself and Maria Trench as 'Arachne' and 'Una' are given alternately in letter form, begins with her own recollections of all the novels; recollections, because she has not 'any of the books in the house except *Romola*'. She puts *Adam Bede* and even the *Mill on the Floss* (though it gave 'no elevating ideas') very high, but finds only 'a few flashes' in *Felix Holt*; (one surely is Mrs. Holt 'curtseying to the cast of a satyr under the impression that he was an eccentric ancestor of the family', which she quotes in *Womankind*). She thought 'the free spontaneous play of imagination and memory ended with the early novels', though there is 'immense power and genius in *Romola*'. She admits to having much enjoyed *Middlemarch*

[1] *Monthly Packet*, 1853, 1855. [2] *Macmillan's*, p. 451.
[3] Coleridge, p. 213.

'when it was coming out' (that is, she read it in its 5*s*. parts), but re-read, 'it leaves a sense of hollowness': 'The ideal gradually became lowered, the imagination tarnished, the purpose stronger perhaps, but more perverted.' G. H. Lewes is adduced as the 'blighting and poisoning' influence. It has to be remembered that she would read *Adam Bede* without knowing who the author was, and she admits to being affected by her knowledge of this: 'we were all taken by storm by Adam Bede, knowing nothing of the authorship', 'most people were bewitched and recommended the book right and left'— 'there were young people set to read it as a kind of sermon, but who found it an admission to the knowledge of evil'. She had herself reviewed it in *The Monthly Packet*,[1] calling it 'a work never meant for the young'; and Aunt Jane accordingly takes it away from Valetta in *Beechcroft at Rockstone*.

Her final conclusion on the author, after reading the *Life*, is what she admits may be thought 'terribly cruel and narrow': that George Eliot is like one of Satan's instruments 'doing all the more harm by their practice of outward virtues'. It *is* narrow, but not cruel—given her own beliefs, she could not think otherwise. Perhaps more to be deprecated is her aesthetic judgement, in a letter of 1896, 'She could represent but could not create'; in *Deronda* 'her ideals were absurd'.[2] However, it is worth remembering how very high she placed the 'representation' in Adam, Dinah, Hetty, and Mrs. Poyser, and that twenty-five years earlier she had said of *Adam Bede*, 'It is full of striking passages, and in almost every respect it is one of those paintings which give their moral by their perfect faithfulness, even as real life does'.[3]

As for minor novelists, I note that she liked writers as different as Bulwer Lytton, Elizabeth Sewell, Lady Georgiana Fullerton, and Jean Ingelow, Anne Thackeray and G. P. R. James (it is Theodora who thinks his novels exactly alike); that her range included Hawthorne's *Transformations*, *Uncle Tom's Cabin* and *Treasure Island*; *The Woman in White* and *East Lynne*, and E. F. Benson's *Dodo*; and finally the 'green railway book' described by Arthur in *Heartsease*: 'where the wife fainted away and broke open a desk with her head. . . . Out came a lot of letters from the old love, a colonel in the

---

[1] July 1859. In January 1859 she had referred to *Scenes of Clerical Life* as 'a clever but uncomfortable book'.
[2] Coleridge, p. 340.
[3] *Monthly Packet*, 1859.

Peninsula.' I am happy to be able to identify this as Mrs. Marsh's *Emilia Wyndham*, a popular success of 1846. And though Arthur is clearly rather a Philistine with regard to literature, in this instance the judgement conveyed by his summary of the plot is not unjust.

Children and Charlotte Yonge

By Ruth Harris

Only a grown-up person could write 'Certainly Adam in
Paradise had not more sweet and curious apprehension of
the world than I when I was a child' and Charlotte Yonge
never quite attained to this maturity. For her, there was no
romance about childhood. She writes about children with the
irritated affection of an elder sister who knows exactly when
the little ones are playing up and doesn't find it at all en-
dearing to be babyish. When Leonard the Lion-Heart wakes
up frightened by 'a little nibbling noise coupled with a
flicker of the fire', he starts screaming—' "They would be
sorry" thought he and he howled and bellowed and he
roared the more'—you can hear the elder sister in the choice
of verbs—'as he told himself there was nobody there to care
and how angry mother would be with them all!' Charlotte's
reaction is typical: 'Foolish boy, he never recollected that he
had brought the people by the horrible noise he was making
and that he had only to unbolt the door to let in company
enough'.

To Traherne 'the gates were at first the end of the world'
but childhood for Charlotte is not a separate country and
Dream Days in terms of the Merrifields is quite unthinkable.
Her children must learn to live in a grown-up world. She had
been educated on Edgeworth principles and to Miss Edgeworth the child is, if not a savage, an ignorant newcomer who
must be taught the rules of good behaviour. Rosamund's
parents almost seem to enjoy her failures and the emphasis
is always on teaching. Children are the products of an
educational system.

Mrs. Sherwood, writing some twenty years later, has more
natural sympathy with children but she too has a healthy
respect for original sin. Lucy, Emily and Henry when under
the eyes of their parents play together nicely, rub the furniture, and fight their besetting sins but when Mr. and Mrs.

71

Fairchild go away for the day, there they are chasing a pig through the muddy lane, half tipsy with cider, and then they are disobedient enough to untie the swing and Emily is nearly killed. Their parents come home to find Emily with her nose, one eye and her lip terribly swollen and missing two teeth, and Lucy and Henry tied to the kitchen table with John, the manservant's blue pocket handkerchief.

Just over 100 years later another Emily, in Richard Hughes' *High Wind in Jamaica*, is as wild as any of Miss Edgeworth's children. She hardly notices saying goodbye to her parents when she leaves Jamaica and she and her contemporaries are natives of another country with a culture that no grown-up can understand.

We are back to almost the same barrier between the child and the adult but with one very important difference. Richard Hughes is passionately interested in the world of childhood. He observes its customs like a careful anthropologist, whereas Miss Edgeworth and Mrs. Sherwood both believe that the child should adapt itself to grown-up rules as smoothly and quickly as possible. Richard Hughes knows that there can be no real communication. Mrs. Sherwood held that a bridge was necessary and that traffic should be only one-way. Miss Yonge would have agreed with her. She preferred the ordered hierarchy of the grown-up world and it was an intellectual decision. Children have their station in life and the distinction of age is as exact as that of sex or class. There are definite rules. 'There is something particularly grievous in a little girl, or a woman of any age, casting off restraint and setting out in the world unprotected and contrary to authority', as Mr. Wardour said to poor Kate when she ran away from her aunts. And Kate knew that he was right. The rules are the same and there is no special court for children. Childhood brings no exemption from the moral law.

I do not know whether Charlotte ever read 'Misunderstood' but no child in any book of hers would have been allowed such a beautiful death-bed without having first expressed repentance for his naughtiness. Humphrey deliberately disobeyed his father by climbing along the branch over the pond and then encouraging his delicate little brother to follow him. Charlotte would never have believed that this was forgetfulness. She was much too near the nursery herself. Infancy for her was not angel infancy and she had no use for clouds of glory. In the death-bed scene in *The Railroad Children* the

point is not that Mary is only five or six but that she is newly
baptized, that she is not so much a child as a child of God.
Compare *Countess Kate* with *Little Lord Fauntleroy*. Cedric
Erroll is seen through the eyes of a grown-up person whereas
Kate is observed by a contemporary who knows exactly when
she is being tiresome. It might be Hary-O writing about
Caroline Lamb. *Little Lord Fauntleroy* grown up is a contra-
diction in terms whereas Kate will clearly have to face the
trials of being an adult Countess. The stories are very much
the same but *Countess Kate* is *Northanger Abbey* to *Little Lord
Fauntleroy*'s *Mysteries of Udolpho*. Compare Dorincourt
Castle with the rather dreary house in Bruton Street, and
Fauntleroy's immediate appeal to everyone from Earl to
footman with Kate's failure to get on with aunts, governess
or maids. *Little Lord Fauntleroy* is one of Kate's own stories,
a perfect example of wish fulfilment. She would have enjoyed
drawing the turreted castle, the old earl with his gouty foot
and Fauntleroy's ringlets but it is a story that Miss Yonge
herself could never have written. She prefers the facts of
everyday life. Countess Kate made no attempt to understand
her great-aunts but even when she was drawing her picture-
letters, she did not escape into another world. Griselda, in
The Cuckoo Clock, was on much better terms with Aunt Grizel
and Aunt Tabitha than Kate ever was with Lady Blanche
and Lady Jane, but she lived on a different plane. Mrs.
Molesworth thought of children as different in kind, whereas
Charlotte thought of them as different in experience; thus
Kate played at being Hermione whereas Griselda really went
through the door of the cuckoo clock into the little snuggery,
something like a saloon railway carriage and lined with rich
mossy-red velvet, and when she'd been to Mandarin land she
found the mandarin shoe inside her bed to prove that it hadn't
been a dream. Charlotte's children could never have made
friends with a cuckoo out of a clock or followed a white rabbit
down a rabbit hole. She attempts the transition from every day
to imaginary in *Little Lucy's Wonderful Globe* but this is not
a success. The setting is promising. Lucy has scarlatina and
is rolled up in her bedclothes and taken away to stay at her
uncle's house where there is a museum containing a crocodile
and stuffed hummingbirds and a poor little fly in amber.
She is fascinated by a pair of globes and traces her finger
over the green South Seas where the black dots call up visions
of coconuts and savages. It might be going to happen, she

might get through to the other side of the looking-glass, but the transition is curiously flat. The room was very warm and Mother Bunch went on talking as she stirred and a steam rose up and by-and-by it seemed to Lucy that she had a sneezing fit and when she looked again into the smoke, what did she see but two little black figures. . . . ' "Mrs. Bunker, Mrs. Bunker", she cried. "What's this? who are these ugly figures?" "Ugly!" said the foremost'—and we are started on the first of a series of geography lessons, instructive and completely down-to-earth.

The only magic story that Charlotte published is *The History of Tom Thumb* and this is history and not imagination. As she writes in her preface 'Originality is the last object aimed at' and she gives us seventy pages of large-print text to forty pages of small-print notes. In fact, she gives us the sources of her fantasy, and Michael Drayton's description of Tom Thumb's armour is better than Miss Yonge's. This she knows herself, explaining that the notes were added 'with the desire of rendering accessible to children some of the choicest passages of English fairy poetry'. She was interested as an historian in 'legitimate English fairy lore' but, just as she found childhood not a separate country but a part of the grown-up system, so fairies remained 'very pretty additions to a tale of wonder'. Her world is not uncharted country of infinite possibilities where by moonlight the tapestry castle comes to life and you can stand 'by the great, strange, silent sea' on the other side of the moon. Her view of life is classical rather than romantic and the *ecclesia dei* is her boundary rather than the *flammentia moenia mundi*. The candles on the altar burn more steadily than will-o'-the-wisps, and she does not look for fairyland just because she believes that here is no abiding city. Nothing is at random: there is a definite scheme of things and, although we are all equal at the altar, there are distinctions of station which it would be wrong to ignore.

Mrs. Sherwood in *The Fairchild Family* took class distinctions as immutable. In Mrs. Fairchild's own story, when she tells her children of her disobedience in stealing cherries, the worst of the fault was that she did it with Nanny, 'a little girl who was employed about the house in weeding and in running errands'. 'Think of the shame and the disgrace of climbing trees in such low company after all the care and pains that we have taken with you, and the delicate manner in which we have reared you!' Although Lucy, Emily and Henry carry down prizes to the schoolchildren, the children remain anonymous but Miss Yonge herself actually taught at Otterbourne and *Langley School* is a study from the life. Miss Edgeworth's *Simple Susan* has an almost Arcadian setting with a be-ribboned pet lamb called Daisy and a harper who plays 'Susan's Lamentation for her lamb', whereas Miss Yonge is writing about the girls that she taught each Sunday. Her children are by Chardin rather than Fragonard. *Langley School* is a book that needs reading several times. The girls are tidily distinguished and you have at first to memorize their various characteristics and look back to make certain that Harriet Cleft was the tall stupid one and Caroline Wallis the terrible chatterer who was always in disgrace—'And this was all from her thoughtlessness—a fault which may seem slight in a child, but which leads to grievous sins'. It is rather like playing with dolls, and the best game is playing school.

Charlotte was never encouraged to visit cottages and so she is not absolutely certain what happens to her girls when they go home. They are to learn to do their duty in that state of life into which it shall please God to call them and class distinctions are very important. Before the days of Marks and Spencer and cheap cleaners, station in life was reflected in dress. 'Miss Dora's white frock and blue sash were very pretty on her because they suited her station, but they would not have been pleasing on any of the children, since these delicate things would not suit with thick heavy shoes, brick floors and hands and faces hardened with rough living or hard work. Another thing to be remembered is that what ladies wear is really good and fine in material, while the imitations that poor girls buy are crude and rough.'

Charlotte accepts the rough living and the crude imitations without question. She is equally practical about parties. 'A young lady does not go to balls till she is 17 or 18 . . . and then only with her mother or some older lady to look after her. Now that would not be thought of for a poor girl who would have to walk home late at night with no one to take care of her.' A girl is a very fragile commodity. Furthermore, it is the duty of young ladies 'to live in society with people of their own station and to be good friends'. The rule is the same for all, to enjoy pleasure if it comes in the way of duty but not to set out on a self-willed frolic of one's own. A lowly station is a safeguard against temptation and it is not always fun to be the gentry. In *Friarswood Post Office* Harold complains 'To think of them little chaps [the boys at Ragglesford School] getting more money for nothing than Paul did in a month by working the skin off his bones' only to be rebuked by his mother and told that 'them little chaps will work hard enough by-and-by: and the money they have now is to train them into making fit use of it then'.

It is difficult perhaps to realize how much the England of Charlotte's youth was a country of two nations. When the Carbonels first went to Uphill, the villagers must have seemed almost as alien as the blacks now do to South Africans. The Betseys and Nannys who worked in the fields, their elflocks escaping from under their rough caps, had almost nothing in common with Mary Carbonel and her two sisters. The Langley stories in fact are based on the class system. Education, cleanliness, refinement are ideas to be pursued and the upper classes should be respected because they embody these ideas. Judith Grey was as good a Christian as Mary Carbonel but because she had less refinement, because she had been a servant, it was right for her to look up to Mrs. Carbonel and to call her 'ma'am'. Miss Yonge's attitude to class was one of her necessary limitations. It was her duty to help the poor but it was also her duty to accept the system that made them her inferiors. She allows that Jack Swing, the machine-breaker, had acted with some generosity, poor young man, 'his head had been turned by foolish notions of liberty for the people'. It would never have occurred to Miss Yonge that there might have been some sense in his folly. With a resignation that is both feminine and quietist, she has made up her mind not to question the system but to make it work.

It is perhaps this sense of limitations, this approval of 'the safest mind' that makes Miss Yonge's books unsympathetic to certain children. Enthusiasm, any impetuous action, is nearly always wrong. When Dora, in *The Carbonels*, exasperated by the fact that her class have again come to school wearing curl-papers, takes the scissors and cuts off their hair, Edmund tells her that she had no right to tyrannize. It is the voice of the grown-ups; Dora knows that he is right and spends the afternoon crying on her bed. Again, in *The Stokesley Secret*, David's obsession with the pig is out of all proportion, but one feels that Miss Yonge is being rather over-scrupulous when she says that David had only been eager to do good when no desire of his own stood in the way. She sees him as an anxious elder sister, wanting to correct him and to put him right.

This moderation and balance is the whole theme of *Patchwork Fever*. Poor Frances! It must have been entrancing work with its mandarin and butterflies and the shaded ribbon of soft geranium colour round the rosebud on a straw-coloured ground. She was only thirteen, she had had all the housework to do and that small sister must have been very tiresome. But Miss Yonge is adamant. Fanny did not put first things first. She thought too much about her patchwork to the neglect of her other duties; she was in the wrong and had to learn her lesson. There is never any question of Fanny's duty towards herself. Her mother, one is glad to know, was touched and pleased by her birthday present, but Fanny ever afterwards hated to see the tablecloth because it reminded her of her enthusiasm.

Miss Yonge herself may have had to learn the same lesson, and Ethel May certainly learnt it when she gave up Greek because it took too much time away from household duties. The child may recognize the argument but it requires a great deal of self-discipline to want to become not only good but ladylike, and being ladylike is so often a part of being good. Miss Yonge was an excellent teacher herself and she is a governess as well as an elder sister. She is as anxious as Mrs. Sherwood to improve her readers but their approach is different. Mrs. Sherwood tells a story to illustrate a lesson and although in *Langley School* Miss Yonge is very near to her, she is more of a historian and less of a moralist.

Her children may be less lively than the dear Fairchilds but even in the Langley stories the ideas exist for the people, not the people for the ideas. Compare the Fairchild's visit to the Nobles with the visit to the Grevilles in *The Stokesley Secret*. The visits are almost identical in plan, but although the visit to the Nobles is more vividly described—who could ever forget Augusta's rose-coloured sash and slippers?—the visit to the Grevilles is much more probable. It is an incident in itself and not a peg on which to hang a moral. In the same way retribution, though sure, is apt to be less violent (and therefore perhaps less satisfactory?). Percy Grafton in *P's and Q's* is punished for his carelessness with a broken arm but proud Augusta Noble is actually burnt to death.

I said just now that children are apt to find most of Miss

Yonge's books a little too cool and moderate, but I think that what they really resent is the feeling that she does not approve of them. Children want to be part of the book that they are reading. Take *The Stokesley Secret*, for an example. What child would identify herself with dear blundering Susan or whiney Bess, who is always bursting into tears and longing for refinement? The eye is too critical. Or take Paulina in *P's and Q's*. When Miss Yonge gives her an immense bush of black, rather rusty hair and a dead mother who had clearly been rather a mésalliance, the poor girl starts at a sad disadvantage. One can sympathize with her resentment at her half-sister's assumption of authority but it is not the instinctive fellow-feeling that one has for Mrs. Molesworth's Rosie, who was jealous of mousey little Bee with far less justification. No child could want to be Paulina Quintal, as Miss Yonge describes her. Even *Countess Kate*, which is perhaps a self-portrait, is written from the outside, but then it is typical of Miss Yonge to be self-critical. In all her children's books I think there is only one character to whom she surrenders completely. From the moment of his first entry into the hall having shot (but not killed) the stag, Richard of Normandy is a hero, the chief person in the story. He is in fact oneself. His reactions are one's own, the weariness of receiving homage and the sudden interest in the little boy of his own age, the tickle of the straw when he is carried out of the castle, these are feelings that one knows and remembers.

Perhaps it would be true to say that some of her stories are written for children by Miss Yonge, the teacher, and others about children by Charlotte, the inventive and conscientious elder sister, but in *The Little Duke* she forgets herself completely. She loves Richard as Fru Astrida loved him, faults and all, and this love gives us a security which makes his story part of our own experience, part of the background of all our minds.

Some Chronological Cruces

By Marghanita Laski

People critically concerned with novels often maintain that
it is the duty of the novelist to know, even if he does not tell,
all there is to be known about his characters. Miss Elizabeth
Bowen, perhaps one of the more improbable people to make
this assertion, once wrote:

'It may sound a commonplace to say that the author
should know his characters: do we grasp, though, what such
knowingness comprehends? First, outwardly, all must be
known *about* them—race, class, heredity, place and date of
birth, the environment of the youth and childhood, education,
profession, amount of salary or income, family life (if any),
place and nature of residence, and careers or adventures up
to the point where the character enters our given story. In
fact, as to each of his men and women the author does well
to compile a dossier, written or otherwise—if not written,
kept ready in the file of the mind.'

What importance this duty has in the novelist's art we
need not today consider. What I will maintain is that among
English novelists no one except Jane Austen has to a greater
extent than Charlotte Yonge this capacity of knowing all
there is to be known about the created characters.

But where Jane Austen often conveys only the assurance
that she knows what there is to be known, Charlotte Yonge
usually tells us what it is, and often this means that she tells
us a very great deal about a large number of people over
many years. I used to suppose that Miss Yonge could have
maintained the consistency of her characters only by com-
piling such dossiers as Elizabeth Bowen spoke of, the
genealogical tables and biographical notes that we, coming
after her, try to compile; and I used to curse Christabel
Coleridge for having, as I supposed, destroyed these with the
other papers she tells us she destroyed after completing her
memoir.

Now, having done some work for this paper, I can see that I was unjust to Miss Coleridge. Charlotte Yonge could never have made biographical notes or drawn up family trees. If she had, she could not have been so inaccurate.

'Inaccurate' is, I grant, an odd word to use of a novelist who has, presumably, the right to do what she wants with her characters, and I must justify my use of it.

Such a novelist as Miss Yonge, such a novelist as Thackeray or Trollope or Louisa Alcott, who creates through several books a social world that we are to accept as co-existent with our own, has made a tacit compact with the readers that the created world will be not only self-consistent within itself—this is a duty of all novelists, including writers of fantasy—but will be equally consistent in relation to the real world, the world we live in. And where this self-consistency inside the imagined world, or the imagined world's consistency with the real world breaks down, then we may as justly speak of an inaccurate novelist as of an inaccurate historian.

My concern is with chronology, with family dates and family relationships, and with our—as I think—reasonable demand that characters shall be consistently related, aged, acted upon and characterized. And I must start by stating my criteria for accuracy, for what counts as a character's 'real' being, what justifies us of speaking of a mistake in relation to what is 'in fact' the case.

In the first place, I take dates in the external world as inescapable. Since Frank Umfraville of *Countess Kate* died in the Indian Mutiny, he died in 1857. Since Henry Ward or Warden of *The Trial* was at the siege of Vicksburg in that spring when poor Minna fell fatally ill, we may be sure that Minna died in 1863. Since Ernly Armytage was wounded at Tel-el-Kebir which was in 1882, the events of *Strolling Players* cannot take place until at least the following year. Since the Jubilee was the year before the events of *The Long Vacation*, that book must cover the period 1888–9. Often, and especially in the later books, this adherence to external chronology is inconvenient; but I do not think it may fairly be evaded.

Secondly, the date of the end of the fictional events must not be later than publication of the book or of its last serial instalment, whichever is the earlier.

Next, as opposed to dates of events in the external world, we must consider the internal fictional dates Miss Yonge so often gives us. It might seem reasonable to accept internal dates with the same rigidity as external ones, but this cannot reasonably be done, and all dates given by Miss Yonge as relating to her characters' lives and unrelated to external events must be looked on with suspicion. I take for an example the list of the Underwood children on the first page of the family Bible. This, which is in Chapter IV of the first volume of the published book—*The Pillars of the House*—was not in the serialized version and so could, presumably, have had the benefit of afterthoughts and adjustments. It is riddled with what I am sure it is proper to call inaccuracies.

Let us take the most important first, the date of the younger twin's birth, for on this the subsequent dating of the book depends. When the book opens Felix is just 16. Wilmet and Alda are 15, Edgar is 14, Geraldine 13; all this is consistent with their birth-dates as given in the table, and so are the ages of the other children as these subsequently appear. Inescapably the book begins in July 1854. Since the younger twins were not born until the following Epiphany, they were born in 1855 and not in 1854 as appears on the table.

But the table has other errors. Wilmet's birthday, on the table, is 11 August; on p. 393 of the first volume it is on 19 August. On the table Clement is born on 23 November, on p. 202 of the second volume he is born in March. (The first date is surely right; it is the Feast Day of St. Clement of Rome.) Lance is born on 16 May on the table, in June on p. 282 of the first volume and on p. 305 specifically on 14 June; and I think we must accept the June date rather than the one on the table since it prevents his getting another year at school and hence an exhibition.

Thus the table may be used as a general guide only, and the same is true of the family tree on p. 353 of the same volume. For instance only a few pages earlier, on p. 349, the Rev. Edward Underwood's father, killed at Waterloo, is called Edward but on the table he is Thomas.

But if we may not trust Miss Yonge's own dates and tables, what may we trust? The answer, I think, must be her creative talent. We must suppose—and we know from her letters and conversations we may justly suppose—that her characters were fully alive for her, and I think we may take it that she looked on them as a great interlocked family whom she knew but could not always perfectly remember. Thus she might, as any of us might with our own families, make occasional

81

mistakes about people's ages or the names of the grand-children. But she would not—at least, not till her later days —make mistakes about people's characters and what happened to them.

In parentheses, I had thought once that this last statement could not be validated in view of the extraordinary behaviour of Harry Merrifield, Lilias's son, in *Strolling Players*, when he so incontinently and embarrassingly pursued Agnes Willing-ham who came to safer harbourage in the arms of cousin David Merrifield, whereupon Harry went off to Ceylon in a huff and married a lady doctor. Could this, I asked, be the thoughtful solicitous son of *Beechcroft at Rockstone*? Had Miss Yonge perhaps confused the two Harry Merrifields, the good and the bad one? Then I re-read *Two Sides of the Shield* and saw that Miss Yonge had not erred. Lilias's Harry had had a flirtation with Constance Hackett, and such a flaw amply fitted the ill-considered pursuit of Agnes and the precipitate marriage.

So apart from the external dates I have in general trusted to Miss Yonge's creative talent rather than to her internal dating. I have taken it that the first establishment of a major character must stand, and subsequent departures from it be inaccuracies, but that where minor characters and events are concerned, we may extend the same tolerance we would allow ourselves if we muddled the names of two distant cousins who went to Australia—or was it New Zealand?—a generation ago. Thus we may forgive Mr. Poulter, the Silver-fold curate and Latin tutor of *Two Sides of the Shield* for becoming Mr. Pollock in *Beechcroft at Rockstone*; Sir Bevil Acton of *Hopes and Fears* becoming Sir Bevil Aston of *Pillars of the House*; we may even forgive the ex-Merrifield` governess Miss Vincent being called Miss Winter in *Modern Broods*. But there are other more troubling errors, and I think I can best refer to these family by family.

The May family is the most consistently all right of any; which is not to say that it is consistently all right. Mrs. Battiscombe's wish, that Dr. May should be under 100 when he died on 24 March 1901, can be satisfied.[1] In *The Daisy Chain* he is forty-six in January 1848, that is, born in 1801 or 1802; in *The Trial* he is fifty-eight in 1859 after Easter, which settles his birth as in 1801, after January and, to please Mrs. Battiscombe, after March; but I am sorry to say that in *The*

[1] See p. 118.

Long Vacation he is eighty years old in 1889, which will *not* do.

The case of Harry May raises an interesting problem relevant to several characters. You will all remember that fifth of May 1852, when Harry, given up for dead, comes home. And this day, we are told, would have been and in fact turned out to be his eighteenth birthday. Now on 5 May 1852, Harry would in fact have been seventeen—'in fact' meaning, as I have indicated, consistently with everything else we know. And the question arises, was it a common practice in that period, or a common practice of Miss Yonge's, to count in the actual day of birth when expressing birthdays in ordinal form? That is, to speak of an eighteenth birthday when someone attained the age of seventeen, a seventeenth birthday when they attained the age of sixteen and so on. Dr. Storr reminds me that in Chapter 48 of the second volume of *The Pillars of the House*, on 6 January 1872, when 'eighteen years ago Father put you two freshly christened babes into my arms' Stella Audley is writing letters that bear the date of 'her eighteenth birthday', though she is in fact seventeen.

That this was not Miss Yonge's invariable practice is made clear from a passage in *Pioneers and Founders*, where she speaks of David Brainerd, who was born—historically—in 1718 as dying in October 1847 'then wanting six months of his thirtieth birthday'. But it certainly seems as if the usage I suggest may sometimes be Miss Yonge's and, if it were, it would rectify some apparent errors.

I do not want to weary you with the many small inaccuracies about age. I will assure you there are sadly many of them and pass on to larger errors. We need not, I think, waste time on the small difficulty of the Miss Ward who married her father's surgical pupil; this was obviously a slip of the pen for the Miss Axworthy who married her father's surgical pupil Mr. Ward, and became the mother of Henry, Averil, Leonard, Minna and Ella. I wonder but cannot say who are the Mackenzie relations Dr. May stayed with in London, sufficiently intimate to be used as an hotel but not, apparently, to be invited back to Stoneborough. I suspect they may be the children of deceased Uncle Mackenzie whose widow lived in Edinburgh; we know that the children of that marriage disliked their parents, which might account for the widowed mother living so far away.

But before leaving the Mays I want to refer to Dickie, or Richard Rivers May, Norman and Meta's eldest son and brother to little Harry and little Ethel. I cannot agree with Mrs. Battiscombe in disavowing his marriage;[1] if Miss Yonge said he was married and never specifically said that he was not, then he was married and that is all there is to it. (Incidentally, Susan de la Poer would have suited him nicely, and another delicate bride in the May family would have been neither here nor there.) But Dickie was, we know from *The Trial*, eight years old when he was sent home in 1863, that is, he was born in 1855, Norman and Meta having been married in January 1854; and for Miss Yonge to tell us, in *The Pillars*, that Dickie was fourteen in 1873, which would make him born in 1859, will not do.

The Mays are not however the only family that stands uncertainly in proximity to the Underwoods. Take the De la Poers. In *Countess Kate*, Lady de la Poer specifically says she has ten children. In that book we learn the names of six—Fanny, the eldest, who apparently turns out the home-bird, since she is still unmarried in 1867; Mary, who did get married; Adelaide, Kate Caergwent's best friend, who married a Scotsman; Grace, who became engaged to and presumably married the Rev. Mr. Pemberton; and of boys, Ernest, who was about Kate's age, that is ten or eleven in 1858; and the baby Cecil, who in 1858 was eighteen months old. Three, then, are unnamed, including Lord Repworth, the heir. Then in *Pillars*, we further learn of Annie and the delicate Susan, and this seems to be the lot, making nine instead of the ten we need. But Annie and Susan are, it appears, younger than Cecil, the baby of *Countess Kate*. Three De la Poers are irrevocably missing.

But the greatest crux peripheral to the Underwoods arises from a discovery of Dr. Storr's, of a piece entitled *A Link between the Castle Builders and the Pillars of the House*.[2] The title is disingenuous, for, far from being a link, it confounds confusion. Miss Yonge says in a note that internal evidence may indicate when it was written, and so it does, giving 1863 or 1864, fourteen years after Lord Herbert Somerville had accepted the living of Dearport.

The matter is as follows: Janet and Cecilia Willoughby, the half-sisters of Constance Somerville and Katharine and Emmeline Berners, are walking near Dearport and discussing

family events since 1850 when *The Castle Builders* ended.
Katharine Berners, we learn, had almost immediately married
Lord Somerville—the ceremony was performed by Uncle
George Willoughby of Dumblethwaite—and Lord Somerville
had become Lord Liddesdale before 1863; by this date they
had had Annie (who married before 1871), little Som, whose
birth-date is varied in *Pillars* and who himself later had sons
and two daughters, Kitty and Constance; and Lord Francis
whose birth-date is also variable and who married Alethea
Merrifield in 1882. Emmeline who, you will remember, had
so recklessly visited a Roman Catholic service with her
friends, the Allens, had had a troubled time. Mr. Montague,
an ill-chosen curate at Dearport, had 'poped' and nearly took
Emmeline over with him. Fortunately Lord Herbert had
founded the Dearport Sisterhood, St. Faith's, just before his
death in 1860, in order to provide an occupation for her whom
he knew would be his widow; and here troubled Emmeline
found peace. Of the rest of the family, both Major-General
Sir Francis Willoughby and his wife had died in the 1850s;
little Alfred, seven years old in *The Castle Builders*, had
provided the longed-for son in the army; Edwin, five years
old in *The Castle Builders*, is reading for Holy Orders and in
1868, when ordained, will become curate to Uncle George at
Dumblethwaite. Of the two girls who give us this information
in improbable discourse, Janet has herself joined the sisterhood; and Cecilia, virtually adopted by Lady Liddesdale, is
about to have her first season.

Now all this matter, agreeable as it is, presents major
difficulties when we try to link it with *The Pillars*, and it does
seem rather casual of Miss Yonge to have printed it in *The
Monthly Packet* at the time when *Pillars* itself was being
serialized. In *Pillars*, in January 1855, Mr. Underwood
remarks that he had met Sister Constance with her husband
at Dearport six or seven years earlier, that is, in 1848 or 1849.
But Constance had married only in 1848 and gone to Dearport
only in 1850. And even if, on this point, we allow for a sick
clergyman's failing memory, larger difficulties still arise,
because in 1855, when Sister Constance came to tend the
Underwoods, she was, according to that book, a Sister and a
widow, whereas according to the *Link*, she could be neither
until 1860.

Then again, in *Pillars* we discover that the priest in charge
of St. Faith's is a Mr. Willoughby, probably rather high,

since in the second volume he is referred to as Father Willoughby. Who is he? He is not Uncle George who, we know from the *Link*, will still be at Dumblethwaite in 1868, nor is he, as I fear Miss Yonge intends him to be, Edwin, who, even if he gave up his intended curacy in the north, was not yet ordained at the required date. These cruces are, I fear, unresolvable. We must live with them.

In *Pillars* itself, most, considering the length of the book, is straightforward. There is considerable confusion over dates in the 1860s but we do more or less come together in 1873 when the story ends. I find some difficulty about Irish ladies. The Rev. Edward's mother was, we are twice told, Irish; so was Felix's great-grandmother, that is the Rev. Edward's grandmother, Lady Geraldine, and with all respect to one of our members, Irish ancestresses in two successive generations seem supererogatory.[1] The Fulmort crux is not, I think, as serious as it has sometimes seemed. It is true that Bertha was only nineteen when she and Miss Fennimore started the school in Brompton; but if we assume that Bertha put up the money and Miss Fennimore, then an elderly sensible lady with grey hair, did the real work, this is not improbable to the point of rejection. There is some difficulty, in relation to the later books, about Alda's family. She is said to have had a daughter a year until at last Adrian arrived—Mary Alda in 1863, Sophia in 1864, Emilia in 1865, Anna in 1866, Franceska presumably in 1867. But Wilmet Felicia, sixteen in *Modern Broods*, cannot have been born until, at the earliest, 1873, and after her come Alda and Joan and, at last, Adrian, born about 1877. What was Sir Adrian senior doing between 1867 and 1873?

But the real crux of the Underwoods is and always has been the question of Gerald's legitimacy. His birth-date is various. When we first meet him in *Pillars* in 1871 he is six or seven, that is, born in 1864 or '65, but a little later on he is five years old, that is, born in 1866. In *The Long Vacation*, which on most of the internal dating dithers between 1884 and 1886, but must, on the external dating of the Jubilee as well as on some of the internal dating, run from 1888 to 1889, Gerald is nineteen at the beginning, that is born in 1867, and has, in March of the second year, been twenty-one for two months, that is, born in 1868. Thus if we take, as I think we should, *Pillars* as establishing Gerald, he was almost certainly born in 1865 or '66; and even if we charitably allow the evidence

[1] Violet Powell denies the difficulty; see Table IV.

of *The Long Vacation* and take for it the latest possible date, he cannot have been born later than the end of January 1868.

Now the only date we have for Giovanni Batista's death is 12 February 1868. If Gerald had been 21 for two months no matter how late in March of 1889, if Zoraya had married Edgar no matter how late in her pregnancy in 1868— remember, subsequent marriage did not then legitimize— Gerald cannot, by at least a fortnight, be legitimate. And in fact—and I think we must take *Pillars* rather than *The Long Vacation* as constituting fact—we know that Edgar married Zoraya in New Zealand soon after 1863. I think we must say of Gerald's death, as Clement said of Angela's, 'O thankworthy!'

None of us is, I know, as interested in Mohuns and Merrifields as in Mays and Underwoods, and though these families provide innumerable cruces, especially in the last books where dating is so wild as to be unestablishable, I will refer only briefly to one or two. The relationship of the Jasper Merrifields to the Stokesley Merrifields presents only superficial difficulty. Old Rear-Admiral Merrifield married twice. By his first marriage he had three children, Sam, who married and had a son who died; Captain, later Admiral H.—may we guess Henry?—Merrifield of Stokesley who married Susanna, an invalid but a long-lived one; and the Reverend John who married Alice. After his first wife's death, the Rear-Admiral married the old Mrs. Merrifield whom we know. She bore a daughter who had died, and one son, Jasper, though she did sometimes speak of her stepson, the Admiral at Stokesley, as her oldest son. She died in the summer of 1883, according to *Beechcroft at Rockstone*, but another find of Dr. Storr's, the story *Come to her Kingdom*[1] badly throws out most of the dates for the Stokesley Merrifields' middle years, including old Mrs. Merrifield's death.

The ageing, or rather the unageing of Gilian or Juliana Merrifield is worth passing attention. She was born at the Cape in the year of Maurice Mohun's marriage, that is 1866, but she is sixteen in the first year of *Two Sides of the Shield*, which sets her birth in 1864. At the beginning of *Beechcroft at Rockstone*, two years later, she is still sixteen, though admittedly nearly seventeen. In *Strolling Players*, which apparently takes place immediately after Beechcroft, that is, in 1884, she meets Ernly Armytage at Rotherwood; we do not

[1] See p. 152.

know her age, but she seems more than seventeen. Then in the first year of *The Long Vacation*, in 1888, she is twenty-two; in *Modern Broods*, which might take place in 1889 but more probably in 1891, she has just gone up to Oxford—not to Lady Margaret Hall, as she had once wished but, apparently without repining, to St. Catherine's. She has, it seems, taken ten years to age from sixteen to twenty-two, and if we cared for her more we might find this disturbing.

But we do not care deeply for Mohuns and Merrifields and I shall not pursue them. Instead I will, as a penultimate point, bring together some old friends from elsewhere. From *Dynevor Terrace*, we meet Lord Ormesfield, once Louis FitzJocelyn, three times: in January 1881 he is at Rotherwood; in 1883 he is spending New Year at Rowthorpe, the Liddesdale home—this time his wife is with him, with her kind motherly face, and we are glad to know they have children; and the next year, in *Strolling Players*, he is at Rotherwood again. From the same book wicked Lady Conway emerges to blast Redgie Mohun's life, persuading her niece Maude to marry rich Lord Clanmacklosky instead of Redgie. From *Three Brides* comes the Reverend Herbert Bowater with his dog Rollo—no relation, so far as I know, to Meta's Newfoundland of that name—to take charge of the next parish to Coalham. From *Magnum Bonum* one or other Dr. Brownlow is forever emerging; the fashionable Dr. Brownlow, as well as the East End one who attends at Whittingtonia and advised Clement's removal to Rockstone in 1888; both Brownlows, as well as Tom May, were recommended for Angela's little ward, Lena Field; and a Dr. Brownlow advises in a very poor dialogue story called 'Mrs. Batseyes' to be found in *More Bywords*. Armine Brownlow, once a curate at Whittingtonia, becomes a curate at Rockquay; and his mother, a friend of Cherry, comes to the Rockquay bazaar. But I do not think that the Mrs. Brownlow of the *Stokesley Secret*, a friend of Mrs. Greville, is connected with this family. The Burnetts, from *Strolling Players*, seem to have belonged originally to Miss Coleridge and to have been born in a book of hers called *Jack O'Lantern*; Miss Yonge, however, took over the Reverend Richard Burnett in *Strolling Players*, a curate at Coalham and not quite a gentleman—an odd comment from a book which describes the class system as 'the infernal system which is responsible for half the evil in the country, and which can be defended on no grounds of Christianity or common justice'.

In *Modern Broods* we hear no more of the Reverend Richard's antecedents; they did not prevent him from becoming incumbent of Coalham, and from there he is to go as Chaplain with the Bishop of Onomootka.

I will end with a thought that sometimes affects me strangely. It is that the last-born children we know of, the twins, little Felix and little Angela, born to Bernard Underwood and Phyllis *née* Merrifield on the last page of *Modern Broods*, must now, in 1965, be over 70 years old.

The Other Miss Yonge

By Alice Fairfax-Lucy

In the early nineteenth century schoolrooms had been going through a dreary patch with *Little Arthur's History of England*, Miss Edgeworth's *Moral Tales* and Mangnall's *Questions*, but by the mid-century *The Christian Year* and Neale's *Stories of the Saints and Martyrs* had supplemented Isaac Watt's doggerel verses and the inanities of *The Peep of Day*. By the middle fifties religious and historical teaching took a fresh gloss, and on schoolroom shelves there was beginning to grow the line of blue-and-gold volumes in which Miss Yonge reclothed the old fairy-tale moralities in historical dress.

In his essay 'Old Books', Hazlitt says that half the pleasure of re-reading one's childhood favourites, lies in the memories they evoke. He calls such books 'links in the chain of our conscious being . . . they transport us over half our lives at a word's notice'. A breath of our childhood comes from between the blue-and-gold covers of Miss Yonge's historical work with the sights and sounds of the quiet schoolrooms and summer gardens in which we first devoured them. It is with mild but real regret that we return them to the shelf, realizing that they were meant to be enjoyed crouched on an attic floor while eating an apple with summer rain drumming on the skylight, or prone in a hayfield where the grass is higher than one's head.

The truth of the matter is that Miss Yonge's historical novels represent the side of her genius that never quite outgrew adolescence, the side of her that from the age of twelve joined fervently in prayers for King Charles the Martyr, and later haloed the memory of Keble and Bishop Paterson with a rainbow of hero-worship—in fact the very same indiscriminate, passionately enthusiastic adolescent she drew in *Countess Kate*.

When Stevenson wrote: '. . . no man lives in external truth . . . but in the warm phantasmagoric chamber of his brain, with the painted windows and the storied walls', he wrote for nearly a century of historical novelists who strove to place on a basis of probability their limited individual conception of the past.

In his Dictionary Dr. Johnson dismissed the word 'chivalrous' as obsolete; Scott resurrected and nobly reanimated it and a host of his imitators did it to death. The fact that nineteenth-century historical fiction was written mainly for young people made for over-simplification and some falsification of character, and was made further unreal, as in the illustrations to Nash's *Mansions of England in the Olden Tyme*, by being varnished with the rich yellow glaze of the idealized past.

Miss Yonge was too intelligent to be unaware of this: in a preface to *Stray Pearls* she says:

'Formerly the Muse of the historical romance was an arbitrary personage who could compress facts, resuscitate the dead, give mighty deeds to imaginary heroes, exchange substitutes for popular martyrs on the scaffold, and make the most stubborn facts subservient . . . but critics have lashed her out of these erratic ways and she has become the meet handmaid of Clio.'

The historical *aperçu*, the gift of being able to place an event or a character in proper relation to time and space, is given to very few. Miss Yonge did not have it. She framed her scenes of chivalry in elaborate descriptions and crammed them with accurate, but irrelevant detail. 'The picture,' she says, 'cannot be exact and is sometimes distorted—nay, sometimes praiseworthy efforts at correctness in detail take away whatever might have been lifelike in the outline.' She was not always able to apply this acuteness of observation to her own work. In the introduction to *The Prince and the Page* she hopes that the dream which has been pleasant to dream may be pleasant to listen to '—there can be no doubt that this style of composition does tend to fix young people's interest and attention on the scenes it treats of and to vivify the characters it describes'.

Miss Coleridge gives us a picture of Miss Yonge in the spring of 1862; she was then thirty-nine, at the age when any woman takes a private farewell of youth and youth's illusions, and braces herself to meet the trials of middle age: 'She told me the story on which she was then engaged; it was, I think, *The Dove in the Eagle's Nest*. She always knew her stories, so to speak, by heart, and would stand still when out walking, and pour them out eagerly and dramatically, claiming sympathy for every detail; or sit on the floor in front of the fire and discuss the characters with unflagging interest. She was at this time very handsome, and when she was at ease a most brilliant talker—talking and writing almost at the same time, with an untiring capacity for interest and enjoyment.' There I think lies the clue to the 'other' Miss Yonge, the historical romancer, bred up on the Waverley novels.[1] 'I am afraid you really thought me cantankerous when I flew out at you the other day,' she wrote to Marianne Dyson who had rashly criticized *The Chaplet of Pearls*. Miss Yonge's 'history people' were as dear to her as were the lords of Angria to the Brontë children.

It would take too long to summarize even briefly the whole twenty-three volumes of straight historical fiction or near-contemporary stories in fancy dress. (*Chantrey House*, *The Carbonels*, *Lady Hester* and perhaps *Love and Life*, come into the second category).

Her first historical venture, *Kenneth, or the Rearguard of the Grand Army*, suffered probably from too much well-intentioned advice from her father. She put it away in a drawer to ripen and it did not see the light till 1850. Its reception must have been encouraging, for *The Little Duke, or Richard the Fearless*, followed in 1854, and immediately established her reputation as an interpreter of history for children.

Kenneth has sunk without a trace, but *The Little Duke* lives, and is the only one of her historical novels that can be re-read with fresh enjoyment every time.

The Lances of Lynwood, a story of France at the time of the Black Prince's conquests, followed in 1855, while at the same time she was embarking on the ambitious project of *Landmarks of History*, intended to supersede Mrs. Markham's 'History', a text-book in the form of questions and answers, which had ruled Victorian schoolrooms for over half a century. Miss Yonge's own reading embraced Hallam's *Constitutional History of England*, and Palgrave's more highly coloured *Truths and Fictions of the Middle Ages* (1837) and, later,

[1] 'You taught us,' Ethel May told her father, 'to love Sir Walter Scott next to our Christian Year, and gave us half-crowns for rehearsing him when other children were learning The Robin's Petition.' This is Miss Yonge speaking for herself, remembering how her own father had rationed her to one chapter of the Waverley novels a day.

Froude and Bishop Stubbs. One can see exactly where she was influenced by Captain Marryat's *Children of the New Forest*, by C. P. R. James's *Life of the Black Prince* and Manzoni's *I Promessi Sposi*. Harrison Ainsworth's *Rookwood* was published in 1834 and his *Tower of London* in 1840, Bulwer Lytton published *Richelieu* in 1839 and *The Last of the Barons* in 1845—and always there was Sir Walter, the fountain-head of all these, for her to turn back to for copious refreshment.

Every reader has his own preference. *The Dove in the Eagle's Nest* (1866), inexplicably Miss Yonge's most popular historical romance, is far too long: it does not touch the heart, as does *The Caged Lion*, or suspend judgement as does *The Little Duke*. But the first words, the description of the view from the wood-carver's house in Ulm in about 1519 is enchanting:

'The upper lattices of a tall narrow window were open and admitted the view of first some richly-tinted vine leaves and purpling grapes, then in dazzling freshness of new white stone the lace-work fabric of a half-built minster spire . . . and beyond, peeping through every crevice of exquisite open fret-work, the intensely blue sky of early autumn'—the scene evoked has all the artless appeal of a shiny picture postcard from abroad. It is doubtful whether Miss Yonge knew anything about the medieval Courts of Love, but she never underestimated a woman's influence. The theme of *The Dove* is the survival of the unfittest. Delicate terrified Christina Sorel is flung into the mountain stronghold of a lawless baron, and by remaining strenuously pure and self-effacing softens him and his followers. We know from the preface that Miss Yonge was of two minds whether to set it in medieval Germany or in Scotland, the scenery of both of which provide unlimited examples of the Awful and Sublime.

Something fervid and repressed in her nature drew her to the mystical gloom and grandeur of German legend. She believed, too, in nurturing the young by beauty and by fear. The cruel pelting to death of the chained wolf cub with hard snowballs by Ebbo, and the description of the snow falling after the death of the old baroness Kunigunde ('the corpse of Kunigunde preserved—we must say the word—salted, was placed in a coffin and laid in the chapel to await the melting of the snow, when the vault could be opened. . . .') are oddly realistic.

Most remarkable is the eventual transformation of the

eagle's nest under the purifying influence of a good woman. Christina was a keen gardener and in no time she had vines running up trellises and pot herbs growing among the rocks (sister under the skin to Wilmet Underwood, who on seeing the bare drawing-room of Vale Leston for the first time remarked 'A little chintz will do a great deal').

Miss Yonge was not so at home in *The Danvers Papers* which followed, but she approached her next novel *The Chaplet of Pearls* with religious and reforming zeal, and poured into the story of the Huguenots in France all her powers of description and exhortation, fed by ardent study of Brantôme. It opens with the words:

'Setting aside the considerations of the risk, the baby-weddings of the Middle Ages must have been very pretty sights,' and goes on to describe the wedding attended by the Court of Catherine de Medici of the child Bérenger de Ribaumont with his baby cousin Marie Eustacie. Miss Yonge loved the de Ribaumonts, through whose eyes she honestly tried to see the religious convulsions of sixteenth-century France in their proper proportion.

Though her descriptions are generally tautologous and overloaded, the adventures of the hunted little bride Eustacie, hidden by old family servants in a ruined castle of the Knights Templars, locally believed to be haunted by *revenants*, and the birth there of her child, are delightfully described:

'Had the little Baronne de Ribaumont been lodged in a tapestried chamber . . . as would have befitted her station, instead of lying on a bed of straw with no hangings to the wall save cobwebs and hay, no curtains to her unglazed window but dancing ivy sprays: no visitors but the two white owls, no provisions save the homely fare that rustic mothers lived upon—neither she nor her babe could have thriven better and probably not half so well. . . . If the April shower beat in at the window, they covered her with cloaks, heaped them with hay, and she took no harm . . . and the little one throve in it like the puff-ball owlets in the hay loft, or the little ring-doves in the ivy whose parents' cooing voice was Eustacie's favourite music.'

Two years later she published *The Caged Lion*. It was never popular and yet one feels that Miss Yonge put a great deal of her heart into it. Keble, the beloved leader of the happy Tractarian colony at Hursley, dawned on the impressionable twelve-year-old daughter of the Yonges like Galahad and

Tristram in one person. Her softened and idealized portrait of Henry V in *The Caged Lion*, thrown into relief by the more sombre character of the Lion, James I of Scotland, was a perhaps unconscious tribute to this gentle and good man. Miss Yonge's endings are often brisk, humorous and unsentimental; not so the falling close of *The Caged Lion*, where the dying priest, Malcolm Stewart, half-tranced, recalls his murdered master:

'I know not whether I slept, but it was to me as though I were again on the river and the hymn of Bernard of Morlaix was sung above and around me, by a voice I never thought to hear again. I looked and behold it was I that was in the boat —my King was there no more. Nay, he stood on the bank and the ghastly wounds I once strove in anguish to staunch shone out like a ruby cross on his breast. . . . He spake not, but by his side stood King Henry, beautiful and spirit-like, and smiled on me, and seemed as though he pointed to the wounds and said: Blessed is the King who dies by his people's hand for withstanding his people's sin! Blessed is every image of the King.'

Mrs. Battiscombe has speculated on what Miss Yonge would have made of Nicholas Ferrar and his following. The parallel between Hursley and Little Gidding should have appealed to her. To the Tractarians Charles I was a Saint and martyr; every year on the 30 January the circle at Hursley joined mournfully in singing Keble's hymn 'Our own, our Royal Saint'. But J. K. Shorthouse's novel *John Inglesant* had been received with such universal praise, especially in ecclesiastical circles, that she perhaps felt that everything had been said on that subject.

The Caged Lion was the peak of her historical books for children.

In 1882 came *Unknown to History*, mined from Miss Strickland's *Queens of England*, which dealt with an unknown daughter of Mary, Queen of Scots, and in the following year, in response to demands for further adventures of the de Ribaumonts, *Stray Pearls*, satisfying, factual, workmanlike books, that could be put into the hands of children without a parental qualm.

All this time the giant shadow of the Author of Waverley had been imperceptibly diminishing. George Eliot wrote as early as 1871: '. . . it is a personal grief, a heart wound to me, when I hear a depreciatory or slighting word about Scott'.

His books were chiefly read by the children and grandchildren of those who remembered the days when he was called the Wizard of the North, and the novels were coming out in three pocket volumes each, a guinea for three. The critics openly voiced their opinions that historical novels for the young had been done to death by a flood of tasteless imitations of Scott, which had deteriorated into mere sensationalism.[1] Without claiming for Miss Yonge the smallest sparkle of his genius, her affection and admiration for Scott's work is shown by her determination to imitate his large imaginative grasp on the past. After Scott's death the passion of intellectual inquiry began to be felt, even in fiction. Bagehot wrote of him: 'The desire to attain a *belief*, which has become one of the most familiar sentiments of heroes and heroines, would have seemed utterly incongruous to the plain sagacity of Scott. Creeds are *data* to his novels; people have different creeds but each keeps his own.' In her historical novels Miss Yonge comes near enough to Scott's generous catholicity and dislike of fanaticism, for Bagehot's pronouncement that Scott 'makes his readers appreciate the full value of natural feelings, plain thoughts and applied sagacity' to apply with equal justice to her.

There followed in 1884 *The Armourer's Prentices*, a pleasing unpretentious chronicle of the times of Sir Thomas More. *A Modern Telemachus*, of 1886, dealt with Jacobite plotting and Algeria. In 1887, came *Under the Storm or Steadfast's Charge*, the experiences of a yeoman's family during the Civil War. *A Reputed Changeling* was published in 1889; and in the same year *The Cunning Woman's Grandson: a Tale of Cheddar 100 years ago*; in 1890 *The Slaves of Sabinas*—a story of the Christian Church under Vespasian and in 1891 *The Constable's Tower, or The Times of Magna Carta*. In 1891 she also published *Two Penniless Princesses* to round off her beloved *Caged Lion*, but the daughters of James of Scotland and Joan Beaufort are neither lovable nor lifelike, and the book is not redeemed by a slight portrait of Henry VI in youth.

In 1893 came *Grisly Grisell—a Tale of the Wars of the Roses*, a subject which twenty-seven years earlier would have been so congenial. In 1894 she published *The Cook and the Captive*,

---

[1] In the years between 1852 and 1860 the historical novel had had a short splendid renaissance with Thackeray's *Esmond*, Kingsley's *Westward Ho!*, Charles Reade's *The Cloister and the Hearth*, George Eliot's *Romola* and Blackmore's *Lorna Doone*—but these were strong meat not intended for children.

or *Attalus the Hostage*, and in 1895 *The Release, or Caroline's French Kindred*, a story of the French Revolution, and her last return to the de Ribaumont family.

She was living by now on her reputation and more and more writing down to younger children. Her historical romances had been the wholesome fare, the porridge and bread and butter, liberally sprinkled with brown sugar, of two generations of Victorian schoolrooms. Clearly while there was a spark left she could not be allowed to stop interpreting the past to a new generation, though she was now nearing the end of her long life, and the burden of it is apparent in the last-mentioned books.

It is too easy to smile at the historical novels: one does not, without reason to do so, re-read them. One is, in fact, inclined to feel they, if anything, mar Miss Yonge's reputation. But when we come to list Miss Yonge's writings, we find that her books with a historical background—her editing of history for schools, her *Aunt Charlotte's Stories* from Greek, Roman, German, French and American History, her *Cameos from English History*, her *Landmarks of History* (from the earliest times to the fall of Napoleon), her biographies of *Historical Worthies and Good Women*, her *18 centuries of the beginnings of Church History*, her *Book of Golden Deeds of all Times and all Lands* (the list is by no means complete for it does not include translations from the French or short stories for periodicals)—we realize that she has as strong a claim to be remembered as an interpreter of history as of her own century.

Serious and Fatal Illness in the Contemporary Novels

By Annis Gillie

I suppose that severe illness and death are shears for tailoring the pattern of a tale. The probability and the sequence of the sickness and the timing of death vary from the arbitrary to the author's interest in the morbid for its own sake and for its effect in shaping reactions of characters and the trend of events.

Charlotte Yonge could be arbitrary when she chose—death is arbitrary often enough in life, after all. But she had a gift for putting down what she must have seen in illness around her, with remarkable observation, sometimes even often unaware of what she was describing. She was free from the accumulated traditions that have long fettered and can still hamper medical thought in classification and in reaching conclusions. She accepted the labelling of many illnesses current in her lifetime, but she described symptoms without adjusting them to fit the names and classifications. She could bend an illness to fit a plot, but not to fit the current theories of the doctors. She was an unprejudiced observer because of her absence of scientific training, and because she was driven by her passionate interest in human lives as a whole.

The evidence that she supplies is incomplete. As my own mother said 'anything wrong with tubes is better not thought about'. There are no surgical emergencies, but there is a little cold surgery. All diseases of the lungs except pneumonia are lumped together as 'consumption'. Koch's discovery of the bacillus of tuberculosis came in the middle 1880s after her main peak of writing. But in the group of chronic chest diseases she gives accounts of illnesses quite other than consumption, and not recognized for what they were by the medical pundits at that time.

I was puzzled as to how a woman of her period and class came by this very intelligent interest, which we should call observational research, if it occurred today. But there is a family tradition of vigorous interest in medicine. The journal of Dr. James Yonge of Plymouth, who died in 1721, was recently published. Mrs. Battiscombe refers to him in the biography as an ancestor of the Yonges. He wrote several medical treatises in the early eighteenth century. His son succeeded him in practice, a Dr. James Yonge again, born in 1671; would he have been grandfather or great-grandfather of Charlotte Yonge's father and her uncle Dr. James Yonge of Plymouth? How many Yonge doctors filled that gap between two generations of practitioners in the West Country?

Dr. James Yonge the first was apprenticed to a naval surgeon at the age of eleven. He travelled all over the world as apprentice, as naval surgeon under Pepys' administration, as prisoner of war, was then in practice in Plymouth, and became Fellow of the Royal Society. The very nature of his early life, when experience not precept trained him, made his professional outlook non-conforming. He had very definite ideas about head and brain and limb injuries, about nutrition and other general aspects of medical work, and he devised a more modern technique in amputations. He wrote well, and put down what he saw (maps included), and what he thought, and how he argued with the leading physicians and surgeons of the day. His journal is excellent reading. I wonder if Charlotte ever read any part of it when she stayed with her uncle James. It would be strong meat for a child at any time. Perhaps her vigorous interest in medical matters generally were inherited alongside the more obvious tradition and training of her father.

There is the survey of chest diseases of Dr. Woolcombe of Plymouth which he made in the mid-nineteenth century. It ranks today as a very important clinical record. Woolcombe and Yonge was the family firm of solicitors. Did this relative have any contacts with Charlotte Yonge in her visits?

And now Charlotte's own case books: I have read little more than half of the contemporary novels and, among those, consumption, fevers and accidents include most of the material. Two problems of obstetrics and two of mentally subnormal children are exceptions to this grouping. Babies usually arrive with little reference to pregnancy, and, with only one brother, her chances of observation in her own family were few. But the description in *Heartsease* of Violet Martindale's condition in great detail before and after the birth of her first child, and

less detailed for the second, gives a picture of anaemia of
pregnancy that is remarkably complete. This condition has
only been recognized as a particular type of anaemia within
my own professional life. Violet's modest but tough little
character had more than solitude and distress to contend
with. Her languor and tendency to faint, her apparently slow
recovery are characteristic.

The death of Bessie Keith in *The Clever Woman* within
twenty-four hours of a short and easy labour is another matter.
If the injury following her fall over a croquet hoop had been
severe enough to account for the fatal collapse I doubt if she
could have had a living child. Here the author's shears were
at work to eliminate a character. A motherless infant was
needed to stimulate Rachel's latent maternal instinct—and
poor Bessie had to go. The unexpected in any first delivery
can give authors and doctors, too, quite enough drama even
today, but that croquet hoop could not in my opinion be
blamed.

Consumption is of course her great field. It was the captain
of the killing diseases of her period. Epidemiology was confused, until the discovery of the tenacious bacillus of tuberculosis with its protective covering; infection from one person to
another was sufficiently variable to excuse the muddles. Among
the thirteen children of the Underwoods in *The Pillars of the
House*, a few infants really would have died of tuberculosis.
But there are descriptions of three cases in the family following
the picture of their father's terminal illness, which itself is
classical in accurate detail. Cherry's chronically inflamed ankle
would at one stage of medical dogma have been attributed to
infected milk, but the connexion with her father's grossly
infected lungs is fair enough. More interesting to me was the
bold step of amputation, so that with an artificial limb below
the knee she was freed from invalidism. That admirable
decision (surely distasteful to many of her readers) smacks of
Dr. James Yonge the first. Then came Lance's long illness
when at school, attributed to sunstroke (a special interest to
Charlotte Yonge, owing to her brother's *coup de soleil*). Lance's
recovery was very slow, and I think that early tubercular
infection sealed off by scarring was reactivated by undue
exposure to the sun. Such a sequence was common in the
1920s, when the newly observed and paradoxical value of sunshine in healing surgical tuberculosis led to its general use in
all forms of the disease at first. It was soon found that even

one long exposure to sun can reactivate a partly healed focus in the lung, and I like to fit Lance's illness to this.

Felix's illnesses are a fascinating complex. We remember his breakdown after his fruitless love for Alice. This was recognized by the family and the doctors as a relapse of an earlier and well-resisted lung infection after measles. General poor condition and persistent cough are noted. The resistance of the Underwood children was high, but relapses in the late teens and early adult life are frequent even in the small number of cases that occur today. They are only exceeded in number by the high proportion of relapses in men in their early forties. Felix made an excellent recovery from the first relapse though I think that his resilience was never quite the same thereafter, though Charlotte attributed this to his disappointment in love.

He was approaching thirty-five at the time of Stella's marriage, and so barely comes into the age group of men peculiarly liable to relapse of pulmonary tuberculosis. The violent haemoptysis that followed his great physical effort in trying to save Theodore from drowning could be explained by the tearing of adhesions which had sealed off a cavity dating from the relapse ten or twelve years before. But the description of his symptoms is very different from those of his earlier illness and does not fit well with a recrudescence of lung infection sufficiently extensive to kill him. 'It seems . . . to me hardly to get better or worse since the mere muscular strain passed off . . . telling chiefly in weakness and lassitude', he said to Mr. Audley. Charlotte Yonge was, I think, describing carcinoma of the lung, two generations before the ubiquity of this condition declared itself, and all unaware that an early history of healed tuberculosis is present significantly often in the history of those who develop cancer of the lung. There is the degree of pain, which would be palliated successfully today, resulting from involvement of the pleura and chest wall. He was young, but not impossibly so, and it has to be remembered that Charlotte Yonge believed that she was describing a third phase of the original illness.

The Rev. Lord Herbert Somervill in *The Castle Builders* was taken to winter in Italy by his wife Constance owing to slow recovery from a chest illness. Letters described his rapid deterioration and Constance's sisters awaited news of his death. Then came a description of a violent attack of what is politely called productive cough followed by rapid recovery.

Surely Charlotte was describing a case of unresolved pneumonia resulting in acute abscess of the lung. Once the pus was coughed up he was saved. But his creator had grouped him as consumptive, and finished him off a year later, as his wife reported to the Underwoods when she came to help the orphans in the first critical weeks of their desolation. The author was unaware of the escape that her own account of the crises of his illness had offered him. The accounts and descriptions of Lucilla Sandbrook in *Hopes and Fears* are convincing enough, of a girl infected early in life but with high resistance and suffering from perhaps fluctuating but contested disease. Wiry, overstimulated, beautiful hair and skin, and precarious well-being, all these are typical characteristics of such cares.

Fevers abound, of course—what did Guy Morville die of? Not typhoid, for that would have been endemic in the Tyrolean villages anyway, and no sudden outbreak of it could have been the hot news that came just before Philip began his walking tour; not cholera or plague, though either would have been possible at that date. The incubation period and the rapidity of those illnesses put them out. Typhus does seem to be a reasonable possibility, though, alas, it is improbable that Guy could have remained so lucid to the end, and we should have to accept that a louse must have leapt from Philip's unconscious form to rest on Guy, to convey the infection. Guy's precautions certainly saved Amy from contracting the disease. Dr. James Yonge contracted typhus, almost certainly when a prisoner-of-war in a Rotterdam gaol. He never became confused or delirious though desperately ill. He described it in detail.

And what of the fevers in *The Young Stepmother*? Typhus again in the town, I think, raging in the Kendal property. The sinister pond suggests seepage from the cesspit contaminating a surface well. Did a typhoid- or dysentery-carrier cook account for some of the names on the Memorial in the Church that Albinia saw for the first time when she went to Mattins on the Sunday after her honeymoon? As illnesses affecting tubes should never be talked about, evidence is not available on which to base a guess. When it comes to the outbreak of diphtheria in *The Clever Woman of the Family*, the details are good. It relates to an area of the body familiar and polite; incubation period, symptoms and slowness of recovery are all convincing, and suggest that Charlotte was intimate with families that had suffered, as so many did until only thirty or forty years ago.

Accidents were relatively no fewer before cars existed, apparently. In *The Daisy Chain* there are so few details about Margaret May's injuries that I can never feel satisfied about the cause of death. But if she was paralysed below the site of injury of a fractured spine, then she survived the accident amazingly long with only home nursing. The eminent Sir Matthew Fleet could not have given his optimistic opinion without adequate examination of the patient, especially when consulting with fellow students and colleagues whose medicine he respected. 'He has known the use of the limbs return almost suddenly after even a year or two', was Dr. May's report of Fleet's opinion who was consulted three months after the accident.

Hysteria does not fit in with Margaret's character. Multiple injuries included a severely fractured pelvis (common in road accidents) in my opinion. This would have made it impossible to walk or stand for all of the three months that had passed, and would justify Fleet's optimism, especially as spinal reflexes were well understood and could rule out damage to the spinal cord if normal. The very slow physical recovery, added to her knowledge of the family responsibilities awaiting her, may have favoured retreat into invalidism. The news of loss of future security and happiness later removed the chief motive to live and her debilitated body could have succumbed to infection easily at any time.

Mrs. Underwood's condition after the fall on the stairs on 2 January, four days before the twins were born, is a complete description of a leak of blood inside the skull causing slow compression of the brain. A subdural hæmatoma is the technical description. 'She got up and made the beef tea' immediately after, but became irritable in manner next day, and by 20 January lay torpid in bed without initiative, and showing 'some weakness of limb'. At this point bleeding must have stopped—weeks later 'Mrs. Underwood was still in the same state'. The clot must have contracted, but damage to the brain after weeks of pressure was permanent and she never regained her initiative and active intelligence. Today operation would have saved both her life and her full normal mentality, and I believe that Dr. James Yonge the first would have urged trephining in his own day in just such a case.

Lord Keith's accident in *The Clever Woman of the Family*

resulted from 'the effects of a blow from the end of a scaffold pole that had been run against him when taking her [Bessie] through a crowded street'. The blow could not have been against his legs when fracture would have been obvious. Shortly after, 'Rachel thought him looking much older than in the autumn—he had little appetite, stooped a good deal, and evidently moved with pain.' Colonel Keith became gravely concerned with his brother's illness; the emphasis is on illness rather than on injury. He swept Lord Keith off to Edinburgh where an operation was performed too late to save his life. Now scaffold poles are manhandled at about waist level. I think that a blow in the loin was the injury, resulting in haemorrhage into the soft tissues round the kidney where deep bruising with a large blood clot is a frequent sequel. Standing up straight would have been difficult and painful, there is intense spasm of the psoas muscle that bends the trunk; infection follows very readily in that area. An abscess (it would be a large one) was evacuated but only when septic-aemia was already established.

And lastly, again in *The Clever Woman*, Ermine Williams's burns ten years before her marriage finally took place resulted in confinement to her chair. When taken for drives in Lady Temple's little carriage, she had to be lifted out and carried into the house by her sister. The contraction of burn scarring over a space of ten years would have been very great; if it was scarring that limited Ermine's capacity to walk, then she could never (even with support) have walked up the aisle in church on her wedding day. 'Only nerves,' said Alison Williams of her sister when Lord Keith's attempt to call on Ermine failed repeatedly.

'In fact Alison was not seriously uneasy about Ermine's health, for these nervous attacks were not without precedent as the revenge for all the excitement of the sensitive mind upon the much tried constitution.' I believe that Ermine could and did walk up the aisle on her wedding day, and could have done as much at any point in the ten previous years had she chosen to do so; the burns, though extensive were superficial—second-degree is the classification—without severe contractures from deep scarring.

I finish with the two mentally subnormal children. Theo Underwood was the child of parents exhausted by procreation. His appearance was not that of a mongol, though his musical capacity was characteristic of that group. All subnormal

children were grouped together, and Charlotte Yonge general-
ized below her usual standard of observation. The case of
Margaret Rivers in *The Daisy Chain* and *The Trial* is a
fascinating one. She was an example of an autistic child with-
drawn from all affectionate relationships, and especially from
any affection from her mother from her birth. 'The first sight
of the baby has put her into such a state of agitation that
we do not know what to do with her', said Mrs. Arnott of
Flora to Dr. May. 'Tell Ethel she will be the best mother to
her—don't call her after me', is evidence of Flora's rejection
of her second daughter a few hours later—and later 'I shall
have very little time with her in that London life. . . . I must
leave her to . . . to the nurses.' These rejected children having
failed to make a normal emotional relationship with their
mother, withdraw in varying degree from all human contacts.
They have a full equipment of intellect but omit to use it,
sometimes actually losing the capacity to communicate, even
though they learned to talk as two-year-olds before the full
damage had been experienced. Margaret Rivers is the most
tragic of Charlotte Yonge's creations.

I have referred to her case-books as though recording the
medicals ups and downs of three-dimensional human beings.
Charlotte Yonge would have been a superb observational
research worker had she lived 100 years later—but then she
would have had no time to write the novels!

Parents

By Catherine Storr

Even the least enthusiastic reader of Miss Yonge's contemporary novels knows what a large part is played in these works by parents. Their regardless fertility, their absolute right to command, their susceptibility to accidents and habit of premature death have been often discussed. What, I think, is not so generally realized is the remarkable diversity which exists between the individual examples. Charlotte Yonge's view of the ideal parent never changed: staunch members of the Church of England and of the professional classes, possessing wisdom, consideration, humour, a high degree of moral courage and an immense sense of family solidarity, these paragons can hardly be expected to survive for long. Many are dead before the book opens. But not all her parents are ideal. She drew many other types, from the saintly to the downright wicked, with many gradations between: the struggling, the mistaken, the careless, the worldly and the weak. For my own amusement I have catalogued them, fitting them roughly into four main categories which are quite arbitrary. These are, *Good* Parents, *Unsympathetic and Misunderstanding* Parents, *Feeble* Parents, and *Learners*. Under these headings I have included characters who, if not parents in physical fact, are in the parental position, generally in virtue of the early decease of the actual father or mother. These are older brothers and sisters of large orphaned families, unmarried aunts, and guardians: the Pillars of the House, Mays, Mohuns and Honora Charlecote.

To begin with the first category, one has to recognize subdivisions even among Good Parents. Those who are so nearly perfect that they are marked for immediate death are Mr. Underwood and Mrs. May; and I should like to add Humphrey Charlecote, who, it is true, never had the charge of younger brothers and sisters or even of nephews and nieces, but who, nevertheless, plays a large posthumous part as a Good

Father, to whose standards both Honora and Phoebe Fulmort constantly refer. Then, Good, but not so good that they may not survive, are Dr. May, too impetuous to be wholly free from blame, Lady Temple, too easily intimidated, Lady Merrifield, whose faulty girlhood was perhaps made too clear to us in *Scenes and Characters* for her to qualify for Class One, Division One, and Mrs. Edmonstone, to my mind the most comfortable and least didactic of all Charlotte Yonge's mothers. Among the proxy parents, Felix Underwood stands high in this class, and is canonized before the end of the book; Margaret May and Claude Mohun are close runners-up. To this first category also belong several minor characters, notably Lord Rotherwood, Mr. Harewood, Lord and Lady de la Poer, Dr. Brownlow and Mrs. Frost.

Category Two contains a very different type. These parents are unsympathetic: sometimes because of misapprehensions, sometimes owing to a flaw, a rigidity, a lack of sympathy in their own characters. Eleanor Mohun has been unsympathetic though always right-minded, because of the weight of private grief depressing her own spirits: the Earl of Ormersfield is unsympathetic because of his fears of his son's apparent levity, and his prejudice in favour of the more apparent virtues of his cousin James Frost. Maurice Mohun suspects Lady Merrifield of the 'sentimental flummery' with which she was imbued when she was silly Lily at seventeen, and removes the reluctant Dolores from her influence. Lady Barbara Umfraville cannot understand Kate Caergwent owing to her own strict and joyless upbringing, and the gap of two generations between them. Beside these well-meaning but harsh elders, there are the more reprehensible ones, all male. Mr. Egremont and Mr. Ponsonby are the outstanding examples, men of dissipated habits and low moral standards, who could not be expected to sympathize with their right-minded young daughters: and on a slightly higher level, Violet Martindale's father, Mr. Moss, a shady solicitor who bullied his wife and thought only of securing grand husbands for his large family of daughters, Mr. Fulmort who could see nothing wrong in making his money out of corrupting the poor by distilling gin in Whittingtonia, Lord Harry Vivien, Colonel Brownlow, and, though he plays a very small part in the book, Mr. Knevett, father of Felix Underwood's first love, the fickle Alice.

The third category is that of Feeble Parents. They exert practically no influence for good over their children, and may even hinder them in their spiritual or worldly aspirations. Sometimes they are nonentities. For all the apparent respect paid to Mr. Mohun, the Baron of Beechcroft, he is a character-less father and a remarkably inefficient one: it is curious that Charlotte Yonge, herself so markedly attached to and in-fluenced by her own father, should have drawn such a colourless picture in her first family saga. Mr. Edmonstone is another ineffective parent though a much more attractive person, but Mrs. Edmonstone and Charles run the family between them, with very little reference to the head of the family; his worst mistakes are always made on impulse when he is beyond their influence. Mrs. Moss, Lady Martindale, Mrs. Curtis, Mrs. Egremont also belong to this class: they know what is right, but are too timid to stand up to any more forceful characters, contrasting strongly with their equally shrinking but more courageous sisters, Violet Martindale and Fanny Temple. Lady Louisa, the Earl of Ormersfield's late wife, must also be included here: we know that, without being wicked, she was frivolous: there were fears that she might not have had strength of mind to resist the temptations of the gay life she enjoyed, and that her early death left a sense of escape rather than regret. Lastly, two mothers unfortunately qualify for the lowest grade of ineffectiveness by the state of their minds: they are poor Mrs. Underwood after the birth of her second batch of twins, and Mrs. Fulmort who has patently never possessed any intelligence at all, and must probably be classified as mentally retarded, like at least one of her daughters.

Finally there are the Learners: and they are in many ways the most interesting because in almost every case they occupy the main theme of the book. The exceptions are Dr. May, whose character changes sufficiently in *The Daisy Chain* for him to be included under this heading as well as under that of Good Parents, and James and Isobel Frost of *Dynevor Terrace* whose change of heart is a subsidiary interest, though in many ways a more convincing theme than the vindication of Louis Fitzjocelyn. But the other Learners, Violet Martin-dale, Albinia Kendal, Carey Brownlow and Honora Charlecote are each the central characters in the books in which they appear. Violet is too good, and conquers her weakness rather too early to hold the reader's interest for the length of the narrative: she rapidly qualifies for the grading Too Good to Live, and when she remarks to Lady Elizabeth Brandon that she has come to the heat and glare of middle life, and it then transpires that she is not yet twenty-two, it seems to presage an early death; I can never quite believe that she survives to appear again in *Last Heartsease Leaves*. But Albinia is a delightfully robust creature; and it is interesting that she stands in age relation to her stepchildren very much as Felix and Wilmet Underwood, Margaret and Richard May and Emily Mohun do to their younger brothers and sisters, and makes much the same sort of mistake. With her own babies she has a much surer hand; nor, by the end of the book, has she quite had time to settle into immovable matriarchal steadiness. For Carey Brownlow of *Magnum Bonum* I have never been able to raise much enthusiasm: but Honora Charlecote is one of the most interesting of all Miss Yonge's characters. We never see her as a quite young girl, either in age or spirits. She is thirty before the main story begins and over fifty at the end of the book: in none of the other novels does the heroine have a comparable age span. She may never encompass what would nowadays be called full psychological maturity, but she is emotionally no green girl. She has known what it is to love both the unworthy object and the worthy: and by the most unrewarding method possible, she knows what it is to be a parent. She has to admit that she has made the same mistake twice, in her feeling for the older and younger Owens: has to recognize that she has undervalued her rejected lover Humphrey, and misunderstood her adopted daughter Lucilla. This is the only novel in which goodness and right intentions do not automatically triumph. It is a much sadder book than *The Heir of Redclyffe*, in spite of Guy's death, and a more truly autobiographical work even than *Countess Kate*. This mother who never achieves actual parenthood, is for me one of the most moving of Charlotte Yonge's characters: the middle-aged woman who is unsuccessful when she takes authority on herself and yet who, by virtue of her age and spinsterhood, has no natural mentor to turn to; and who has gradually to recognize authority and superior wisdom in a much younger generation. *Hopes and Fears* is, as far as I remember, the only novel in which the heroine is left declining rather than ascending, resigned rather than hopeful. But then, Miss Yonge wrote nothing quite comparable: the books which immediately precede and follow this novel, written when she herself was still under forty, are in a different and more familiar idiom. In them—*Dynevor Terrace* and *The Young Stepmother*—the emphasis is on the young adult: middle age, unless we accept Violet Martindale's placing of it, is hardly touched on.

There is one parent who, I must confess, I cannot fit into any category: and this is Mrs. Charnock-Poynsett of *The Three Brides*. She was not unsympathetic: we are told her boys brought to her sick bed all their troubles. Charlie had the habit so strongly that he had rushed in and told her of the train crash in which Frank might be involved, before his more restrained brothers had thought of dissuading him. She was certainly not feeble: in spite of her ostensible efforts to withdraw to the dower house, she remains in control of the household throughout the book and is to continue there in the future. She was no learner: she already knew all the answers. Was she then, Good? Charlotte apparently thought so. Yet if Charlotte's great literary gift was to make goodness attractive, Mrs. Charnock-Poynsett must be one of the exceptions to prove the rule. Her illness was clearly hysterical; her hold over her sons abnormally strong, and her influence on her daughters-in-law catastrophic. It would surely be better to be the child of a real Baddy like Mr. Egremont than such an outrageous Goody as this.

It is to this extraordinarily heterogeneous collection of parents that Charlotte Yonge's heroes and heroines owe their noted filial obedience. I need not weary you with examples of the lengths to which this primary duty drives many of the characters, because you will know them already. The more unreasonable and intolerable the parent, the higher, it seems, is implicit obedience valued: and even minor acts of schism, concealment of romantic understandings, marriage with consent but not approval, are terribly severely punished: Laura Edmonstone and Lucy Kendal have harassed married lives, Alda Vanderkist and Flora Rivers are downright wretched. Our country right or wrong, could be translated, for Charlotte Yonge, into my parent, right or wrong. I believe this is because the authority of the human parent was intimately equated with the divine authority of the Anglican Church. It was not only the fifth commandment which persuaded Miss Yonge that fathers and mothers should be honoured—and certainly the early death of so many of her most estimable characters hardly bears out the promise that their days shall be long in the land; it was her feeling that the family unit was very little less sacred than the Church: to belong to both was necessary for spiritual and worldly safety. But because she was reticent about religion—Mrs. Battiscombe has pointed out that the word God does not appear once in *The Daisy Chain*—she expressed her emotions through the medium of the family unit. It is the relationships and readjustments with the family which constitute the main themes of the books. It is not that outside events do not occur: surprisingly often we meet with fire, forgery, sudden death, fatal or near fatal accidents, even murder: but they are subsidiary, rather than essential, to the real plot, and the subsequent narrative emphasizes the resulting change in the family pattern at least as much as the alteration in the protagonists. When disobedient little Ada Mohun blows herself up with her brother's illicit store of gunpowder, she is scorched and Phyllis is wrongfully blamed; but after the true story of the accident has been disclosed, it is not Ada, or Phyllis or Maurice who is fundamentally altered, it is the place they hold in the family esteem. When Guy Morville dies, the character of his widow is unchanged: but the Edmonstone family circle is disrupted. Amy takes the elder sister's place, with the added dignity of her title. Laura and Philip are indeed reinstated, but at a far lower rating than they originally held. One could quote innumerable examples: but whether it is Arthur Martindale's threatened bankruptcy, Cecil Charnock's bid for the emancipation of women, juvenile alcoholism in Stoneborough School, or the various vicissitudes of the less satisfactory Underwoods, it is the family unit which suffers or benefits in consequence. The characters involved rebel against the family, stray away from the family, betray the family: repent, return, are incorporated into the family again. Behind all these events is the shadow of the Anglican Church: and often the orthodoxy to both church and family is closely correlated in the narrative. Lilias Mohun neglects her churchgoing and her home duties during the same Lenten period; Edgar Underwood learns to despise all religious observances while he is proving a most unsatisfactory brother and adopted son; and it is clear that Mr. Kendal will never take his proper place as father of the family until the long-delayed confirmation has been performed.

Charlotte Yonge could be described perhaps as ardent, but not passionate. She was no Saint Theresa. It was not the mystical, the ecstatic, the erotic aspect of religion which inspired her; the more prosaic pleasures of parental approval

111

and affection were the attractions and rewards she found within the Anglican Church. So it is not surprising that her characters undergo no spectacular spiritual conversions; their regeneration is a gradual awakening to the full meaning and everyday applicability of the creed to which they already belong. In the secular field the same holds true: the emphasis, in her treatment of romantic love, is not on its irrational, unpredictable course, but on the necessity for it to fit in with the existing family pattern. James and Isobel Frost set up house with his grandmother and sister: and fond as they are of each other, their marriage is never completely successful until the family feud is solved and they have also adopted James' unsympathetic and paralysed uncle. Alethea Western, when she marries William Mohun, automatically takes charge of her father-in-law and seven or eight younger members of her husband's family; and Hector Ernescliffe is known, by Aubrey, to have married Blanche mainly for the pleasure of calling himself son to Dr. May. It is interesting that one can carry this parallel between loyalty to the Anglican church and the concerns of the heart a degree farther. Two of Miss Yonge's characters are, at one point in the respective narratives, in danger of losing their faith; but both Norman May and Rachel Curtis are reclaimed by the love of a steadfast member of the church. Emma Brandon nearly suffers an equally terrible fate: immediately before her flirtation with the Scarlet Woman, she has been infatuated with one of Miss Yonge's most desperate villains, that wolf in sheep's clothing, Mark Gardiner. To have gone over to Rome, like her friend Theresa, or to have married Mark as the lost Georgina did, would equally, one feels, have been fates worse than death.

It was not change, taking risks, the bold individual *sorties* of the body or the spirit which interested Charlotte Yonge: obedience, stability, tradition and the *status quo* were what she valued. No wonder she applauded the Oxford Movement, with its new enthusiasm for the established past. God the Father and the Mother Church remain unalterably themselves: how fortunate for us that Charlotte Yonge's gifts of invention and observation prevented her from casting every parent in that same immutable mould!

Miss Yonge's Taste in Dress

By Violet Powell

In compliment to our surroundings[1] I would like to begin this paper—which I have called *Miss Yonge's Taste in Dress* —by a quotation from *The Three Brides*.

' "When the Backsworth engines and the soldiers came up it was like the Prussians at Waterloo."

' "Take care, my grandfather was in the Light Division."

' "And my uncle in the Guards," said the curate.'

Luckily there was a diversion before what Miss Yonge calls the 'Waterloo Controversy' could be pursued farther. The curate was Hector Bowater, and he was reporting to his rector's wife on a fire which had destroyed the slums of Willansborough. This newly-arrived bride is Lady Rosamund Charnock and the vivid contrast of her clothes with those of her sisters-in-law gives a picture of the three brides and their characters. Indeed this book is remarkable throughout for the way the author uses clothes to underline personalities. Cecil, bride of the eldest son, first appears correctly dressed for dinner in crisp worked muslin with blue ribbons. Anne, wife of the absent sailor, shows her puritanical upbringing by her Quaker-like dress of closely fitting dove-coloured silk. Rosamund, on the other hand, 'displays a long thing that had once been a curl falling onto the shoulder of a white tumbled bodice worn over a grey skirt that looked as if it had done solitary duty for the five weeks since the marriage.' Nowadays one would say that Rosamund was wearing rather grubby separates, and at the risk of intruding personally I have always been made uneasy by Miss Yonge's low opinion of the standard of grooming prevalent among the daughters of Irish earls. At the meeting to discuss the rebuilding of the town, the only practicable scheme for employing the homeless is produced by the sandy-haired Mrs. Duncombe. She is

[1] This paper was read at a meeting held at the Guards' Club.

a brilliant figure in a gorgeous many-coloured gold-embroidered oriental mantle and a Tyrolean hat tipped over her forehead, with cord and tassels of gold. (Incidentally Tyrolean hats seem to have been emblems of feminine revolt to Miss Yonge, for Angela Underwood wears one for the historic arrival at Vale Leston.)

To return to Mrs. Duncombe: she dresses her little boys in Highland dress, which must have ill accorded with their long red hair, and when Ducky Duncombe is picked from the gutter he is found to have holes in his boots. Thereafter one cannot be surprised when this Mrs. Jellaby of a mother is punished for her efforts to introduce drains where none were before by precipitating an epidemic which polishes off several of the more hard-pressed characters. Her friend Mrs. Tallboys, an American lecturer on women's rights, makes a brief but smashing appearance in 'a robe of sheeny sky blue' with a plumed 'coronal of gold and sapphire' on her head. Lady Rosamund's clothes cause more trouble later as her ball dress is so low-necked that the priggish Cecil refuses to be seen with her. This matter is put to rights, but Rosamund is a glutton for pleasure, and insists on going to the tough local race-meeting in mauve silk and a bonnet 'just large enough to contain one big water lily'. This un-shady bonnet is an additional handicap to her in the course of a hot and disastrous afternoon which ends by her having to rescue her neglected baby from a low haunt where little Julia was being drugged with Godfrey's Cordial. Luckily the results were not fatal as they were with Flora's daughter, Leonora Rivers, in *The Daisy Chain*.

Most of the clothes that I have described have been in good taste whether pretty or striking, but Miss Yonge also uses clothes to demonstrate vulgarity. *The Young Stepmother*, Albinia Kendal, having decided that her first appearance as a widower's bride is no moment for display, dresses for church in a dark silk and a cashmere shawl, only to find that her stepdaughters have been garishly fitted out in sea-green mantillas topped by pink bonnets. Incidentally I have always wondered what a tarn cap could be. It was Albinia's only wedding bonnet and she was invisible in it.[1] However, when Albinia had taken her stepdaughters in hand Lucy learns to look charming in a white evening dress trimmed with cerise,

[1] The Oxford English Dictionary describes a tarn cap as 'A magic cap, securing the invisibility of the wearer'.

though Géneviève, the little French governess, appears to more advantage in her old black silk whenever she and Lucy are seen together. In fact, though Lucy is a flirt, Géneviève is a menace, and finally she marries the only young man who might have taken on poor neurotic Sophy with her slipped disc. Sophy, a great self-torturer, dresses the French girl's hair with a spray of holly, given to Géneviève by her betrothed, and does it with such skill that the only wounds are in her own hands and heart.

On the question of hairdressing and bonnets Miss Yonge has strong opinions as to what is seemly. Shade over the face is essential and, as we have seen, Rosamund was instantly punished for exposing her countenance to the sun and to idle gazers. Rachel Curtis—*The Clever Woman of the Family*—accepts a wreath of white roses to please her mother although she considers herself to be past such vanities. She does however condescend to wear it at Lord Keith's ball where the fascinating Bessie Keith wears an eagle's feather in her hair, clasped by a large emerald which seems to have been looted from Lucknow by her father. In *The Heir of Redclyffe* wreaths of real jessamine are worn by Laura and Amy Edmonstone when they go to Lady Kilcoran's ball, but it is a wreath of feather flowers from Madeira presented to Violet Martindale in *Heartsease* by her brother-in-law John which has such a soothing effect on her nerves and complexion. She wears it with a dress given to her by Arthur, her husband, in an unsuccessful attempt to atone for his strictures on her family's lowly station. He is more successful in buying her a hat which is admired by the smooth, sinister but taste-conscious Jane Gardner; as Violet wears this hat for riding this is presumably not an example of the backsliding headgear on the evils of which Ethel May is for once able to enjoy a cosy feminine chat with her sister Flora.

To mention the Mays brings one, of course, to what I think may be called the linked novels, in which characters from one book reappear to play important subsidiary parts in others; in some cases—Lilias Mohun is an example—beginning as barely grown-up and ending as grandparents. Lilias Mohun herself, when she has become Lady Merrifield, lightens her grey gown with touches of carnation ribbons, which is one of Miss Yonge's favourite colours, pink bows being the first sign that Wilmet might be going to yield to John Harewood's proposals. Major Harewood, an ideal husband and particularly delightful about clothes, soon cures Wilmet of her economical attitude to the vanities of life. Already at Bagnères she appears in a blue and brown striped silk with a velvet jacket, and decks her little sister Robina with a rosy snood and streamers. When she next meets her twin, worldly Lady Vanderkist, she is far the more blooming, and equally smart in a Parisian rosebud bonnet. She is finally seen at the houseparty for her sister Stella's wedding to the younger Charles Audley dressed in the black velvet which her husband, with the good taste that equals his generosity, has always urged on her. The unhappy Alda Vanderkist, also in black velvet, has regained the palm of beauty, but is suffering deeply from the jealous brutality of Sir Adrian. He rightly suspects her of retaining her love for Fernan Travis, jilted years before when the Travis fortunes were in eclipse. Particularly galling to Alda is the sight of the bouquet of emerald leaves and diamond flowers which Fernan is now in a position to give Stella as a wedding present. In keeping with her character as one of the least lovable of Miss Yonge's more priggish girls, Stella has persuaded Charlie to agree to her finishing her year's mourning for her brothers and also gets her way over dressing her bridesmaids in white with the green leaves of the Star of Bethlehem as their only colour. In spite of the doting attitude adopted towards her by her brothers and sisters, one suspects their relief at getting rid of this rapidly developing power-maniac must have been considerable.

On the other hand any priggishness of Stella's pales beside the behaviour of Phoebe Fulmort, that Cinderella of *Hopes and Fears*, who did not have to wait for a prince but was rescued by the egregious Miss Charlecote. Having dwelt lovingly on this perfect girl, gliding through the woods in her favourite robin-redbreast uniform of brown suit and red cravat, or insisting on a particularly pure shade of sea-green silk for her ball gown, Miss Yonge has some qualms. She even goes so far to admit that Phoebe's assistance in her brother Robert's love-affair was sometimes ill-judged. Lucilla, the heroine of this romance, is an irresponsible fairy whose final abandonment of Robert Fulmort is instrumental in the foundation of Saint Matthew's Whittingonia. Lucilla owes many of her troubles to her taste for pretty clothes, and Robert refuses to press his suit when she appears in a double-skirted silk gown trimmed with many-coloured fishing flies. As she was wearing a coronal trimmed with real flies complete with hooks, Robert has some reason for keeping his distance.

The crinoline, into one of which Ethel May was forced on the occasion of her sister Blanche's wedding, is condemned by Miss Yonge as an inconvenient machinery of inflation. Early in *The Trial* she sends Mary May to rescue Averil Ward from 'a mountain of mohair upborne by an overgrown steel mouse-trap', although Flora, famous for her impeccable taste, must presumably have given her sanction to the wearing of hoops. Flora's taste is underlined at the Saint Kitt's Head picnic where Mrs. Fulbert Underwood wears what one of the Somerville boys aptly calls a 'stunning tile' decorated with 'a foreign pheasant's plume from whose tip hung glass dew-drops'. At Flora's own wedding the bridesmaids, including the infant Gertrude, are dressed in blue merino trimmed with white swansdown, for which Doctor May has a penchant. It may be this predilection of her father's that explains Gertrude's appearance in the same outfit when she pays a grown-up visit to Vale Leston, as it is unlikely that she was still wearing out her elder sister's bridesmaid's dresses. There is praise from Felix for her pink silk and wreath of clematis, again chosen by Flora, which does indeed sound more attractive than Gillian Merrifield's white tarlatan on which at a later date Geraldine, now married to the faithful Grinstead, paints blue nemophilas. I must however make one protest about Flora's taste. Considering the well-known sallowness of Ethel's complexion I feel that she would have been ill-suited by the blue-and-white shot silk brought back from Paris by Mrs. Rivers as a gift to her sister. Far better if Ethel had stuck to the useful silk chosen for her by Doctor May and described as 'just the colour of a copper tea-kettle when it turns purple'.

Finally, I am well aware that I should apologize for many omissions both of characters and their varied clothes. I can only say how grateful I am for this opportunity to examine an aspect of Charlotte Mary Yonge's writing, for which it appears to me she had herself some of the warmth that Doctor May felt for white swansdown.

How It All Ended: or, Last Links of
'The Daisy Chain'

BY GEORGINA BATTISCOMBE

Miss Yonge solemnly promised that she would never, never
kill off Doctor May. We, however, are under no such obligation. You will remember that Dickie and Aubrey found the
initials R. M. scratched on the leads of the Minster tower with
the date 1820. By the beginning of the new century, therefore,
Doctor May could not have been less than ninety years of age.
The old man had no long illness. His son Harry, we know,
had married that delightful creature, Phyllis Mohun, left the
Navy, and settled in New Zealand. In the spring of 1901
Harry came over to England alone, leaving his family behind.
Doctor May had always had a special fondness for Harry—
'the flower of them all', as he declared to Doctor Spencer—
and he had been greatly looking forward to this visit. The day
after Harry's arrival was warm and sunny, and in the afternoon father and son went out for a stroll. On returning Doctor
May sat down in his fireside chair in the drawing-room we all
know so well—by the way, the expensive French paper chosen
by Flora thirty years previously was still nearly as good as
new—and there, ten minutes later, Harry found him dead.
The date was 24 March 1901, the day that Miss Yonge died
at Otterbourne.

All Doctor May's surviving children attended his funeral,
with the exception of Norman and Aubrey. Norman, of course,
was a Bishop in the Antipodes, whilst Aubrey, now a Major-
General, was on active service in South Africa. (Aubrey, we
know, was over fifty but Major-Generals were older in those
days than they are now.) Although he had had a successful,
almost brilliant, military career, Ethel had been right in
thinking that his real vocation had been for Holy Orders, not
for the Army. Aubrey was much too sensitive and also much
too clever for nineteenth-century soldiering, although he might

118

have found himself quite at home in the more intelligent Army
of today. All he could do to satisfy his intellectual bent was
to write admirable articles on military affairs for *The
Pursuivant*. Now he was sending home to Ethel rather unhappy letters which betrayed his doubts as to the justice of
the British case against the Boers and his uneasiness at the
general confusion and incompetence prevailing at Head-
quarters. One of the things I cannot tell you is whether in fact
Aubrey had ever married, or whether his wife had died very
young, leaving him a childless widower.

Over one marriage I have indeed been very mistaken, and
that is the marriage of Norman and Meta's son, Dickie. You
remember that when George Rivers was killed in a carriage
accident Flora made over to Dickie his mother's old home,
Abbotsford Grange. I thought I knew that he lived there as
a rich and aesthetic bachelor, exquisite in velvet jackets and
flowing bow-ties, a collector of blue-and-white china and
Japanese prints. Dickie, in short was, very *fin de siècle*. But
on page 33 of *The Long Vacation* Gertrude speaks of Flora as
having 'young Mrs. Dickie on her hands'. All I can say is that
personally I find it very hard to believe in the existence of
any such person.[1]

Doctor May's funeral service was of course taken by
Richard, who had been for many years Vicar of St. Saviour's,
the great church built by Doctor Pusey in the slums of Leeds.
It is a matter of history that the early years of St. Saviour's
were much disturbed by quarrels over ritualistic practices and
by defections to Rome. At first Richard's position had not
been an easy one but his gentleness and quiet good sense had
proved to be the very qualities needed to restore peace and
amity in this troubled parish.

The funeral was at Cocksmoor. You will remember that
when Stoneborough cloister had been closed for further burials
Charles Cheviot had meanly refused to make an exception
which would have allowed Doctor May to lie there beside his
wife and daughter, and that the Doctor had then expressed a
wish to be buried in Cocksmoor churchyard. When Cheviot
moved from Stoneborough to be Headmaster of a Woodard
school in the Midlands the Doctor had decided not to reopen
the matter, thinking it more Christian to acquiesce quietly
in the original ruling. Charles Cheviot, of course, was present
at the funeral with his wife Mary, who had certainly not been

[1] See p. 82.

improved by matrimony. Her pleasant plumpness had turned
to rather unhealthy fat, and her good-temper had not survived the trials of life as a Headmaster's wife and the mistress
of a large household, a position which had proved altogether
too much for her very moderate abilities. As for Charles
Cheviot, he had all too soon discovered that his wife was
almost entirely lacking in brainpower and he lived in a state
of scarcely concealed irritation at her stupidity.

Tom's marriage too had not been altogether successful,
belying Doctor May's high hopes of its happiness. 'I like
people to rub one another brighter', he had declared, but
unfortunately Averil rubbed all her in-laws up the wrong way,
so that everyone was secretly relieved when Tom turned up
alone for the funeral, his wife having decided that she was
far too unwell to attend. Fond as Ethel was of Tom, she had
not been altogether sorry when, after years of wifely nagging,
he had at last decided to do as Averil had always wished, and,
cutting loose from Stoneborough, set up as a specialist in
Harley Street. He did not, however, take this step until
Lance and Gertrude's son Felix, who had followed the May
family tradition and studied medicine at Edinburgh, was fully
qualified and ready to take over the Stoneborough practice
from his uncle.

Felix's parents were now living at Vale Leston, only twelve
miles from Stoneborough. Clement Underwood had died at a
comparatively early age as the result of an illness brought on
by overwork, and after his death Lance had moved from Bexley
to take up his own rightful place as Squire at Vale Leston.
Geraldine still made her home at the Priory, where Gertrude
was glad to have her sister-in-law's help with what was to her
the somewhat uncongenial task of housekeeping. In old age
Doctor May had grown more and more fond of Lance, who
seemed to be the person best able to fill the place of the absent
Harry, and to the May family he was now just as much a son
of the house as ever Hector Ernescliffe had been.

Hector's marriage to Blanche had proved happy and
prosperous. He was now a Deputy-Lieutenant, a J.P. and the
Chairman of a dozen committees, including, of course, the
local Conservative Association, so that no one was surprised
when, a few years after Doctor May's death and just before
the great Tory débâcle of 1906, he was raised to the peerage as
Baron Ernescliffe of Maplewood. Blanche was the ideal help-
meet for such a pillar of society. She had borne him a large

brood of children, some blondes, some redheads, none of them very exciting but all of them highly satisfactory. In middle age she was still a very pretty woman, always neatly turned out in good expensive clothes, but somehow lacking in that real flair for dress so characteristic of her sister Flora, whom at one time she had been thought to resemble.

Flora herself had grown in beauty with the years. The haggard, anxious air which had once marred her looks had vanished and she was now an exceptionally lovely woman, remarkable in any company for 'the ease and sweetness of manner and the perfect fitness of her dress' which had so impressed Felix at that long-ago picnic on the Kitten's Tail. We know that Lance counted twenty-four pigeon-holes in her desk with a Society for each, but from her appearance no one would have supposed her a woman whose life was chiefly devoted to good works. Of all Doctor May's children she had been the one who most often made time to run down to see him at Stoneborough. As for Ethel, she found herself relying more and more not only on Flora's good sense and judgement but also on the warmth of her affection and sympathy.

The funeral over, Dickie carried Harry off to spend the night with him at Abbotstoke. There was not much love lost between uncle and nephew but they had news of their New Zealand relatives to talk over together. Hector and Blanche were obliged to hurry off to catch the last train that would get them home that night as a big Conservative bazaar was to be held next day at Maplewood. Miss Yonge herself places Stoneborough in Herefordshire, on the far side of the Malverns, so that if Maplewood were really in Shropshire, as *The Daisy Chain* has it, the journey would be an easy one, but were it in Dorset, where it is located in *The Trial*, Blanche and Hector would have to spend a tediously long time in travelling. Lance also had an engagement next day at Bexley, a meeting of the Board of Directors of *The Pursuivant*, so that he and Gertrude were off as soon as possible in his De Dion Bouton, the very first car ever to be seen in the streets of Stoneborough. Lance's pleasure in this new toy, said Geraldine, reminded her of the delight he used to take in the 'velocipede' of Bexley days. Ethel had been in hopes that Mary would be able to stay on for a day or two. Nowadays she saw far too little of this sister; Charles Cheviot did not encourage Stoneborough visits, and for many years now Ethel herself had been unable to leave her father even for a day's shopping in Whitford. Charles, however, had to leave that evening, and Mary, fretful and fussy as ever, was set on leaving with him. She complained bitterly of the troubles awaiting her at home, but home she would go. Ethel realized with a pang that Mary, who had once been such a devoted daughter and sister, was now so taken up with her own affairs that she cared little for the troubles of her family.

So it was only Richard, Flora, Ethel and Tom who found themselves together that evening around the drawing-room fire. Ethel was disappointed, as she herself put it, 'not to have the teacups riding in double again'—meal-times at Stoneborough had never altered and tea was still served late in the evening, not at four o'clock of an afternoon. There was, however, a pleasant intimate feeling about the small gathering, just as there had been in the old days, whenever the elders had had the chance to enjoy a few quiet moments together, free of their more boisterous juniors. Now, however, there were serious matters to decide. What was to become of their old home, and, more important still, what was to become of Ethel?

Long ago, you will remember, Doctor May had made a will leaving the Stoneborough property to Tom who was to succeed him in the medical practice, and when Tom had moved to London the doctor had not thought to change this arrangement. Young Felix Underwood, happily settled in Doctor Spencer's old abode at the bottom of the garden, had no wish at all to rent the big house from Tom. Ethel could not afford to live on there alone, even if she could face the loneliness of such an existence, and, with the exception of Flora, all her brothers and sisters had too many commitments of their own to be able to help financially with the upkeep of the family home.

Although he was the eldest Richard was never one to make the first move, and he left it to Tom to put the question.

'Well, two things we must settle. Since I have gone to live in London, giving up the practice here, I feel I have no moral right to the ownership of this house. Properly speaking, it belongs to us all. What do you want me to do with it? If none of us wishes to take it over I am afraid it must be sold. And if that were to happen, where would you, Ethel, wish to live?'

Ethel said nothing. She had just lost the father who had always been the centre of her life, and now, it seemed, she must lose her home also. She had been born in the old house,

lived there all her life, and she could not imagine herself
transplanted to any other place. Both Richard and Flora, she
knew, would be only too glad to have her live with them, but
even with Flora London life would be a desolation, especially
in her present state of mind. She felt that as her father had
once said, 'sorrow weighs more heavily in the town than in
the country'. As for Leeds, she had never even seen the place,
and dear and good though Richard was, he was not quite the
companion with whom she would wish to live alone in the
alien North, cut off from all her other friends and interests.
If Leeds were her duty, to Leeds of course she would go, but
she could not help hoping that the path of duty lay elsewhere.

'Ethel!' It was Flora who spoke. 'Would you perhaps
allow me to come and live with you here, in this house? It
would be such happiness to come home again, for good. It's
a big place, I know, for us two old sisters, but I hope the others
would come and stay, just as they have always done, so that
Papa's children and grandchildren would still have a family
centre, here in Stoneborough.'

'Oh, Flora, what a wonderful idea! But I can't have you
leave your own home just for me. And all your London
charities—what would become of them?'

'There are plenty of people only too anxious to take them
over, if only for the sake of the social kudos. Besides, they
have never been as near to my heart as Cocksmoor is. And
you know, I have always rather hated the Park Lane House
since—since—' Flora could not finish her sentence, but Ethel
knew that she was thinking of the tragic death of her first
baby. 'Oh, Ethel, say that you will have me, and that I may
come home!'

'Flora, Flora, as if I could ever thank you enough!'

'Nonsense! it is I who should be thanking you. And I'll
promise you I'll not be the old, domineering Flora; it shall be
your house, always. And one thing more—if *my* heart is in
Stoneborough, part of *yours* is with Norman in New Zealand.
Now's your chance to visit him and Meta. You could travel
with Harry when he goes back at the end of the summer.'

'Oh, I have dreamed and dreamed of such a thing, but
never thought it could come true! But what would you do?'

'Well, I've more money than I know what to do with and
I should enjoy spending some of it on the old house—'

'Yes, and you would make it pretty and cosy again, as it
was when Mamma was alive. Somehow, it has never looked

quite right all these years; I've no taste, I know, about that sort of thing.'

'You have lots of gifts which are much more important than taste. But I really should enjoy myself, spending next winter here, and getting the place ready against your return, seeing to the re-decoration, putting in a bathroom—'

'A bathroom!'

'Yes, and lighting as well; not gas, but the new electricity; I'm too much of a Londoner to stand these old-fashioned oil lamps. But I promise you the house shall be the *same* house when you come back, only rather more comfortable to live in. You can trust me not to spoil it.'

'Flora, Flora, I never thought to be so happy again!' And Ethel leant her head on Flora's shoulder and shed a few of what Miss Yonge describes as 'her rare tears'.

I wish I could stop there, leaving it a story with a happy ending, but then it would not be a true story. Ethel's trip to New Zealand was indeed the greatest success. With Harry to look after her the voyage out was a delightful experience, and the months spent with Norman and Meta were the perfect fulfilment of her dreams. On her return however, she found a sadly changed Flora. The two sisters enjoyed a few quiet months together in their old home, which was now prettier and more comfortable than ever Ethel could remember it, but towards the end of the year poor Flora died of cancer. And what happened to Ethel herself? Well, Miss Yonge would not kill Doctor May—I *cannot* kill Ethel.

A Vale Leston Luncheon

BY RACHEL TOWNSEND

(This luncheon, identical with that provided by the Underwoods for the Archeological Society in the late summer of
1867, was set before the Society on 8 October 1964.)

A piece of hung beef

Mrs. Froggatt's parting gift of hams

Grouse Pie from Marilda

Venison Pasties from Marilda

Wilmet's and Krishnu's jellies and creams

Marilda's best fruit

    The table was decorated with Wilmet's 'formal glories of
purple and crimson quilled dahlias, obscured', in Cherry's
taste, 'by loose streamers of passion-flower and hoary clematis',
the tablecloth being 'bestrewn with green leaves and fallen
fuchsia bells'.

PART THREE

Pieces by Miss Yonge

To choose, among Charlotte Yonge's shorter pieces, the ones we wanted for this book was surprisingly easy. The first three chose themselves. Among people devoted to her works, demand for the hard-come-by *Last Heartsease Leaves* has hardly slackened since the first would-be reader inquired for it in *The Monthly Packet* in 1862. *A Link*—and *Come to her Kingdom* both provide necessary information about the characters we are concerned with in the linked novels. But one should warn newcomers that these stories, whose interest is solely for devotees, do not show Miss Yonge at her best.

The last two pieces were chosen for the light they throw on Miss Yonge as a writer, in relation to both her own early influences and her attitude to her profession.

Last Heartsease Leaves[1]

MAY we be allowed a glimpse of Martindale House in the present spring?

The drawing-room is no stiff or stately apartment, but a pleasant room, full of comfort and prettiness. It is late in the evening, and the seats are vacant that stand so cosily round the central table, covered with tokens of occupation—work-box, basket, books, pencil, and paper adorned with schoolboy drawings. A low chair and small rosewood table have a candle-lamp to themselves, and by the fire is a large arm-chair, where a little dog lies *perdu*, sunk among the cushions like a presuming pet.

Two figures are lingering over their good-nights before the fire. That slight youth, fair-haired and dark-eyed, of delicate complexion and features of feminine purity and regularity, is John, third Baron Martindale. Gentle as is his manner, and fragile as is his appearance, he has no lack of moral strength, and his handsome, high-spirited brothers and sisters look up to him as to a father. He has gained high honours at school and college; but there is one who thinks most of his having passed through those trials without injury to the innocence and sweetness of his disposition. It is she who stands beside him in her black dress; her tall and graceful figure so youthful, her cheek and brow so exquisitely smooth and fair, and her dark brown eyes so clear and soft, that she would hardly be supposed to be the mother of a grown-up son. He thinks her unrivalled in loveliness, and indeed the trust and affection between those two is as intense as it can be without idolatry.

'Johnnie' (for she has not learnt to call him Martindale: his grandmother says they ought, and his sisters try, but Johnnie is always the readiest name), 'Johnnie, you took no part in discussing the festivities. You must not be shy at these years, my dear!'

'I do not think it is shyness, mamma. I will try to do what

1 See *Bibliography*, p. 210.

is expected of me; but I want to know what you think. It seems to me that I cannot ask people to rejoice at my coming of age, when it only reminds them of those who would have been in my place.'

'I know that feeling, dear Johnnie, but I think we must conquer it. Your grandmamma would be vexed, as at an impropriety, if we had not rejoicings.'

'And if she wishes it no one could object. But I did not expect her to like it, and I know you do not, mamma.'

'Yes, I shall, for'—with a sweet smile—'I shall think of your dear father's and uncle's pleasure in their boy. And although it may be punishment to his lordship himself, how the rest will enjoy it, and what a family gathering it will be! I am glad of anything to bring us the Fotheringhams.'

'One thing is certain, I will go to Wrangerton and fetch the grandmamma that is there. She *shall* not be afraid of railways with me to take care of her!''

'Oh, Johnnie, if you can but bring her! I really think she would consent. She will never refuse you, and once here, how happy she will be! That is an excellent thought.' She kissed him, and he, thinking it the good-night, continued—

'Can you stay a little longer? There is something I have been wishing to say to you.'

'Well?'

'That property of Mrs. Nesbit's,' he said, casting down his eyes.

'Yes,' and she sighed.

'My uncle, not long before his death, talked over family matters, and told me the history of its being settled on me.'

'I am glad you know it—it was on my mind to tell you.'

'What a frightful injustice it was! I have been considering a good deal lately, and this seems to be the right way. I find it is not much less than 150,000*l*. Now I suppose if the poor old lady had acted as most people would, it would have been divided between the three, and my Aunt Theodora has a clear right to her third part. Could you persuade Uncle Percy to see it is only fair they should have it?'

'I hope he will,' said Mrs. Martindale. 'No one can doubt that it is just, and they will be particularly glad to be able to live in England now that their children are old enough to want education, and with that little Marcia Gardner on their hands too—adopting her as they have done with no dependence for the future.'

'What is her connexion with them, mamma? I am sure the name of Mr. Gardner is one that I used to hear in old times.' He suddenly paused, as there was a look of pain on his mother's face; but she calmly answered,

'He has been dead a long time, poor man. He married a sister of Lady Fotheringham's, a great friend of your Aunt Theodora, spent all her property, used her very ill, and at last deserted her and this little girl at Dresden, where your Uncle Percy found them in great poverty and distress. Mrs. Gardner had been maintaining herself by teaching English——'

'But surely Lady Fotheringham must have helped her?'

'Lady Fotheringham was never a very warm-hearted person. I believe she thought the Gardners were—were undeserving, and she makes her son her one object. Poor Mrs. Gardner said she had wearied out her sister's kindness, and now her health was failing, and she only begged that Mr. Fotheringham would, after her death, see the child safely sent to Worthbourne, as her sister could not refuse the care of the poor little thing.'

'Did she not die in their house?'

'Yes, your aunt took her home, and nursed her till her death. They had been great friends, and there was much that made it a satisfaction to Theodora.'

'And did not the Worthbourne people accept the little girl? With no daughter of their own, I should have thought they would have been glad.'

'No; Lady Fotheringham meant to send her to some institution. She thought it undesirable that she should be brought up with her son, lest any expectations should be excited. Thereupon Uncle Percy answered, that all expectations were equal in their family, and that his little girls could not part with their playfellow.'

'Was anything ever heard of the father?'

'Yes, Percy traced him out, and found that he had died in a hospital in Paris. So the poor little thing is, to all intents and purposes, like their own.'

'There is nothing I look forward to so much as knowing Uncle Percy? I wonder if I really remember him. I am so glad this is their due. You will break it to him, will you not, mamma?'

'Will I not, my dear!'

'I will ask Uncle Christopher to have the papers ready to be signed. Well then, my father's share would have gone to my brothers and sisters, and so it shall, and then their fortunes will be a little more respectable. And now, taking myself to stand in my Uncle Martindale's place, there is 50,000*l*. left. Don't you think it might go towards Church matters in the West Indies?'

'Have you thought of it well, my dear?'

'I have been considering it continually these six months,' said Lord Martindale. 'Will that do? Ah, I see you are not going to tell me it is my duty to keep it.'

'No, indeed, I should never dare to say so.'

'That is very kind of you, mamma. I was afraid it might not seem to older folks as it does to me, and I cannot bear to keep that money.'

'I can hardly judge,' she said, laying her hand fondly on his arm. 'There was so much pain connected with that property I never believed it could give me half the pleasure it does now.'

It is the interval between the villagers' dinner and the arrival of the county neighbours. The glorious sunshine of early spring is on the avenue where the school children are at play, and the party staying in the house are watching them, and regaling themselves with tea and cake.

'Now, mamma, do go in and rest like a wise person.' Thus speaks the young lord, who, with a small, frail, worn, but very sweet-looking old lady in deep mourning leaning on his arm, has just found his mother busied in hospitable cares. 'Think of all you have to do by and by, and pray go and rest. Grandmamma is going to look at the old women at tea in the lodge, and then she will come to you. Won't you conduct her in, Uncle Percy, and not let her fly off to anything else?'

'What is everyone to do? I can rest to-morrow. I cannot leave everyone to their own devices.'

'Oh! grandmamma is with the grandees in the drawing-room,' declares a tall bright girl. 'Helen and I will see to the rest. Do go in, mamma. Johnnie and I will take care this grandmamma comes to no harm.'

'They are a great deal too kind to me,' says Mrs. Moss, as Anna drew her other arm into hers; 'only pray rest, my dear Violet.'

Mr. Fotheringham, who looks somewhat gray, but hearty and merry as ever, holds out his arm as if it was her fate, and they turn towards the house. She turns round and says, 'I suppose I need not talk of Theodora's resting. Where is she?'

'Don't you see her? There, on the slopes,—she is teaching little Antony to climb the old scraggy thorn where her governess once captured her. Now have I not brought her home as buxom, blithe, and debonair a dame as you would wish to see?'

'I have been wondering at her. She is so much fatter and handsomer than ever before, and her spirits so high! Why, she used to be the gravest person!'

'There is a great deal in having found one's vocation, and running after wild boys is hers. I leave them to her, and take the female department. Ha! Marcia!' catching hold of the joyous child who races after him, calling, 'Papa! papa! come, that lady is showing us an English game we want you to play!'

'Learn it well. Perhaps I shall come by and by, and see if you are perfect. Only don't overwhelm Miss Brandon.'

'Oh no, papa, she has kept hold of my hand all day. She wants me to come and see her at her house, but I said I could not go without Dolly.'

'Now run back to her then! If you compliment my wife, Violet, I am quite as much amazed at your friend Emma Brandon. I never thought to see her look so blooming, or of so much consequence. I am glad good old Lady Elizabeth has lived to see this happy development.'

'Yes, Emma thrives on being active in all that is good. We tell her she is a person of weight in the county, and really her example has worked wonders in the tone of the neighbourhood.'

'Not hers alone, perhaps! This house, such as it has been of late years, must have a very different influence from the pinnacle of state it used to be.'

'Did you see Emma's orphans—the nicest looking children here?'

'What I did see was the instinct that pounced on Marcia from among the whole contemporary bunch of Violets, and indeed the child is very like her father.'

'I suspect if you want to keep Marcia to yourself you will have a battle to fight.'

'Hem! No, no, we could not spare her—the prettiest thing in the family,—Dolly would break her heart, and mamma, too! No, no, not just as we have something for the creatures to live on.'

'I am very glad to hear you say that. I trusted you were not going to mortify Johnnie.'

133

'Theodora thought with me that it was best to look on it as an act of restitution; and as to any previous feelings on the matter, I believe the hands it comes through are enough to sweeten it.'

'Johnnie came into my room early this morning to tell me he thought you would be kind.'

'It is not a difficult kindness. Antony's schooling is becoming imminent, and family men can't be proud. I do not deny that I am very much obliged to him.'

'And you will live at the cottage?'

'And be only too glad to make Englishwomen of the girls.'

'You will help Johnnie and me. We shall want your advice very often, for it is a great responsibility for so young a head of the family. The dear boys are as good and affectionate as possible, and we have never had the least difficulty, but Johnnie is very little older to be in authority.'

'I don't think you and he likely to break down. I was impressed the other day, when Arthur was talking nonsense, with the quiet effective way in which Johnnie set him down —a great big fellow taller than himself. I thought it indicated a most wholesome state of affairs.'

'Yes, Arthur looks up to Johnnie with all his heart. Is he not a fine fellow, so exactly like his father?'

'He puts me in mind of him continually.'

'The same sort of sweet, rough manner! *He* used always to say these two would be the same John and Arthur over again, without the disadvantages.'

The saddened voice was checked by the appearance of a brilliant-looking young lady, very tall, beautifully formed, with jet black hair, splendid dark eyes, and a glowing complexion. 'Mamma! I had lost you. I went to see if you were housed, and only found grandmamma anxious you should rest; so Lord St. Erme went one way, and I the other, to look for you.'

'Thank you, dear Helen, I am on my road. Take care of every one. Lady Lucy is your charge, you know.'

'Oh, mamma!' stopping her, 'was not dear Johnnie's speech beautiful!' Then coming near enough to whisper, 'Lord St. Erme was so struck with it!' And, with a happy pressure of the hand, she hastens off, and they saw her soon joined by another figure.

'Your prediction verified!' observes Violet, smiling.

'Tell me the whole story. I long to hear how it came about.'

'It is a short story—it was curious. That coal-pit adventure took a strong hold of Helen's mind as a little child, and it always was the event of her life that she had seen the hero. When she was about seven years old she met with his poems on her grandmamma's shelves; the melody of them caught her imagination, and she used to sit poring over them till she could say whole pages by heart. I remember her ecstasy at discovering that her dear ballad of the Troubadour had an author, and he the colliery hero. You always said I had a feudal feeling for him, and she got it, I don't know how. Her papa used to laugh so see her light up if any one said Lord St. Erme had been speaking in the House; and when she was quite a little thing, she really stole away and read his pamphlet on emigration, blushing so desperately when I found her with it that I would not take any notice. This enthusiasm was only because he was a live model of poetry and benevolence. She had never seen him since she was five years old, and did not remember him in the least.'

'When did they meet?'

'Three years ago, when dear grandpapa and grandmamma set their hearts on her having a season in London, and seemed to think it quite wrong she should not be presented. I did not like it: hers had been a character so difficult to manage, and I feared the effect of admiration.'

'You thought of her aunt?'

'I did. But all was safe; this enthusiasm was to be her protection. She had no idea of flirtation, and it never seemed to enter her mind to be excited by the admiration she met with. It only teazed her to be interrupted in her greatest delight, sitting by me or her grandmamma and hearing Lord St. Erme talk to us; and by and by she used to put in some observation, and she is so much the cleverest and best read of us, that it always was to the purpose. Dear child! she had no notion—she was so perfectly simple and open about her enthusiasm. Annie and Violet used to come and ask her if she had seen Lord St. Erme and the Duke, regarding both as the same sort of spectacle. Indeed, there was a standing dispute among the sisters, when Helen would call her Earl the greatest man of the age.'

'And pray when did the Earl begin to be smitten?'

'Much sooner than I imagined. He was always talking to me, and I, thinking it the old malady, used to pity him, while he, it seems, thought himself old, and beneath the notice of such a creature as Helen, since he could not succeed with her aunt in his best days. So it went on, and I don't know when we should have come to an understanding if——. At last, you know, he carried the bill he had been working at for years.'

'The colliery children?'

'Yes, it was the triumph of his life. We had been thinking a great deal of it. Helen and I were going to a breakfast, and while she was dressing she was only wild to read the debate. Little Theodore was set to watch for the *Times*, and bring it to her the moment grandpapa had done with it. I can see Helen glowing over it, and her sisters wondering if she would meet him. "Oh no," she said, sighing, "he will be at no such foolish affair. If I could but stay at home for the chance of his coming to talk it over with grandpapa!"'

'Of course you did meet him?'

'Yes; there was a fine young guardsman, a son of Mrs. Bryanstone's, talking to us, and Helen looking grave and wearied, when we saw Lord St. Erme coming, and—it was too transparent! Helen's black eyes were dancing and sparkling, and her cheeks in a glow. I know she felt as if she was meeting a conqueror after a victory, as if the honour was in his notice. Their eyes met as she held out her hand, and then the change was in an instant; the colour spread and deepened, her eyes were cast down, and for him, he blushed as he used to do in Theodora's time. Poor Mr. Bryanstone! I pitied him, and tried to talk to him.'

'When did he speak?'

'He came to me the next morning and told me how he had thought it impossible he should ever form another attachment, but now Helen had gone beyond all his visions. I cannot tell you what he said. I could only remember your declaring he had a gift of perpetual youth. Not that it was foolish, but so ardent, and so well understanding dear Helen, except that he fancied himself too old for her, and that his position was against him.'

'Did you say—Try?'

'I thought it best to speak to Helen myself. Poor dear! she fairly burst into tears, because she said it was too much, and he did not know what a wilful, headstrong temper she had; but it was great joy all the time.'

'And this was three years ago? I had no idea of it.'

'As she was so very young, we thought it best to be in no haste to make it known, lest it should only be her bright fancy.

Johnnie and I were sure it was a real deep attachment, but it seemed safer to wait, and besides, I could not wish anyone to be married as young as I was. Lord St. Erme was very good and patient, and I think he has been rewarded. Grandpapa was very much pleased; it seemed to relieve his mind as to us. And you cannot think how rejoiced I have been, that a girl like Helen, whose elder brother is so little older, should have some one to look up to so entirely, far better than if he had been nearer her own age.'

'Three years! a trial! Has she never faltered? I suppose she had her coquetry out at five years old, when she was an arrant little piece of vanity?'

'It was so evident as to be well pulled up. All self-complaisances were absorbed in the sense of inferiority to him, and her faults the more resolutely conquered in the desire to be worthy of him. Oh! there has not been a moment's doubt! If the romance is less, there has been a deeper, quieter affection and confidence.'

'I am proud of my prediction.'

'I like to remember her papa's answer. It is like his consent. How he liked to stroke Helen's head, and call her Theodora's deputy!'

A silence, broken by Mr. Fotheringham—'How do you think Lady Martindale? She looks very well.'

'Yes, she lives in her grandchildren. Yours, as being younger than mine, will be a renewal of delight.'

'I wonder whether I shall ever see the warmth you all ascribe to her; she seems to me to be as grand and impassive as ever.'

'That is an outward habitual manner, but if you had seen her in grief, or had it to share with you—Oh! grandmamma and I could never get on without each other; we have come quite to lean on each other now, and there are such bonds between us,—the buried links are the firmest, as you once wrote.'

'I think they are. I dare say you still wear my sister's cross.'

'That I do;' her hand on the chain; 'it has had a double value since it used to lie on dear John's little table. One of the last things he said was to thank me for lending it; but that he had learnt not to look on it only as the memorial of frail earthly love, but as the token of the endless love that gives hope and joy.'

'He was very happy, you said. How I longed to be with him!'

'Quite happy; it put me in mind of what he said of your sister's peaceful sinking. Once he told me it was the way he had always wished it to end. And I was so thankful he was spared to form and guide Johnnie.'

'I should not have spoken of these things on a day like this.'

'Do not say so. To have you and Theodora with whom to talk over dear Arthur and John, is a new pleasure to me, and to-day this talk has been especially comfortable.'

'Is it a trying day?'

'No, it is very gratifying, and this talk with you has been one of its pleasantest parts.' And understanding a kind look of solicitude, 'Yes, I am very happy. If life is a long hot summer's day, the sunshine is very cheerful, and there are pleasant way-side shades, as well as, above all, the one shadow of the "Great Rock in a weary land." '

'Weary?'

'Now and then, but there is plenty of heartsease to be found in it.'

A Link Between 'The Castle Builders' and 'The Pillars of the House'[1]

FOURTEEN years from the period of Lord Herbert Somerville's acceptance of the living of Dearport, Janet and Cecilia Willoughby were wandering on the green slopes of Bayhurst. Janet was of a short slight homely figure, and her dark-complexioned face without pretensions to beauty, though interesting from its kind good expression, and its grave deep reflective cast; and her dress was that of a Sister of Mercy. Her companion, three or four years younger, was considerably taller, and with an air of fashion and elegance; her face was bright and fair, not exactly beautiful, but very pleasant to look upon in its freshness and vivacity.

'You delightful old Dearport!' said she; 'I am so sorry to be going away! The longer one stays, the more pity it seems to have to go, because one gets so entirely into your ways.'

'Yes; and we miss you the more. It would not be right to try to keep you entirely, because Kate must want you.'

'And after she has had the trouble of me when I was little, it would not be fair to desert her now that I can be of some use to her. No, indeed! Rowthorpe is my home, and I would not leave Katherine and the children, even for my sisters here. It was only the thought of London.'

'Your first season! I wonder how you will like it!'

'You never tried, did you, Janet?'

'No; you know I have always felt myself dear Herbert and Constance's child, and it was not in their line.'

'It is not much in Katherine's,' said Cecilia; 'but she must go into society, and she says I am a help to her.'

'And you like it?'

'Tolerably; it is amusing, and it is great fun to talk it over afterwards with her and Lord Liddesdale; but I am spoilt by those delightful evenings at Rowthorpe, with all the children at high romps with their papa! And the walks we take all together, with the donkeys and ponies, and picking up Lady

[1] *The Monthly Packet*, December, 1871

139

Frances from her cottage! We are so very happy, I don't wonder at Emmie's telling me to beware of making a world of my Rowthorpe home, and an idol of little Franky. I suppose we shall not get you to come and see us in London.'

'Hardly; there is so much to do here. But Kate promises to come here, and bring the children. It is half a year since we saw any of them.'

'Janet, I wish you would tell me about the old times. Just after the death of dear Frank. I know about him from Katherine and Edwin.'

'Has Edwin ever talked of him?'

'Once; he told me all he remembered. He has a most distinct recollection of the accident, but he cannot talk about it. Katherine says he is exactly like Frank, in all his ways.'

'Oh yes, so they all say; and I can see it a little. Uncle Willoughby says having him in the holidays is so like the old days that he is continually catching himself calling him Frank.'

'He wrote to Katherine that he only wishes to live to see Edwin Curate of Dumblethwayte.'

'Oh! that he will. He is as hearty and strong as ever, and Edwin will be old enough in four years.'

'He looks to it just as they say Frank did,' said Cecilia. 'It is curious, is it not, that Alfred should be in the army, and be as our poor father intended for his eldest son? Now comes what I wish to hear about, only I do not like to ask Katherine. It was not a very happy home—was it?—when we came back from India.'

'I was not happy, but that was my own fault. I was not engaging, and I brooded over neglect, and almost hated everyone except Frank and Miss Townsend. I remember sitting curled up in the corner of the nursery, feeding myself with a fierce bitter wish that any of them had been drowned rather than Frank.'

'What was wrong?' said Cecilia.

'Our mother's habits were Indian; she had bad health, and the climate had taken away her energy; and my father was— I can hardly tell—he was much fonder of the boys than of me.'

'But there were our sisters?'

'We never took to each other in those days. I was too disagreeable, I suppose; and besides, Emmeline has told me that she was to blame. She was neglectful, and not as considerate as she ought. She was very young, you know, and there was nobody to direct her; and she says she has bitterly lamented things that happened in that first year.'

'Emmeline!' exclaimed Cecilia. 'I thought no one ever had been as good and wise as Emmie! She has always been like the head of the family. I think I look up to her more than even to my own Katherine, or to Constance. She is a better person for a deep talk.'

'Yes; but she was not always what she is now. She has gone through a great deal. Her cleverness and strong feeling was a great temptation, she was excitable and unstable, and discontented—at least so she tells me—and nothing rectified her, or gave her what she calls the key of life, but Herbert's coming home and preparing her for Confirmation.'

'She must have been very old for Confirmation.'

'She had missed opportunities, from fear, and not rightly understanding; and that, she says, was what did her the great mischief. She says she has felt the consequences ever since.'

'It is a comfort to hear that Emmeline ever was foolish!'

'The blessing above all, as she and I have often said to each other, was that dear Herbert's life was spared for those ten years. Where should we have been but for him and Constance? Their arrival was the opening of life to me!'

'You went to live with them at once?'

'Our father and mother had to go abroad on business, and it seemed afterwards as if it had been the great turning-point in our sister's life, that they gave up Paris for the sake of their Confirmation. Constance offered to take charge of me, and you and Edwin had the French *bonne*.'

'Ah! you need not tell me of her. How cross she used to be! especially to Edwin. Those were our first miseries. You were lucky to be out of her clutches.'

'Lucky indeed! Soon after the Confirmation, we all went to pay a visit at Rowthorpe.'

'You, and my other sisters, and Herbert? Was that *the* visit?'

'It was. I did not know what was going on, but there was great sport among the others, and old Lord Liddesdale used to prompt me with impertinent speeches. Ask Lady Frances to tell you about all that.'

'I know there's some joke against Katherine about his age, but they seem just the same age now.'

'Oh no, Cecilia; Kate does not look five-and-forty!'

'No; but he does not seem a bit older than she does.'

141

'I fancy the great fun was that he was very much in love, and thought no one guessed it, whereas everybody did, except Kate herself. Lady Frances says it came of his having made friends with her when he thought her only a child, and did not suspect her of intending to marry him against his will, as he did all other young ladies; and old Lord Liddesdale declared he knew how it would be, ever since he had come home despising Herbert for marrying a school-girl. He was afraid Kate would think him too old, and never be able to like him, and was resolved to find out before he asked her. So one day when some of them were riding, he got her alone, and tried to fish out her opinion of some novel where there was the same sort of disparity of age; but he had put her on a spirited horse, and in the midst it ran away with her, and threw her, and her ankle was sprained. They were out of sight of the others, and he had to pick her up, and put her on horseback, and lead the horse home. But he did not speak till the next day, when the rest were out, and she lying on the sofa. Somehow, there was a confusion. You know it is sometimes hard to tell whether he is in jest or earnest.'

'I know it is. It used to frighten me, but now I have learnt to look for a mischievous wrinkle under his eye before I am taken in,' said Cecilia.

'Well; Kate fancied he was making fun, and made an answer which he took as rejection. So he went away.'

'Oh! poor Kate!'

'Then she understood; but she could not escape to her room, for she could not walk; and it was lucky, for old Lord Liddesdale came in. He was very fond of her, and tried to find out what distressed her. He said he never heard his little Katie, as he used to call her, so piteous, as when she sighed out, "Oh! I never guessed that he really meant it." And he petted her, and talked it over, and settled with her what she ought to do, just as if he had been her father instead of his; and then he went and quizzed his son, for talking so much nonsense that he could not be believed when he was most in earnest.'

'So it was all right?'

'Yes; Herbert used to teaze them about its being like the catastrophe in a religious novel, which the Quarterly Review says always ends by the heroine being rewarded by an evangelical young duke.'

'But how came the wedding to be at Rowthorpe?'

'Our poor father had been much broken by grief at the loss

142

of Frank, and after he went abroad he grew worse. He was not able to come to England, but it was thought that as there was no severe illness, it was a pity to put off the wedding; I remember Lord Liddesdale saying his son could not afford to grow any older. Constance had undertaken to manage the breakfast in "twelve foot square," when the old Marquis begged to have it at his home. It was so delightful! Uncle Willoughby married them, and Herbert gave her away, and we feasted the whole parish. I shall never forget the kind old Lord calling to me, "Come here, you small bridesmaid," and holding me up in his arms to see them drink my sister's health. It was such a happy day to everyone, except poor Emmie.'

'Ah! Kate must have been a great loss to her!'

'They had always been together, like twins, and had everything in common; you know they tell us we can't understand what it is to be such sisters as they were. And it was not only the having no longer the same home, but Emmie had to go away the next day to attend on Papa. Poor Emmie, she never suffered so much, she told me, as that last night before she parted with Kate. Constance says her behaviour was so very beautiful—such affection and self-command! Well, Emmie set out for Nice with Uncle Willoughby and Miss Townsend; but Constance still was so kind as to keep me.'

'Oh! there my remembrances begin; Edwin and I were so glad when they came. How kind Emmeline was! I used to go to her in all my troubles; I can just recollect our life abroad. We used to dread going into the room where the elders sat, because it was a chance whether we were made much of, or told we were naughty. I chiefly recollect Papa in a dressing-gown, and sometimes his driving out with Mamma. Our treat used to be to get Emmeline to walk with us, or to tell us a story. No one ever was such a story-teller as Aunt Emmie, as Kate's children and the orphans have found out. It must have been a forlorn time for her.'

'Yes; I used to hear Herbert and Constance talk about it, and say how much responsibility and care she had, and how admirably she managed. She had to think and contrive, and persuade Papa, and soothe him, and make Mamma comfortable. It was very hard work, and she had no time for her own pursuits, and no conversation or companionship, except now and then a little talk with Miss Townsend. And only think of her never seeing Constance or Kate for three years!'

'Was it as long as that? I know it seems as if we had been an immense time travelling about! I first recollect Katherine standing on the stairs in the house in St. James's Place, with her little baby in her arms. Emmeline and I had gone to the early service the morning after we came to London; it was the first time I ever went into an English church, and there we met the Somerville party, all but Katherine—little Som was only two months old, I think.'

'Yes; how happy his grandfather was when he was born!'

'So we went home with them. I know Emmie pinched my hand *so* tight, and I heard Lady Frances saying she had turned quite pale. Lord Somerville went on before, to tell his wife; and when we came in, there she stood with the dear little baby!'

'Then we all came up as from Dearport,' said Janet. 'I recollect thinking you the most beautiful little sister that ever was! and I came to live at home again. But that was the last of our very happy days, for Papa was getting so much worse.'

'Yes, yes,' said Cecilia. 'It is one of the things one cannot forget, that day when we sat shivering, and listening, till Emmeline came to tell us all was over.'

'How beautifully she managed!' said Janet. 'I really think Alfred and Edwin have ever since looked up to her, as if she was father and mother both at once.'

'That they have!' said Cecilia, 'and she really has had to settle for them a great deal. Mamma left everything to her; and though she could get plenty of advice from our brothers-in-law, she was the one to determine.'

'Besides, she had to keep order at home,' said Janet, 'and capitally she did it. People used to wonder to see two such great rough boys under control of a gentle slender-looking young lady.'

'It must have been a wearing tiresome sort of life,' said Cecilia.

'That it was, going wandering about from watering-place to watering place. As soon as she had made friends and occupations, she was sure to be carried off somewhere else; but she submitted so cheerfully, and always made the best of things, and managed to be of use wherever she went.'

'Oh! don't you recollect, Janet, how we all worked one evening because we found the clergyman's wife at one sea place wanting some clothes for some poor emigrants? And there was the night when she sat up painting some prints to be hung up in the school.'

'She made a great deal to send to us here.'

'All that together with the constant attendance on Mamma! She used to read to her so much, and sit working in her room. She never could do anything there but work, for Mamma thought it unsociable for her to read to herself.'

'She never read except by sitting up at night. And, oh! the tiresome little evening parties! I think those must have tried her patience most of all. I remember once, when I had just come back from a visit here, pouring out to her what a miserable useless do-nothing sort of life it was. I was quite angry at the change. She was writing invitations for one of these little parties. I believe there were to be cards! I was vehement, and thought from force of contrast it was wicked, and I nearly told her so.'

'How old were you?'

'Thirteen. You know I always was a little old woman.'

'What did she answer?'

'She told me she did not think it hurt *me*, and asked me if I thought she did it for her pleasure. I was cross, and said I supposed so. Indeed, I am afraid I was foolish enough to think her frivolous and worldly compared with Constance, or with what I meant to be. The tears came into her eyes, and I was so vexed with myself, she spoke so gently and humbly. "Dear Janet," she said, "I know that this is not the best and holiest course of life; I wish I had the privilege of turning from these vain empty wearisome things, and waiting on the poor as they do at happy Dearport." She said she had had her day-dreams of holier happier ways of life, but they had been only day-dreams which had led her out of the plain path, and they had made her unworthy of the higher walks of a Christian maiden's life, so that now she was thankful that an evident duty of waiting on our mother, and pleasing her, was set before her. After that I could say no more, but only try to help her as well as my awkwardness would allow. We began to have talks, and it was very nice when she said I was growing up to be something like a Kate to her, and lessening her loneliness. I could talk to her as I could to Constance, and did not long quite so much to be at Dearport.'

'But you were there a great deal?'

'Yes. You know dear Herbert liked to call me their child, and I seemed to belong there. I never was a year without being with them, but they thought it right I should call my home with Mamma.'

145

'Then came that long year of her illness! That must have fallen very heavily on Emmie, for you know poor Mamma was so nervous, that she could not bear for anyone else to wait upon her.'

'Oh yes; Emmie was dreadfully tried, body and mind. She kept up, calm and firm to the last; but you know how ill she was at Rowthorpe afterwards, so entirely worn out and exhausted. I don't think she recovered the tone of her health for a year; everything knocked her up, and the quiet and rest seemed perfectly wonderful to her.'

'So we were divided amongst them!'

'Yes, Constance wanted to have had us both; but since dear old Lord Liddesdale's death, and Lady Frances giving up the house, Kate had so much more on her hands, that she could not teach Som and Annie herself, and was glad to have Miss Townsend, and she begged to have you too.'

'How kind they all have been! Alfred says he has so many homes, he does not know which is *home* above the others; and Katherine—she is everything to me! We have been very well off!'

'But there is one sad time we have said nothing about,' continued Janet, 'Emmeline's worst trial.'

'I thought I knew all about that,' said Cecilia gravely. 'We like to talk of dear Herbert.'

'It was not his death that I meant,' said Janet. 'It was what went before; and I think you ought to know the whole history now.'

'Tell me. This is a place to speak of him, looking down upon the town, and seeing his churches lifting up their heads. One —two—three—four—and the hospital chapel. Yes, and the three schools, and the "home for the aged," and our own dear nest of orphans.'

'Yes,' said Janet; 'but it is strange to recollect that, fourteen years ago, there was only the one old church, and the chapel in the new town. And no service but on Sunday. Now, every day from six to twelve, from three to seven, there is service going on in one or other of the churches. You are disappointed that more people are not there, but you little know how few would join when he first came! You would know what fruits he gave his life for!'

'Janet! You don't mean—?'

'Yes, I do mean. It was a hard up-hill task he had set himself, from the first. People misunderstood, and accused, and

146

thwarted him. And the poor were very bad and ungracious; but he went on his own quiet way, and was getting over the worst of the opposition, after the first six or seven years. People began to understand and trust him; and though there was plenty of bad, there was visible good to cheer one up.'

'And after the cholera time, the great difficulties with the poor were conquered.'

'But then came the trouble of troubles,' said Janet. 'Do you remember Mr. Montague?'

'The Curate who became a Roman Catholic?'

'It came out, afterwards, that his opinions had not been quite settled when he came, and he ought to have told Herbert so. He lived in the severest, most self-denying way, but he would make himself conspicuous, and give offence, just as if for the purpose of startling people. Herbert used to say he did not know what to do, and would come in saying, "I wish Montague had some sense of the ridiculous!" Then if people complained, they generally did it in such a bad spirit that Herbert was forced to take his part, though he was vexed with him for having brought it on himself. The only time Uncle Willoughby and Herbert had any difference of opinion was about Mr. Montague.'

'Lord Liddesdale used to laugh sometimes, I remember; though I never quite understood.'

'Well; then came Emmeline. You know she always meant to give herself, and all she had, up to the service of the poor or the Church. It had always been her vision through all those long years. Now Emmie liked Mr. Montague very much, and looked up to him more than she did to Herbert.'

'O Janet—impossible!'

'I'll tell you how it was. Emmeline has one of those minds that are always straining for some ideal of perfection, always seeking for something beyond. Well, Herbert was not entirely her *beau ideal* of a clergyman. I don't mean that she did not love and respect him exceedingly, but he was not quite her model. He was too like other people, he went on quietly, without going beyond the Prayer Book; and though no one ever exercised more self-denial and self-devotion than he did, he could not, with his health, live in the ascetic hermit sort of way she used to fancy. And then he was so merry! And he never would hear things said disparaging to the English Church, or her services. Mr. Montague came much nearer Emmie's notion, and they were always talking. Emmie once

147

when she was a girl had gone to a Romanist chapel, and she
had never got it out of her head. He used to lend her books,
and they conversed on those subjects till he confused her
head, like his own, and she began to think the English Church
was no more her ideal of a Church than Herbert was of a
priest.'

'O Janet, how can you say such things?'

'I am only telling them as they happened. It was a sad time
for poor Emmeline; and whenever foolish people cried out at
right doings, she fancied it was the fault of Anglicanism, and
read Romanist books till she thought her vision was to be
found in Rome. At last, suddenly, Mr. Montague went to
London, and wrote from thence to announce his being received
into the Romish Church! It was a great blow, and it did a
grievous quantity of harm. Several people, who had been his
great admirers, followed him; and many more said it only
shewed Lord Herbert's real tendencies, and flew out into
worse opposition than ever. Everything seemed unsettled;
Mr. Montague had a great influence over the younger clergy,
and Herbert was anxious about several of the curates. Mr.
Redlands was his great help and stay. Then it came out how
much harm Mr. Montague had done Emmeline. O Cecilia! you
in your school-room at Rowthorpe little thought what a time
of trouble and perplexity it was here! Even those gay spirits
of dear Herbert's gave way, and he grew grave and silent. I
don't mean that he did not often laugh, and when a great
Festival day came, he would put it all aside, and be like his
old self; but he would sit for half an hour in the evening,
thinking in silence, or look so very melancholy over his letters.
He had long talks with Emmie, and that made it worse; and
Emmeline was so very wretched, that if Constance had not been
always calm and gentle and cheerful, it would have been a
sad house. All the time Herbert was working harder than ever;
and that winter, one frosty evening when there was a funeral, he
caught cold. He was quite laid up for a fortnight, and never
lost the cough, or was well again. He did as usual all the
summer, but he grew thinner and thinner, and the troubles
went on. I remember how dead tired he used to be those hot
summer evenings, and the hollow cough. He would lie down
on the sofa a little while, quite worn out, then stir himself
up to answer one of the letters that were always pestering, or
perhaps have a Confirmation class, or be obliged to talk
matters over with one of the curates. Or poor Emmeline kept

on growing more unhappy; she worked very hard at parish work, and read half the night, and looked like a ghost.'

'Did she read all the controversy?'

'Yes. Herbert thought it right she should, as she had head enough. He used to look out books, Romish and Anglican, for her, and help her with the Latin. But, after all, it was feeling more than argument that had unsettled her for the time. She said the English Church had grown no great Saints; and oh! what a list of quiet, homely, self-denying people they answered her with; and then Herbert said how laxity and lukewarmness had indeed once fallen on our Church, but how as soon as her services and ordinances were bestowed more abundantly, her children had thriven and grown, and begun to do mighty things again. And, oh! as I looked at his bright calm eyes, and pale face with its deep red spots, and his grave melancholy smile, I felt as if Emmie had not far to seek for a true son of her Mother, with all the martyr spirit.'

'And it succeeded!' said Cecilia.

'Well,' said Janet, 'spring came, and the storm began to die away. Things grew more settled, and he was better! I thought all would be happy again, and oh! the joy that there was that Sunday, when he took part in the service again! But it had gone too far. He went to Rowthorpe, you know. She had been reading some book he had given her, and was not satisfied!'

'Lord Liddesdale always thought going abroad would have saved him,' sighed Cecilia.

'Yes; but you don't know why he would not go? He thought his name and station kept off what the young curates might not have patience to bear, and he knew he could restrain them from bringing it on themselves in his absence. He talked it over with Constance, after the doctors had advised him to go abroad; and they settled that if it was any other time, it would be right to go, but now everything might depend on his remaining at his post as long as he could. Constance told me how they had decided, and why; and though when she was alone with me she cried very much, she would not say a word against it. So dear Herbert was shut up all the winter, and did no duty, but was the head that settled everything, and he saw people, and arranged matters. He used sometimes to be very ill at night, but no one knew that but Constance.'

'Ah! and then we saw how fearfully he was changed!'

'Yes; nothing did him good, and we came home. But the battle was over; Emmeline had told him she believed the

English Church was Catholic, and that it was her duty to hold to it, and that it would only have been a wandering after castles in the air to leave it. Oh! he was very happy again, though so very weak and ill, that evening we came home. He made fun again as he used, and enjoyed everything all through those three months that he was growing worse and worse. No suffering seemed able to take away his spirits.'

'Yes, so they all said.'

'And then the people knew how they loved him! O Cecilia, I should like to tell you—only I can't—how the roughest sailor people, and the bitterest of those half-dissenters, gave up their animosity; how they enquired for him, and even some of them cried like children when they heard there was no hope. And the little children—the orphans, and the school. But I can't talk of that! I must tell you how bright his room used to be, and how pleased he was to hear all the little bits of news we brought him. Then he so much enjoyed planning St. Faith's for Constance's work and comfort for life. The last great pleasures to him were a promise of Mr. Redlands having the living, and his brother and sister coming. And then came that last day, the last Communion. I wish you had been there, and old enough, Cecilia! He saw Emmeline first, and asked her again if her faith was sure. "Oh, yes," she said, it was; and he looked up at her, and held her hand, and said, "Emmeline, on the faith of a dying priest, the Church of England is a branch of the Holy Catholic Church, and the way of Salvation is in her." She said she did believe it; and he told her once more, now her mind was settled, never to shake it or unsettle it with controversy again. "You crave after perfection, Emmeline," he said. "Do the *work* here, and fix your dreams beyond the grave; and there will be their fulfilment, without the drawbacks we have had here." And then, Cecilia, he thanked me—dear Herbert!—for having been as a daughter to him, and hoped I should go on to be the same to Constance! Then came Mr. Redlands, and the rest! After that we all kissed him, and took leave of him; and I saw him no more till it was all over.'

'Yes, I know,' said Cecilia, in a low reverent voice. 'And, oh! surely you are doing as he would have you here. Constance gathering her nursing Sisterhood about her, her house full of the orphans and the sick; and you and Emmeline among her first Sisters.'

'Emmeline says it is such a life as she used to fancy, though

150

she never took the drawbacks into her account. But she said those little sacrifices are the trial. And now it has gone on four years, so that we feel really established in our way of life.'

'And a happy way it is.'

'Yes: Emmeline is its very life and soul. Her day-dreams have turned to brighten the daily course of life, since she has been content, as Herbert taught her, to make them be of Heaven.'

Come to Her Kingdom[1]

'TAKE care! Oh, take care!'

Whisk, swish, click, click, through the little crowd at
Stokesley on a fine April afternoon, of jocund children just
let loose from school, and mothers emerging from their
meeting, collecting their progeny after the fashion of old
ewes with their lambs; Susan Merrifield in a huge, carefully
preserved brown mushroom hat, with a big basket under one
arm, and a roll of calico under the other; her sister Elizabeth
with a book in one hand, and a packet of ambulance illustrations; the Vicar, Mr. Doyle, and his sister likewise loaded,
talking to them about the farmer's wedding of the morning, for
which the bells had been ringing fitfully all day, and had just
burst out again. Such was the scene, through which, like a
flash, spun a tricycle, from which a tiny curly-haired being in
knickerbockers was barely saved by his mother's seizing him
by one arm.

'A tricycle!' exclaimed the Vicar.

'A woman! Oh!' cried Susan in horror, 'and she's stopping
—at the Gaps. Oh!'

'My dear Susie, you must have seen ladies on tricycles
before,' whispered her sister.

'No, indeed, I am thankful to say I have not! If it should be
Miss Arthuret!' said Susan, with inexpressible tones in her
voice.

'She was bowing right and left,' said the Vicar, a little
maliciously; 'depend upon it, she thought this was a welcome
from the rural population.'

'Hark! here's something coming.'

The Bonchamp fly came rattling up, loaded with luggage,
and with a quiet lady in black seated in it, which stopped at
the same gate.

'The obedient mother, no doubt,' said Elizabeth. 'She looks
like a lady.'

[1] In the Christmas number of *The Monthly Packet*, 1889; reprinted 1890
in *More Bywords*.

There had been a good deal of excitement at Stokesley about the property known by the pleasing name of the Gap. An old gentleman had lived there for many years, always in a secluded state, and latterly imbecile, and on his death in the previous year no one had for some time appeared as heir; but it became known that the inheritrix was a young lady, a great niece, living with a widowed mother in one of the large manufacturing towns in the north of England. Her father had been a clergyman and had died when she was an infant. That was all that was known, and as the house had become almost uninhabitable, the necessary repairs had prevented the heiress from taking possession all this time. It was not a very large inheritance, only comprising a small farm, the substantial village shop, four or five cottages, and a moderate-sized house and grounds, where the neglected trees had grown to strange irregular proportions, equally with the income, which, owing to the outgoings being small, had increased to about £800 or £900 a year, and of course it was a subject of much anxiety with Admiral Merrifield's family to know what sort of people the new-comers would prove.

Of the large family only the two eldest daughters were at home; Susan, now nearly forty, had never left it, but had been the daughter of all work at home and lady of all work to the parish ever since she had emerged from the schoolroom; her apricot complexion showing hardly any change, and such as there was never perceived by her parents. The Admiral, still a light, wiry, hale man, as active as ever, with his hands full of county, parish, and farming business; and his wife a thoroughly homely yet ingrained lady, an invalid for many years, but getting into that health which is 'la jeunesse de la vieillesse'.

Elizabeth had, from twenty-five to thirty-two, been spared from home by her father to take care of his step-mother in London, where she had beguiled her time with a certain amount of authorship under a *nom de plume*, and had been introduced to some choice society both through her literary abilities and her family connections.

Four years previous the old lady had died, leaving her a legacy, which, together with her gains, would have enabled her to keep such a home in town as to remain in touch with the world to which she had been introduced; but she had never lost her Stokesley heart enough for the temptation to outweigh the disappointment she would have caused at home, and the satisfaction and rest of being among her own people. So she only went up for an occasional visit, and had become the brightness of the house, and Susan's beloved partner in all her works.

Her father, who understood better than did her mother and sister what she had given up, had insisted on her having a sitting room to herself, which she embellished with the personal possessions she had accumulated, and where she pursued her own avocations in the forenoon, often indeed interrupted, but never showing, and not often feeling, that it was to her hindrance, and indeed the family looked on her work sufficiently as a profession, not only to acquiesce but to have a certain complacency in it, though it was a kind of transparent fiction that MESA was an anagram of her initials and that of Stokesley. Her mother at any rate believed that none of the neighbours guessed at any such thing.

Stokesley was a good deal out of the world, five miles from the station at Bonchamp, over hilly, stony roads, so that the cyclist movement had barely reached it; the neighbourhood was sparse, and Mrs. Merrifield's health had not been conducive to visiting, any more than was her inclination, so that there was a little agitation about first calls.

The new-comers appeared at church on Sunday at all the services. A bright-faced girl of one-and-twenty, with little black eyes like coals of fire, a tight ulster, like a riding habit, and a small billy-cock hat, rather dismayed those who still held that bonnets ought to be the Sunday gear of all beyond childhood; but the mother in rich black silk was unexceptionable.

Refusing to be marshalled up the aisle to the seat which persistent tradition assigned to the Gap in the aristocratic quarter, daughter and mother (it was impossible not thus to call them) sat themselves down on the first vacant place, close to a surviving white smock frock, and blind to the bewildered glances of his much bent friend in velveteen, who, hobbling in next after, found himself displaced and separated alike from his well-thumbed prayer and hymn book and the companion who found the places for him.

'It ain't fitty like,' said the old man confidentially to Susan, 'nor the ladies wouldn't like it when we comes in with our old coats all of a muck with wet.'

'The principle is right,' said Bessie, when this was repeated to her; 'but practice ought to wait till native manners and customs are learnt.'

The two sisters offered to save their mother the first visit—

leave her card, or make her excuses; but Mrs. Merrifield held that a card thus left savoured of deceit, and that the deed must be womanfully done in person. But she would not wait till the horses could be spared, saying that for near village neighbours it was more friendly to go down in her donkey chair; and so she did, Bessie driving her, and the Admiral walking with them.

The Gap had, ever since Bessie could remember, been absolutely shrouded in trees, its encircling wall hidden in ivy bushes, over which laburnums, lilacs, pink thorns, and horse chestnuts towered; and the drive from the seldom-opened gate was almost obstructed by the sweeping arms of laurels and larches.

It was obstructed now, but by these same limbs lying amputated; and 'chop, chop!' was heard in the distance.

'Oh, the Arbutus!' sighed Bessie.

'Clearing was much needed,' said her father, with a man's propensity for the axe.

The donkey, however, thought it uncanny, 'upon the pivot of his skull, turned round his long left ear,' and planted his feet firmly. Mrs. Merrifield, deprecating the struggle by which her husband would on such occasions enforce discipline, begged to get out; and while this was going on, the ulstered young lady, with a small axe in hand, came, as it were, to the rescue, and, while the donkey was committed to a small boy, explained hastily, 'So overgrown, there is nothing to be done but to let in light and air. My mother is at home,' she added; 'she will be happy to see you,' and, conducting them in with complete self-possession—rather, as it occurred to Bessie, as the Queen might have led the way to the Duchess of Kent, though there was a perfect simplicity and evident enjoyment about her that was very prepossessing, and took off the edge of the sense of conceit. Besides, the palace was, to London eyes at least, so little to boast of, with the narrow little box of a wooden porch, the odd one-sided vestibule, and the tiny ante-room with the worn carpet; but the drawing-room, in spite of George IV furniture, was really pretty, with French windows opening on a well-mown lawn, and fresh importations of knickknacks, and vases of wild flowers, which made it look inhabited and pleasant. There was no one there, and the young lady proceeded to fetch her mother; and the unguarded voice was caught by Bessie's quick ears from the window.

'Here are Admiral and Mrs. Merrifield, and one daughter.

155

Come along, little mammy! Worthy, homely old folks—just in your line.'

To Bessie's relief, she perceived that this was wholly unheard by her father and mother. And there was no withstanding the eager, happy, shy looks of the mother, whose whole face betrayed that after many storms she had come into a haven of peace, and that she was proud to owe it to her daughter.

A few words showed that mother and daughter were absolutely enchanted with Stokesley, their own situation, and one another, the young lady evidently all the more because she perceived so much to be done.

'Everything wants improving. It is so choked up,' she said, 'one wants to let in the light.'

'There are a good many trees,' said the Admiral, while Bessie suspected that she meant figuratively as well as literally; and as the damsel was evidently burning to be out at her clearing operations again, and had never parted with her axe, the Admiral offered to go with her and tell her about the trees, for, as he observed, she could hardly judge of those not yet out in leaf.

She accepted him, though Bessie shrewdly suspected that the advice would be little heeded, and, not fancying the wet grass and branches, nor the demolition of old friends, she did not follow the pair, but effaced herself, and listened with much interest to the two mothers, who sat on the sofa with their heads together. Either Mrs. Merrifield was wonderful in inspiring confidence, or it was only too delightful to Mrs. Arthuret to find a listener of her own standing to whom to pour forth her full heart of thankfulness and delight in her daughter. 'Oh, it is too much!' occurred so often in her talk that, if it had not been said with liquid eyes, choking voice, and hands clasped in devout gratitude, it would have been tedious; but Mrs. Merrifield thoroughly went along with it, and was deeply touched.

The whole story, as it became known partly in these confidences, partly afterwards, was this. The good lady, who had struck the family at first as a somewhat elderly mother for so young a daughter, had been for many years a governess, engaged all the time to a curate, who only obtained a small district incumbency in a town, after wear and tear, waiting and anxiety, had so exhausted him that the second winter brought on bronchitis, and he scarcely lived to see his little daughter, Arthurine. The mother had struggled on upon a pittance eked out with such music teaching as she could procure, with her little girl for her sole care, joy, and pride— a child who, as she declared, had never given her one moment's pang or uneasiness.

'Poor mamma, could she say that of any one of her nine?' thought Bessie; and Mrs. Merrifield made no such attempt.

Arthurine had brought home all prizes, all distinctions at the High School, but—here was the only disappointment of her life—a low fever had prevented her trying for a scholarship at Girton. In consideration, however, of her great abilities and high qualities, as well as out of the great kindness of the committee, she had been made an assistant to one of the class mistresses, and had worked on with her own studies, till the wonderful tidings came of the inheritance that had fallen to her quite unexpectedly; for since her husband's death Mrs. Arthuret had known nothing of his family, and while he was alive there were too many between him and the succession for the chance to occur to him as possible. The relief and blessing were more than the good lady could utter. All things are comparative, and to one whose assured income had been £70 a year, £800 was unbounded wealth; to one who had spent her life in schoolrooms and lodgings, the Gap was a lordly demesne.

'And what do you think was the first thing my sweet child said?' added Mrs. Arthuret, with her eyes glittering through tears. 'Mammy, you shall never hear the scales again, and you shall have the best Mocha coffee every day of your life.'

Bessie felt that after this she must like the sweet child, though sweetness did not seem to her the predominant feature in Arthurine.

After the pathos to which she had listened there was somewhat of a comedy to come, for the ladies had spent the autumn abroad, and had seen and enjoyed much. 'It was a perfect feast to see how Arthurine entered into it all,' said the mother. 'She was never at a loss, and explained it all to me. Besides, perhaps you have seen her article?'

'I beg your pardon.'

'Her article in the *Kensington*. It attracted a great deal of attention, and she has had many compliments.'

'Oh! the *Kensington Magazine*,' said Mrs. Merrifield, rather uneasily, for she was as anxious that Bessie should not be suspected of writing in the said periodical as the other mother was that Arthurine should have the fame of her contributions.

157

'Do you take it?' asked Mrs. Arthuret, 'for we should be very glad to lend it to you.'

A whole pile was on the table, and Mrs. Merrifield looked at them with feeble thanks and an odd sort of conscious dread, though she could with perfect truth have denied either 'taking it' or reading it.

Bessie came to her relief. 'Thank you,' she said; 'we do, some of us have it. Is your daughter's article signed A. A., and doesn't it describe a boarding-house on the Italian lakes? I thought it very clever and amusing.'

Mrs. Arthuret's face lighted up. 'Oh, yes, my dear,' slipped out in her delight. 'And do you know, it all came of her letter to one of the High School ladies, who is sister to the sub-editor, such a clever superior girl! She read it to the headmistress and all, and they agreed that it was too good to be lost, and Arthurine copied it out and added to it, and he—Mr. Jarrett —said it was just what he wanted—so full of information and liveliness—and she is writing some more for him.'

Mrs. Merrifield was rather shocked, but she felt that she herself was in a glass house, was, in fact, keeping a literary daughter, so she only committed herself to 'She is very young.'

'Only one-and-twenty,' returned Mrs. Arthuret triumphantly, 'but then she has had such advantages, and made such use of them. Everything seems to come at once, though, perhaps, it is unthankful to say to. Of course, it is no object now, but I could not help thinking what it would have been to us to have discovered this talent of hers at the time when we could hardly make both ends meet.'

'She will find plenty of use for it,' said Mrs. Merrifield, who, as the wife of a country squire and the mother of nine children, did not find it too easy to make her ends meet upon a larger income.

'Oh, yes! indeed she will, the generous child. She is full of plans for the regeneration of the village.'

Poor Mrs. Merrifield! this was quite too much for her. She thought it irreverent to apply the word in any save an ecclesiastical sense; nor did she at all desire to have the parish, which was considered to be admirably worked by the constituted authorities, 'regenerated,' whatever that might mean, by a young lady of one-and-twenty. She rose up and observed to her daughter that she saw papa out upon the lawn, and she thought it was time to go home.

Mrs. Arthuret came out with them, and found what Bessie

could only regard as a scene of desolation. Though gentlemen, as a rule, have no mercy on trees, and ladies are equally inclined to cry, 'Woodman, spare that tree,' the rule was reversed, for Miss Arthuret was cutting, and ordering cutting all round her ruthlessly with something of the pleasure of a child in breaking a new toy to prove that it is his own, scarcely listening when the Admiral told her what the trees were, and how beautiful in their season; while even as to the evergreens, she did not know a yew from a cedar, and declared that she must get rid of this horrid old laurustinus, while she lopped away at a Portugal laurel. Her one idea seemed to be that it was very unwholesome to live in a house surrounded with trees; and the united influence of the Merrifields, working on her mother by representing what would be the absence of shade in a few months' time, barely availed to save the life of the big cedar; while the great rhododendron, wont to present a mountain of shining leaves and pale purple blossoms every summer, was hewn down without remorse as an awful old laurel, and left a desolate brown patch in its stead.

'Is it an emblem,' thought Bessie, 'of what she would like to do to all of us poor old obstructions?'

After all, Mrs. Merrifield could not help liking the gentle mother by force of sympathy; and the Admiral was somewhat fascinated by the freshness and impetuosity of the damsel, as elderly men are wont to be with young girls who amuse them with what they are apt to view as an original form of the silliness common to the whole female world except their own wives, and perhaps their daughters; and Bessie was extremely amused, and held her peace, as she had been used to do in London. Susan was perhaps the most annoyed and indignant. She was presiding over seams and button-holes the next afternoon at school, when the mother and daughter walked in; and the whole troop started to their feet and curtsied.

'Don't make them stand! I hate adulation. Sit down, please. Where's the master?'

'In the boys' school, ma'am,' said the mistress, uncomfortably indicating the presence of Miss Merrifield, who felt herself obliged to come forward and shake hands.

'Oh! so you have separate schools. Is not that a needless expense?'

'It has always been so,' returned Susan quietly.

'Board? No? Well, no doubt you are right; but I suppose it is at a sacrifice of efficiency. Have you cookery classes?'

'We have no apparatus, and the girls go out too early for it to be of much use.'

'Ah, that's a mistake. Drawing?'

'The boys draw.'

'I shall go and see them. Not the girls? They look orderly enough; but are they intelligent? Well, I shall look in and examine them on their special subjects if they have any. I suppose not.'

'Only class. Grammar and needle-work.'

'I see, the old routine. Quite the village school.'

'It is very nice work,' put in Mrs. Arthuret, who had been looking at it.

'Oh, yes, it always is when everything is sacrificed to it. Good-morning, I shall see more of you, Mrs. —— ahem.'

'Please, ma'am, should I tell her that she is not a school manager?' inquired the mistress, somewhat indignantly, when the two ladies had departed.

'You had better ask the Vicar what to do,' responded Susan.

The schoolmaster, on his side, seemed to have had so much advice and offers of assistance in lessons on history, geography, and physical science, that he had been obliged to refer her to the managers, and explain that till the next inspection he was bound to abide by the timetable.

'Ah, well, I will be one of the managers another year.'

So she told the Vicar, who smiled and said, 'We must elect you.'

'I am sure much ought to be done. It is mere waste to have two separate schools, when a master can bring the children on so much better in the higher subjects.'

'Mrs. Merrifield and the rest of us are inclined to think that what stands highest of all with us, is endangered by mixed schools,' said Mr. Doyle.

'Oh!' Arthurine opened her eyes; 'but education does all *that.*'

'Education does, but knowledge is not wisdom. Susan Merrifield's influence has done more for our young women than the best class teaching could do.'

'Oh, but the Merrifields are all so *bornés* and homely; they stand in the way of all culture.'

'Indeed,' said the Vicar, who had in his pocket a very favourable review of MESA's new historical essay.

'Surely an old-fashioned squire and Lady Bountiful and their very narrow daughters should not be allowed to prevent improvement, pauperise the place, and keep it in its old grooves.'

'Well, we shall see what you think by the time you have lived here long enough to be eligible for—what?'

'School manager, guardian of the poor,' cried Arthurine.

'We shall see,' repeated the Vicar. 'Good-morning.'

He asked Bessie's leave to disclose who MESA was.

'Oh, don't!' she cried, 'it would spoil the fun! Besides, mamma would not like it, which is a better reason.'

There were plenty of books, old and new, in Bessie's room, magazines and reviews, but they did not come about the house much, unless any of the Rockstone cousins or the younger generation were staying there, or her brother David had come for a rest of mind and body. Between housekeeping, gardening, parish work, and pottering, Mrs. Merrifield and Susan never had time for reading, except that Susan thought it her duty to keep something improving in hand, which generally lasted her six weeks on a moderate average. The Admiral found quite reading enough in the newspapers, pamphlets, and business publications; and their neighbours, the Greville family, were chiefly devoted to hunting and lawn-tennis, so that there was some reason in Mrs. Arthuret's lamentation to the Vicar that dear Arthurine did so miss intellectual society, such as she had been used to with the high school mistresses—two of whom had actually been at Girton!

'Does she not get on with Bessie Merrifield?' he asked.

'Miss Bessie has a very sweet face; Arthurine did say she seemed well informed, and more intelligent than her sister. Perhaps Arthurine might take her up. It would be such an advantage to the poor girl.'

'Which!' was on Mr. Doyle's tongue, but he restrained it, and only observed that Bessie had lived for a good many years in London.

'So I understood,' said Arthurine, 'but with an old grandmother and that is quite as bad as if it was in the country; but I will see about it. I might get up a debating society, or one for studying German.'

In the meantime, Arthurine decided on improving and embellishing the parish with a drinking-fountain, and meeting Bessie one afternoon in the village, she started the idea.

'But,' said Bessie, 'there is a very good supply. Papa saw that good water was accessible to all the houses in the village street ten years ago, and the outlying ones have wells, and there's the brook for the cattle.'

'I am sure every village should have a fountain and a trough, and I shall have it here, instead of this dirty corner.'

'Can you get the ground?'

'Oh, anyone would give ground for such a purpose! Whose is it?'

'Mr. Grice's, at Butter End.'

The next time Susan and Bessie encountered Arthurine, she began—

'Can you, or Admiral Merrifield, do nothing with that horrid old Grice! Never was any one so pig-headed and stupid.'

'What? He won't part with the land you want!'

'No; I wrote to him and got no answer. Then I wrote again, and I got a peaked-hand sort of note that his wife wrote, I should think. "Mr. Grice presented his compliments" (compliments indeed!), "and had no intention of parting with any part of Spragg's portion." Well, then I called, to represent what a benefit it would be to the parish, and his own cattle, and what to you think the old brute said, "That there was a great deal too much done for the parish already, and he wouldn't have no hand in setting up the labourers, who were quite impudent enough already. Well I saw it was of no use to talk to an old wretch like that about social movements and equal rights, so I only put the question whether having pure water easily accessible would not tend to make them better behaved and less impudent as he called it, upon which he broke out into a tirade. "He didn't hold with cold water and teetotal, not he. Why, it had come to *that*—that there was no such thing as getting a fair day's work out of a labouring man with their temperance, and their lectures, and their schools, and their county councils and what not!" Really I had read of such people, but I hardly believed they still existed.'

'Grice is very old, and the regular old sort of farmer,' said Bessie.

'But could not the Admiral persuade him or Mr. Doyle?'

'Oh, no,' said Susan, 'it would be of no use. He was just as bad about a playground for the boys, though it would have prevented their being troublesome elsewhere.'

'Besides,' added Bessie, 'I am sure papa would say that there is no necessity. He had the water analysed, and it is quite good, and plenty of it.'

'Well, I shall see what can be done.'

'She thinks us as bad as old Grice,' said Susan, as they saw her walking away in a determined manner.

The next thing that was heard was the Admiral coming in from the servants' hall, whither he had been summoned by 'Please, sir, James Hodd wishes to speak to you.'

'What is this friend of yours about, Bessie?'

'What friend, papa?'

'Why, this Miss Arthur—what d'ye call her?' said the Admiral (who on the whole was much more attracted by her than were his daughters). 'Here's a deputation from her tenant, James Hodd, with "Please, sir, I wants to know if 'tis allowed to turn folks out of their houses as they've paid rent for reg'lar with a week's notice, when they pays by the year." '

'You don't mean it!' exclaimed Mrs. Merrifield and Susan together.

'Poor old Mrs. West,' said the mother.

'And all the Tibbinses!' exclaimed Susan. 'She can't do it, can she, papa?'

'Certainly not, without the proper notice, and so I told James, and that the notice she had sent down to him was so much waste-paper.'

'So at least she has created a village Hampden,' said Bessie, 'though, depend upon it, she little supposes herself to be the petty tyrant.'

'I must go and explain to her, I suppose, to-morrow morning,' said the Admiral.

However, he had scarcely reached his own gate before the ulstered form was seen rushing up to him.

'Oh! Admiral Merrifield, good-morning, I was coming to ask you——'

'And I was coming to you.'

'Oh! Admiral, is it really so—as that impudent man told me—that those horrid people can't be got out of those awful tumble-down, unhealthy places for all that immense time?'

'Surely he was not impudent to you? He was only asserting his right. The cottages were taken by the year, and you have no choice but to give six months' notice. I hope he was not disrespectful.'

'Well, no—I can't say that he was, though I don't care for those cap-in-hand ways of your people here. But at any rate, he says he won't go—no, not any of them, though I offered to pay them up to the end of the time, and now I must put off

163

my beautiful plans. I was drawing them all yesterday morning —two model cottages on each side, and the drinking-fountain in the middle. I brought them up to show you. Could you get the people to move out? I would promise them to return after the rebuilding.'

'Very nice drawings. Yes—yes—very kind intentions.'

'Then can't you persuade them?'

'But my dear young lady, have you thought what is to become of them in the meantime?'

'Why, live somewhere else! People in Smokeland were always shifting about.'

'Yes—those poor little town tenements are generally let on short terms and are numerous enough. But here—where are the vacant cottages for your four families? Hodd with his five children, Tibbins with eight or nine, Mrs. West and her widow daughter and three children, and the Porters with a bed-ridden father?'

'They are dreadfully over-crowded. Is there really no place?'

'Probably not, nearer than those trumpery new tenements at Bonchamp. That would be eight miles to be tramped to the men's work, and the Wests would lose the washing and charing that maintains them.'

'Then do you think it can never be done? See how nice my plans are!'

'Oh! yes, very pretty drawings, but you don't allow much outlet.'

'I thought you had allotments, and that they would do, and I mean to get rid of the pig-sties.'

'A most unpopular proceeding, I warn you.'

'There's nothing more unsanitary than a pig-sty.'

'That depends on how it is kept. And may I ask, do you mean also to dispense with staircases?'

'Oh! I forgot. But do you really mean to say that I can never carry out my improvements, and that these people must live all herded together till everybody is dead?'

'Not quite that,' said the Admiral, laughing; 'but most improvements require patience and a little experience of the temper and habits of the people. There are cottages worse than these. I think two of them have four rooms, and the Wests and Porters do not require so much. If you built one or two elsewhere, and moved the people into them, or waited for a vacant one, you might carry out some of your plans— gradually.'

'And my fountain?'

'I am not quite sure, but I am afraid your cottages are on that stratum where you could not bring the water without great expense.'

Arthurine controlled herself enough for a civil 'Good-morning!' but she shed tears as she walked home and told her pitying mother that she was thwarted on every side, and that nobody could comprehend her.

The meetings for German reading were, however, contrived chiefly—little as Arthurine guessed it—by the influence of Bessie Merrifield. The two Greville girls and Mr. Doyle's sister, together with the doctor's young wife, two damsels from the next parish, and a friend or two that the Arthurets had made at Bonchamp, formed an imposing circle—to begin.

'Oh, not on Wilhelm Tell!' cried Arthurine. 'It might as well be the alphabet at once.'

However, the difficulties in the way of books, and consideration for general incompetency, reduced her to Wilhelm Tell, and she began with a lecture first on Schiller, and then upon Switzerland, and on the legend; but when Bessie Merrifield put in a word of such history and criticisms as were not in the High School Manual, she was sure everything else must be wrong—'Fraülein Blümenbach never said so, and she was an admirable German scholar.'

Miss Doyle went so far as to declare she should not go again to see Bessie Merrifield so silenced, sitting by after the first saying nothing, but only with a little laugh in her eyes.

'But,' said Bessie, 'it is such fun to see any person having it so entirely her own way—like Macaulay, so cocksure of everything—and to see those Bonchamp girls—Mytton is their name—so entirely adoring her.'

'I am sorry she has taken up with those Myttons,' said Miss Doyle.

'So am I,' answered Susan.

'You too, Susie,' exclaimed Bessie—'you, who never have a word to say against anyone!'

'I dare say they are very good girls,' said Susan; 'but they are——'

'Under-bred,' put in Miss Doyle in the pause. 'And how they flatter!'

'I think the raptures are genuine gush,' said Bessie; 'but that is so much the worse for Arthurine. Is there any positive harm in the family beyond the second-rate tone?'

'It was while you were away,' said Susan; 'but their father somehow behaved very ill about old Colonel Mytton's will— at least papa thought so, and never wished us to visit them.'

'He was thought to have used unfair influence on the old gentleman,' said Miss Doyle; 'but the daughters are so young that probably they had no part in it. Only it gives a general distrust of the family; and the sons are certainly very undesirable young men.'

'It is unlucky,' said Bessie, 'that we can do nothing but inflict a course of snubbing, in contrast with a course of admiration.'

'I am sure I don't want to snub her,' said good-natured Susan. 'Only when she does want to do such queer things, how can it be helped?'

It was quite true, Mrs. and Miss Arthuret had been duly called upon and invited about by the neighbourhood; but it was a scanty one, and they had not wealth and position enough to compensate for the girl's self-assertion and literary pretensions. It was not a superior or intellectual society, and, as the Rockstone Merrifields laughingly declared, it was fifty years behindhand, and where Bessie Merrifield, for the sake of the old stock and her meek bearing of her success—nay, her total ignoring of her literary honours—would be accepted. Arthurine, half her age, and a new-comer, was disliked for the pretensions which her mother innocently pressed on the world. Simplicity and complacency were taken for arrogance, and the mother and daughter were kept upon formal terms of civility by all but the Merrifields, who were driven into discussion and opposition by the young lady's attempts at reformations in the parish.

It was the less wonder that they made friends where their intimacy was sought and appreciated. There was nothing underbred about themselves, both were ladies ingrain, though Arthurine was abrupt and sometimes obtrusive, but they had not lived a life such as to render them sensitive to the lack of fine edges in others, and were quite ready to be courted by those who gave the meed of appreciation that both regarded as Arthurine's just portion.

Mr. Mytton had been in India, and had come back to look after his old relation to whom he and his wife had paid assiduous attention, and had been so rewarded as to excite the suspicion and displeasure of the rest of the family. The prize had not been a great one, and the prosperity of the family was further diminished by the continual failures of the ne'er-do-well sons, so that they had to make the best of the dull, respectable old house they had inherited, in the dull, respectable old street of the dull, respectable old town. Daisy and Pansy Mytton were, however, bright girls, and to them Arthurine Arthuret was a sort of realised dream of romance, raised suddenly to the pinnacle of all to which they had ever durst aspire.

After meeting her at a great 'omnium gatherum' garden party, the acquaintance flourished. Arthurine was delighted to give the intense pleasure that the freedom of a country visit afforded to the sisters, and found in them the contemporaries her girl nature had missed.

They were not stupid, though they had been poorly educated, and were quite willing to be instructed by her and to read all she told them. In fact, she was their idol, and a very gracious one. Deeply did they sympathise in all her sufferings from the impediments cast in her way at Stokesley.

Indeed, the ladies there did not meet her so often on their own ground for some time, and were principally disturbed by reports of her doings at Bonchamp, where she played at cricket, and at hockey, gave a course of lectures on physiology, presided at a fancy-dress bazaar for the schools as Lady Jane Grey, and was on two or three committees. She travelled by preference on her tricycle, though she had a carriage, chiefly for the sake of her mother, who was still in a state of fervent admiration, even though perhaps a little worried at times by being hurried past her sober paces.

The next shock that descended on Stokesley was that, in great indignation, a cousin sent the Merrifields one of those American magazines which are read and contributed to by a large proportion of English. It contained an article called 'The Bide-as-we-bes and parish of Stick-stodge-cum-Cadgerley,' and written with the same sort of clever, flippant irony as the description of the mixed company in the boarding-house on the Lago Maggiore.

There was the parish embowered, or rather choked, in trees, the orderly mechanical routine, the perfect self-satisfaction of all parties, and their imperviousness to progress—the two squires, one a fox-hunter, the other a general reposing on his laurels—the school where everything was subordinated to learning to behave oneself lowly and reverently to all one's betters, and to do one's duty in that state of life to which it *has* pleased Heaven to call one—the horror at her tricycle, the impossibility of improvement, the predilection for farmyard odours, the adherence to tumble-down dwellings, the contempt of drinking fountains—all had their meed of exaggeration not without drollery.

The two ancient spinsters, daughters to the general, with their pudding baskets, buttonholes, and catechisms, had their full share—dragooning the parish into discipline—the younger having so far marched with the century as to have indited a few little tracts of the Goody Two-Shoes order, and therefore being mentioned by her friends with 'bated breath as something formidable, 'who writes,' although when brought to the test, her cultivation was of the vaguest, most discursive order. Finally, there was a sketch of the heavy dinner party which had welcomed the strangers, and of the ponderous county magnates and their wives who had been invited, and the awe that their broad and expansive ladies expected to impress, and how one set talked of their babies, and the other of G.F.S. girls, and the gentlemen seemed to be chiefly occupied in abusing their M.P. and his politics. Altogether, it was given as a lesson to Americans of the still feudal and stationary state of country districts in poor old England.

'What do you think of this, Bessie?' exclaimed Admiral Merrifield. 'We seem to have got a young firebrand in the midst of us.'

'Oh, papa! have you got that thing? What a pity!'

'You don't mean that you have seen it before?'

'Yes; one of my acquaintances in London sent it to me.'

'And you kept it to yourself?'

'I thought it would only vex you and mamma. Who sent it to you?'

'Anne did, with all the passages marked. What a horrid little treacherous baggage!'

'I dare say we are very tempting. For once we see ourselves as others see us! And you see 'tis American.'

'All the worse, holding us, who have done our best to welcome her hospitably, up to the derision of the Yankees!'

'But you won't take any notice.'

'Certainly not, ridiculous little puss, except to steer as clear of her as possible for fear she should be taking her observations. "Bide as we be," why, 'tis the best we can do. She can't pick a hole in your mother though, Bess. It would have been hard to have forgiven her that! You're not such an aged spinster.'

'It is very funny, though,' said Bessie; 'just enough exaggeration to give it point! Here is her interview with James Hodd.'

Whereat the Admiral could not help laughing heartily, and then he picked himself out as the general, laughed again, and said: 'Naughty girl! Bess, I'm glad that is not your line. Little tracts—Goody Two-Shoes! Why, what did that paper say of your essay, Miss Bess? That it might stand a comparison with Helps, wasn't it?'

'And I wish I was likely to enjoy such lasting fame as Goody Two-Shoes,' laughed Bessie, in a state of secret exultation at this bit of testimony from her father.

Mrs. Merrifield, though unscathed, was much more hurt and annoyed than either her husband or her daughter, especially at Susan and Bessie being termed old maids. She *did* think it very ungrateful, and wondered how Mrs. Arthuret could have suffered such a thing to be done. Only the poor woman was quite foolish about her daughter—could have had no more authority than a cat. 'So much for modern education.'

But it was not pleasant to see the numbers of the magazine on the counters at Bonchamp, and to know there were extracts in the local papers, and still less to be indignantly condoled with by neighbours who expressed their intention of 'cutting' the impertinent girl. They were exactly the 'old fogies' Arthurine cared for the least, yet whose acquaintance was the most creditable, and the home party at Stokesley were unanimous in entreating others to ignore the whole and treat the new-comers as if nothing had happened.

They themselves shook hands, and exchanged casual remarks as if nothing were amiss, nor was the subject mentioned, except that Mrs. Arthuret contrived to get a private interview with Mrs. Merrifield.

'Oh! dear Mrs. Merrifield, I am so grieved, and so is Arthurine. We were told that the Admiral was so excessively angry, and he is so kind. I could not bear for him to think Arthurine meant anything personal.'

'Indeed,' said Mrs. Merrifield, rather astonished.

'But is he so very angry?—for it is all a mistake.'

'He laughs, and so does Bessie,' said the mother.

'Laughs! Does he? But I do assure you Arthurine never meant any place in particular, she only intended to describe the way things go on in country districts, don't you understand? She was talking one day at the Myttons', and they were all so much amused that they wanted her to write it down. She read it one evening when they were with us, and they declared it was too good not to be published—and almost before she knew it, Fred Mytton's literary friend got hold of it and took it to the agency of this paper. But indeed, indeed, she never thought of its being considered personal, and is as vexed as possible at the way in which it has been taken up. She has every feeling about your kindness to us, and she was so shocked when Pansy Mytton told us that the Admiral was furious.'

'Whoever told Miss Mytton so made a great mistake. The Admiral only is—is—amused—as you know gentlemen will be at young girl's little—little scrapes,' returned Mrs. Merrifield, longing to say 'impertinences,' but refraining, and scarcely believing what nevertheless was true, that Arthurine did not know how personal she had been, although her mother said it all over again twice. Bessie, however, did believe it, from experience of resemblances where she had never intended direct portraiture; and when there was a somewhat earnest invitation to a garden party at the Gap, the Merrifields not only accepted for themselves, but persuaded as many of their neighbours as they could to countenance the poor girl. 'There is something solid at the bottom in spite of all the effervescence,' said Bessie.

It was late in the year for a garden party, being on the 2nd of October, but weather and other matters had caused delays, and the Indian summer had begun with warm sun, and exquisite tints. 'What would not the maple and the liquid amber have been by this time,' thought the sisters, 'if they had been spared.' Some of the *petit noblesse*, however, repented of their condescension when they saw how little it was appreciated. Mrs. Arthuret, indeed, was making herself the best hostess that a lady who had served no apprenticeship could be to all alike, but Arthurine or 'Atty,' as Daisy and Pansy were heard shouting to her—all in white flannels, a man all but the petticoats—seemed to be absorbed in a little court of the second-rate people of Bonchamp, some whom, as Mrs. Greville and Lady Smithson agreed, they had never expected to meet. She was laughing and talking eagerly, and by-and-by ran up to Bessie, exclaiming in a patronising tone—

'Oh! my dear Miss Bessie, let me introduce you to Mr.

Foxholm—such a clever literary man. He knows everybody—all about everybody and everything. It would be such an advantage! And he has actually made me give him my autograph! Only think of that!'

Bessie thought of her own good luck in being anonymous, but did not express it, only saying, 'Autograph hunters are a great nuisance. I know several people who find them so.'

'Yes, he said it was one of the penalties of fame that one must submit to,' returned Miss Arthuret, with a delighted laugh of consciousness.

Bessie rejoiced that none of her own people were near to see the patronising manner in which Arthurine introduced her to Mr. Foxholm, a heavily bearded man, whose eyes she did not at all like, and who began by telling her that he felt as if he had crossed the Rubicon, and entering an Arcadia, had found a Parnassus.

Bessie looked to see whether the highly educated young lady detected the malaprop for the Helicon, but Arthurine was either too well-bred or too much exalted to notice either small slips, or even bad taste, and she stood smiling and blushing complacently. However, just then Susan hurried up. 'Bessie, you are wanted. Here's a card. The gentleman sent it in, and papa asked me to find you.'

Bessie opened her eyes. The card belonged to the editor of one of the most noted magazines of the day, but one whose principles she did not entirely approve. What could be coming?

Her father was waiting for her.

'Well, Miss Bessie,' he said, laughing, 'Jane said the gentleman was very urgent in wanting to know when you would be in. An offer, eh?'

'Perhaps it is an offer, but not of *that* sort,' said Bessie, and she explained what the unliterary Admiral had not understood. He answered with a whistle.

'Shall you do it, Bessie?'

'I think not,' she said quietly.

The editor was found waiting for her, with many apologies for bringing her home, and the Admiral was so delighted with his agreeableness as hardly to be able to tear himself away to bring home his wife.

The offer was, as Bessie expected of excellent terms for a serial story, terms that proved to her what was her own value, and in which she saw education for her sister Anne's eldest boy.

'Of course, there would be a certain adaptation to our readers.'

She knew what that meant, and there was that in her face which drew forth the assurance.

'Of course nothing you would not wish to say would be required, but it would be better not to press certain subjects.'

'I understand,' said Bessie. 'I doubt——'

'Perhaps you will think it over.'

Bessie's first thought was, 'If I forget thee, O Jerusalem, then let my right hand forget her cunning.' That had been the inward motto of her life. Her second was 'Little Sam! David's mission room!' There was no necessity to answer at once, and she knew the periodical rather by report than by reading, so she accepted the two numbers that were left with her, and promised to reply in a week. It was a question on which to take counsel with her father, and with her own higher conscience and heavenly Guide.

The Admiral, though not much given to reading for its own sake, and perhaps inclined to think ephemeral literature the more trifling because his little daughter was a great light there, was anything but a dull man, and had an excellent judgement. So Bessie, with all the comfort of a woman still with a wise father's head over her, decided to commit the matter to him. He was somewhat disappointed at finding her agreeable guest gone, and wished that dinner and bed had been offered.

Mrs. Merrifield and Susan were still a good deal excited about Arthurine's complimentary friend, who they said seemed to belong to Fred Mytton, of whom some of the ladies had been telling most unpleasant reports, and there was much lamentation over the set into which their young neighbour had thrown herself.

'Such a dress too!' sighed Mrs. Merrifield.

'And her head-mistress has just arrived,' said Susan, 'to make her worse than ever!'

'How comes a head-mistress to be running about the country at this time of year?' asked Bessie.

'She has been very ill,' said Mrs. Merrifield, 'and they wrote to her to come down as soon as she could move. There was a telegram this morning, and she drove up in the midst of the party, and was taken to her room at once to rest. That was the reason Miss Arthuret was away so long. I thought it nice in her.'

'Perhaps she will do good,' said Bessie.

Dinner was just over, and the Admiral had settled down

with his shaded lamp to read and judge of the article that
Bessie had given him as a specimen, when in came the
message, 'Mrs. Rudden wishes to speak to you, sir.'

Mrs. Rudden was the prosperous widow who continued the
business in the village-shop, conjointly with the little farm
belonging to the Gap property. She was a shrewd woman,
had been able to do very well by her family, and was much
esteemed, paying a rent which was a considerable item in the
Gap means. The ladies wondered together at the summons.
Susan hoped 'that girl' did not want to evict her, and Bessie
suggested that a cooperative store was a more probable peril.
Presently the Admiral came back. 'Do any of you know Miss
Arthuret's writing?' he said.

'Bessie knows it best,' said Susan.

He showed a letter. 'That is hers—the signature—' said
Bessie. 'I am not sure about the rest. Why—what does it
mean?'

For she read—

'The Gap, Oct. 2nd.

'MRS. RUDDEN,

'You are requested to pay over to the bearer, Mr.
Foxholm, fifty-pounds of the rent you were about to bring
me to-morrow.

'I remain, etc.,

'ARTHURINE ARTHURET.'

'What does it mean!' asked Bessie again.

'That's just what Mrs. Rudden has come up to me to ask,'
said the Admiral. 'This fellow presented it in her shop about
a quarter of an hour ago. The good woman smelt a rat. What
do you think she did? She looked at it and him, asked him to
wait a bit, whipped out at her back door, luckily met the
policeman starting on his rounds, bade him have an eye to
the customer in her shop, and came off to show it to me. That
young woman is demented enough for anything, and is quite
capable of doing it—for some absurd scheme. But do you
think it is hers, or a swindle?'

'Didn't she say she had given her autograph?' exclaimed
Susan.

'And see here,' said Bessie, 'her signature is at the top of the
sheet of note paper—small paper. And as she always writes
very large, it would be easy to fill up the rest, changing the
first side over.'

'I must take it up to her at once,' said the Admiral. 'Even if it be genuine, she may just as well see that it is a queer thing to have done, and not exactly the way to treat her tenants.'

'It is strange too that this man should have known anything about Mrs. Rudden,' said Mrs. Merrifield.

'Mrs. Rudden says she had a message this morning, when she had come up with her rent and accounts, to say that Miss Arthuret was very much engaged, and would be glad if she would come to-morrow! Could this fellow have been about then?'

No one knew, but Bessie breathed the word, 'Was not that young Mytton there?'

It was not taken up, for no one liked to pronounce the obvious inference. Besides, the Admiral was in haste, not thinking it well that Mr. Foxholm should be longer kept under surveillance in the shop, among the bread, bacon, cheeses, shoes, and tins of potted meat.

He was then called for; and on his loudly exclaiming that he had been very strangely treated, the Admiral quietly told him that Mrs. Rudden had been disturbed at so unusual a way of demanding her rent, and had come for advice on the subject; and to satisfy their minds that all was right, Mr Foxholm would, no doubt, consent to wait till the young lady could be referred to. Mr. Foxholm did very decidedly object; he said no one had any right to detain him when the lady's signature was plain, and Admiral Merrifield had seen him in her society, and he began an account of the philanthropical purpose for which he said the money had been intended, but he was cut short.

'You must be aware,' said the Admiral, 'that this is not an ordinary way of acting, and whatever be your purpose, Mrs. Rudden must ascertain your authority more fully before paying over so large a sum. I give you your choice, therefore, either of accompanying us to the Gap, or of remaining in Mrs. Rudden's parlour till we return.'

The furtive eye glanced about, and the parlour was chosen. Did he know that the policeman stationed himself in the shop outside?

The dinner at the Gap was over, and Miss Elmore, the head-mistress, was established in an arm-chair, listening to the outpouring of her former pupil and the happy mother about all the felicities and glories of their present life, the only

174

drawback being the dulness and obstructiveness of the immediate neighbours.

'I thought Miss Merrifield was your neighbour—Mesa?'

'Oh, no—quite impossible! These are Merrifields, but the daughters are two regular old goodies, wrapped up in Sunday schools and penny clubs.'

'Well, that is odd! The editor of the —— came down in the train with me, and said he was going to see Mesa—Miss Elizabeth Merrifield.'

'I do think it is very unfair,' began Arthurine; but at that moment the door-bell rang. 'How strange at this time!'

'Oh! perhaps the editor is coming here!' cried Arthurine. 'Did you tell him *I* lived here, Miss Elmore?'

'Admiral Merrifield,' announced the parlour-maid.

He had resolved not to summon the young lady in private, as he thought there was more chance of common-sense in the mother.

'You are surprised to see me at this time,' he said; 'but Mrs. Rudden is perplexed by a communication from you.'

'Mrs. Rudden!' exclaimed Arthurine. 'Why, I only sent her word that I was too busy to go through her accounts to-day, and asked her to come to-morrow. That isn't against the laws of the Medes and Persians, is it?'

'Then did you send her this letter?'

'I?' said Arthurine, staring at it, with her eyes at their fullest extent. 'I! fifty pounds! Mr. Foxholm! What does it mean?'

'Then you never wrote that order?'

'No! no! How should I?'

'That is not your writing?'

'No, not that.'

'Look at the signature.'

'Oh! oh! oh!'—and she dropped into a chair. 'The horrible man! That's the autograph I gave him this afternoon.'

'You are sure?'

'Quite; for my pen spluttered in the slope of the A. Has she gone and given it to him?'

'No. She brought it to me, and set the policeman to watch him.'

'What a dear, good woman! Shall you send him to prison, Admiral Merrifield? What can be done to him?' said Arthurine, not looking at all as if she would like to abrogate capital punishment.

'Well, I had been thinking,' said the Admiral. 'You see he did not get it, and though I could commit him for endeavouring to obtain money on false pretences, I very much doubt whether the prosecution would not be worse for you than for him.'

'That is very kind of you, Admiral,' exclaimed the mother. 'It would be terribly awkward for dear Arthurine to stand up and say he cajoled her into giving her autograph. It might always be remembered against her!'

'Exactly so,' said the Admiral; 'and perhaps there may be another reason for not pushing the matter to extremity. The man is a stranger here, I believe.'

'He has been staying at Bonchamp,' said Mrs. Arthuret. 'It was young Mr. Mytton who brought him over this afternoon.'

'Just so. And how did he come to be aware that Mrs. Rudden owed you any money?'

There was a pause, then Arthurine broke out—

'Oh, Daisy and Pansy can't have done anything; but they were all three there helping me mark the tennis-courts when the message came.'

'Including the brother?'

'Yes.'

'He is a bad fellow, and I would not wish to shield him in any way, but that such a plot should be proved against him would be a grievous disgrace to the family.'

'I can't ever feel about them as I have done,' said Arthurine, in tears. 'Daisy and Pansy said so much about poor dear Fred, and every one being hard on him, and his feeling my good influence—and all the time he was plotting this against me, with my chalk in his hand marking my grass,' and she broke down in child-like sobs.

The mortification was terrible of finding her pinnacle of fame the mere delusion of a sharper, and the shock of shame seemed to overwhelm the poor girl.

'Oh, Admiral!' cried her mother, 'she cannot bear it. I know you will be good, and manage it so as to distress her as little as possible, and not have any publicity.'

'I will do my best,' said the Admiral. 'I will try and get a confession out of him, and send him off, though it is a pity that such a fellow should get off scot-free.'

'Oh, never mind, so that my poor Arthurine's name is not brought forward! We can never be grateful enough for your kindness.'

It was so late that the Admiral did not come back that night, and the ladies were at breakfast when he appeared again. Foxholm had, on finding there was no escape, confessed the fraud, but threw most of the blame on Fred Mytton, who was in debt, not only to him but to others. Foxholm himself seemed to have been an adventurer, who preyed on young men at the billiard-table, and had there been in some collusion with Fred, though the Admiral had little doubt as to which was the greater villain. He had been introduced to the Mytton family, who were not particular; indeed, Mr. Mytton had no objection to increasing his pocket-money by a little wary, profitable betting and gambling on his own account. However, the associates had no doubt brought Bonchamp to the point of being too hot to hold them, and Fred, overhearing the arrangement with Mrs. Rudden, had communicated it to him—whence the autograph trick. Foxholm was gone, and in the course of the day it was known that young Mytton was also gone.

The Admiral promised that none of his family should mention the matter, and that he would do his best to silence Mrs. Rudden, who for that matter probably believed the whole letter to have been forged, and would not enter into the enthusiasm of autographs.

'Oh, thank you! It is so kind,' said the mother, and Arthurine, who looked as if she had not slept all night, and was ready to burst into tears on the least provocation, murmured something to the same effect, which the Admiral answered, half hearing—

'Never mind, my dear, you will be wiser another time; young people will be inexperienced.'

'Is that the cruellest cut of all?' thought Miss Elmore, as she beheld her former pupil scarcely restraining herself enough for the farewell civilities, and then breaking down into a flood of tears.

Her mother hovered over her with, 'What is it? Oh! my dear child, you need not be afraid; he is so kind!'

'I hate people to be kind, that is the very thing,' said Arthurine. ('Oh! Miss Elmore, don't go)—while he is meaning all the time that I have made such a fool of myself! And he is glad, I know he is, he and his hateful, stupid, stolid daughters.'

'My dear! my dear!' exclaimed her mother.

'Well, haven't they done nothing but thwart me, whatever I wanted to do, and aren't they triumphing now in this abominable man's treachery, and my being taken in? I shall go away, and sell the place, and never come back again.'

'I should think that was the most decided way of confessing a failure,' said Miss Elmore; and as Mrs. Arthuret was called away by the imperative summons to the butcher, she spoke more freely. 'Your mother looks terrified at being so routed up again.'

'Oh, mother will be happy anywhere; and how can I stay with these stick-in-the-mud people, just like what I have read about.'

'And have gibbeted! Really, Arthurine, I should call them very generous!'

'It is their thick skins,' muttered she; 'at least so the Myttons said; but, indeed, I did not mean to be so personal as it was thought.'

'But tell me. Why did you not get on with Mesa?'

'That was a regular take-in. Not to tell one! When I began my German class, she put me out with useless explanations.'

'What kind of explanations?'

'Oh, about the Swiss being under the Empire, or something, and she *would* go into parallels of Saxon words, and English poetry, such as our Fraulein never troubled us with. But I showed her it would not *do*.'

'So instead of learning what you had not sense to appreciate, you wanted to teach your old routine.'

'But indeed, she could not pronounce at all well, and she looked ever so long at difficult bits, and then she even tried to correct *me*.'

'Did she go on coming after you silenced her?'

'Yes, and never tried to interfere again.'

'I am afraid she drew her own conclusions about High Schools.'

'Oh, Miss Elmore, you used to like us to be thorough and not discursive, and how could anybody brought up in this stultifying place, ages ago, know what will tell in an exam?'

'Oh! Arthurine. How often have I told you that examinations are not education! I never saw so plainly that I have not educated you.'

'I wanted to prepare Daisy and Pansy, and they didn't care about her prosing when we wanted to get on with the book.'

'Which would have been the best education for them, poor girls, an example of courtesy, patience, and humility, or *getting on*, as you call it?'

'Oh! Miss Elmore, you are very hard on me, when I have just been so cruelly disappointed.'

'My dear child, it is only because I want you to discover why you have been so cruelly disappointed.'

It would be wearisome to relate all that Arthurine finally told of those thwartings by the Merrifields which had thrown her into the arms of the Mytton family, nor how Miss Elmore brought her to confess that each scheme was either impracticable, or might have been injurious, and that a little grain of humility might have made her see things very differently. Yet it must be owned that the good lady felt rather like bending a bow that would spring back again.

Bessie Merrifield had, like her family, been inclined to conclude that all was the fault of High Schools. She did not see Miss Elmore at first, thinking the Arthurets not likely to wish to be intruded upon, and having besides a good deal to think over. For she and her father had talked over the proposal, which pecuniarily was so tempting, and he, without prejudice, but on principle, had concurred with her in deciding that it was her duty not to add one touch of attractiveness to aught which supported a cause contrary to their strongest convictions. Her father's approbation was the crowning pleasure, though she felt the external testimony to her abilities, quite enough to sympathise with such intoxication of success as to make any compliment seem possible. Miss Elmore had one long talk with her, beginning by saying—

'I wish to consult you about my poor, foolish child.'

'Ah! I am afraid we have not helped her enough!' said Bessie. 'If we had been more sympathetic she might have trusted us more.'

'Then you are good enough to believe that it was not all folly and presumption.'

'I am sure it was not,' said Bessie. 'None of us ever thought it more than inexperience and a little exaltation, with immense good intention at the bottom. Of course, our dear old habits did look dull, coming from life and activity, and we rather resented her contempt for them; but I am quite sure that after a little while, every one will forget all about this, or only recollect it as one does a girlish scrape.'

'Yes. To suppose all the neighbourhood occupied in laughing at her is only another phase of self-importance. You see, the poor child necessarily lived in a very narrow world, where examinations came, whatever I could do, to seem everything,

179

and she only knew things beyond by books. She had success enough there to turn her head, and not going to Cambridge, never had fair measure of her abilities. Then came prosperity——!'

'Quite enough to upset any one's balance,' said Bessie. 'In fact, only a very sober, not to say stolid, nature would have stood it.'

'Poor things! They were so happy—so open-hearted. I did long to caution them. "Full cup, steady hand." '

'It will all come right now,' said Bessie. 'Mrs. Arthuret spoke of their going away for the winter; I do not think it will be a bad plan, for then we can start quite fresh with them; and the intimacy with the Myttons will be broken, though I am sorry for the poor girls. They have no harm in them, and Arthurine was doing them good.'

'A whisper to you, Miss Merrifield—they are going back with me to be prepared for governesses at Arthurine's expense. It is the only thing for them in the crash that young man has brought on the family.'

'Dear, good Arthurine! She only needed to learn how to carry her cup.'

Lifelong Friends[1]

WHEN did I begin story weaving? I can hardly tell. I know that in almost baby days, for want of companions, I imagined ten boys and eleven girls living in an arbour in the garden, but I can remember nothing about them except that two were Caroline and Lucy. Dolls were my delight, to be treated as children of a family. I did not like them to be in costumes or in baby fashion, but as children to be naughty, or to be set up in rows to do their lessons; and, in the same way, all attempts at drawing and all interest in 'pictures' were of the dramatic kind. A scene of a wood, or a lane with a child going along it, would be the theme of a mental story.

Not being taught to write nor allowed to scribble very early, prevented any writing out of these attempts, but I was an omnivorous story reader, from the time when, at four years old, I first discovered that I could read the letterpress in a great quarto edition of *Robinson Crusoe*, close to the point where the print shewed him clinging to a rock among the breakers. Miss Edgeworth's tales were a real delight; also *Children as They Are, Anna Ross, Ornaments Discovered;* and Miss Strickland's *Rival Crusoes*, the *Perambulations of a Mouse*, and the *Village School*—all old-fashioned books. Mrs. Hofland's tales, which were then much admired, never pleased me; her children grew up and fell in love far too soon for the childish mind.

Fairy tales were discouraged. It was a treat to pick one up from time to time, and a book with selections from Grimm, by Edgar Taylor, illustrated by Cruikshank, belonging to my cousins, was a special favourite. I strongly hold to such moderation being wiser and better for the imagination than continual feeding on them.

The first volume of the *Fairchild Family* was delightful for the outrageous naughtiness, though neither in this nor anything else were the improving portions read, except, perhaps,

[1] In *The Monthly Packet*, December, 1894.

those in Maria Hack's charming books, *Winter Evenings, Harry Beaufoy, Stories from Ancient and Modern History.*

How soon it began, I cannot tell, but there were perpetual dreams of romance going on, in which somebody was always being wounded in the Peninsular War, and coming home with his arm in a sling; and one generation after another had to be moved back for the reigning hero to be eligible and youthful enough, for thirty was then old age.

Writing began when my old French master wanted me to write original letters. These ran into a story. As Scott's yearning for Border chivalry led to his poems, so did my solitude and longing for young companions develop into tales of large families. We were then anxious about the building of a school, and trying to raise money by a bazaar. Sundry translations into French, corrected by old M. de Normanville, were wrought into the story that had grown up by the title of the 'Château de Melville,' and sold at what I fear was an extortionate price. This was when I was about fifteen. The curious thing is that the *dramatis personæ* have been more or less my companions through life. I took them up again, much modified, with some names changed, six or eight years after in *Scenes and Characters*, and again in the *Two Sides of the Shield*. The indolent sister was always Emily, but the lively and the inquisitive sisters remain with me still. History never failed to have great power over my imagination. This, and the desire to supply good tales to my school children, and the pleasure of living, as it were, with large families, were three separate fields of delight in which my mind could expatiate.

Alison's *History of Europe*, giving an account of the retreat from Moscow, with the episode of the mother forsaking a young child, and likewise the story of Marshal Ney, made a strong impression. I romanced about it to my mother. She told my father. He said it might be a fine story, and tried to bring it into shape, looking over a page of foolscap a night. But it was like trying to mould a piece of wax too slight to bear manipulation from strong fingers. He could criticise, but not compose, and by the time a sentence of the unformed capacity of eighteen was tortured into good English, all the life was gone out of it, and the attempt on 'Shiverydown,' our pet name for it, was given up.

Translating Manzoni's *I Promessi Sposi* for him to read did more good to power of language than anything else. Meantime school-child literature was being begun by my dear friends Mrs. and Miss Dyson, and Miss Anne Mozley. Several short stories, beginning with *Midsummer Day,* were the consequence; also *Langley School,* in the *Magazine for the Young.*

Mrs. Mozley's *Fairy Bower* was the starting-point of a certain style of writing for the young. There was something—together with the wonderful cleverness of portraiture—in the reticence of Grace to her mother, that certainly set me to demonstrate the contrary habit, and, I suspect, had a like effect on Miss Sewell. *Amy Herbert* was her work, *Abbey Church* mine. My mother told the story of the latter to Mrs. Keble, and this led to the manuscript being most kindly considered and recommended to Mozley.

My grandmother, who was nearly ninety, was an old-fashioned person, who thought the publication of the *Château de Melville* rather shocking, but she had since died. I cannot forget, however, my father, before taking any steps about *Abbey Church,* gravely putting it before me that there were three reasons for which one might desire to publish—love of vanity, or of gain, or the wish to do good. I answered, with tears, that I really hoped I had written with the purpose of being useful to young girls like myself. The matter of gain we were old-fashioned enough to hold as quite out of the question; and for a long time it seemed a point of honour, and perhaps of duty, with me to spend none of it on myself. As to vanity, for many years all was anonymous, and one or two funny encounters about *Abbey Church* were the consequence. There was a good deal of unnecessary allusion in it, but my head was overflowing with ideas. Nor must it be forgotten that Mr. and Mrs. Keble looked over it, and Mr. Keble suggested that the way in which perfect candour on the girl's part could be combined with a sudden discovery would be to let her confess to her gentle stepmother, who will not worry the father at an inopportune time. That the clerical family should discourage the Mechanics' Institute, instead of taking the lead in the mental cultivation, is a curious memorial to the tone of mind at that period.

Scenes and Characters was the next work, and *Shiverydown* was re-written in a manner that could endure the criticising ordeal, and came out by the title of *Kenneth; or, the Rear Guard of the Grand Army.* Being asked to help in the revivification of the *Churchman's Companion, Henrietta's Wish* and the *Two Guardians* were the result.

From very early times, Scott had become a delight; the poems first, and afterwards the novels, beginning with the *Talisman,* and they produced all the enthusiasm and delight belonging to the teens and more advanced years. One chapter a day was the allowance, though it was allowable to read back. No doubt these moulded the plan of *The Little Duke,* and they also made history become a series of character studies, and of material for romance. To begin a historical tale seems to me like taking a microscope to look into the times withal. I cannot write what I do not believe to be possible. Of course there are mistakes and anachronisms, but I did not know them to be such at the time. The worst are, perhaps, in the *Prince and Page,* the supposing all the Knights of St. John to have been priests, and likewise the omitting that the Order of Redemptorists was the chief means in the ransoming of *The Modern Telemachus;* but that was the fault of my authority, an old history of shipwrecks, which evidently thought it right to omit all mention of a Roman Catholic Order.

I do not go farther. I have told the history elsewhere of my dear friend Miss Dyson, suggesting the main character of Guy; and with the *Heir of Redclyffe,* when I was about thirty years old, authorship ceased, in a manner, to be a simple amusement, and became a vocation, though never less of a delight, and I hope I may say of a conscience.

Authorship[1]

WE sometimes hear of amateur authors. What this means at the present day there is no knowing. In former times it was clear enough. It was the persons who had something to say and were desirous of saying it to the public at their own cost; nay, who thought it almost derogatory to accept any remuneration. Horace Walpole was the type of these.

But now there is no one who is not willing to obtain, if not appropriate, the profits of the sale that is hoped for as a testimony of success; and there are great numbers of writers, not always dependent on their earnings, but finding them an important addition to their income, and thus becoming more and more professional.

There is really no rule as to whence the impetus comes that leads to success. It is not always the sheer love of the expression of thoughts, or of setting the puppets of one's imagination to work, though this was so entirely my own case that I long believed it essential to the commencement of original composition that (as Mr. Keble used to say) one could not help it. But to dwell on women alone, how different was the motive in each case. Fanny Burney, Jane Austen, and the Brontë sisters, were all instances of the same kind of instinct, of need of expression; but Maria Edgeworth was the exponent of her father's thoughts, and her earlier works were exercises under his superintendence. Mrs. Trollope, now almost forgotten, but a considerable power in her day, wrote under the most unfavourable circumstances, late in life, for actual maintenance, and at the bedsides of a dying husband and son. Yet her factory tale was in its way almost as effective a protest against white slavery as *Uncle Tom's Cabin* was against black slavery; and Mrs. Beecher Stowe really only began to write by the advice of her mother-in-law, who thought her strength and ability wasted in trying to make puddings and mind three

---

[1] In *The Monthly Packet*, September, 1892, reprinted 1893 in *Ladies at Work*.

baby children at the same time. It was from no burning partizanship of the negroes that she began the story, but the facts grew on her after the serial was started. Her other books show her to have had real power and imagination. Mrs. Gaskell began as a distraction to her mind after a heavy domestic grief, when her youth was over, and thus learnt the charm and developed the faculty. Breadwinning actuated George Eliot's earlier work, so likewise Dinah Muloch (Mrs. Craik) and Louisa Alcott, both of whom worked up through mere 'pot-boilers' to success. Miss Alcott was found a year or two ago to be the most popular author in America, judging by the amount of sales, but it remains to be proved how far this was an ephemeral matter.

One very unpalatable piece of counsel I would give. Do not try to publish very early in life. Many people have a gift of narration, and when they have plenty of leisure, they are much inclined to use it; and there is no reason against their practising it in home MSS. and competitions, but at the very best, they are really incapable of using it to the fullest effect without some experience. Their knowledge of life cannot help being limited, and if taken from books, their work is imitative. They may have indeed the noble freshness that depicts a character after an ideal standard, but if they make him and his doings impossible, the effect is destroyed. Or else they ramble into the commonplace for want of knowing that the notions, to them pathetic and lovely, are the most hackneyed. The real idea, if there be any good and original germ in it, is wasted by being put forward with inadequate powers, and cannot be used for fear of repetition when after-years have given the faculties needful for carrying it out.

Meantime, it is quite well to write. Translation is excellent practice. I once translated the whole of Manzoni's 'Promessi Sposi' for a very fastidious man to read and enjoy it. When I returned to writing original stories, I found my facility of correct composition greatly improved. Translation, as regards the purse, is not apt to be profitable, and those who expect to depend on it are often sorely disappointed; but if carefully executed, not too literally, yet not too freely, it is excellent training. It has the advantage, too, of drawing the translator out of habits of slip-slop.

Almost all the writers we have enumerated had the training of letter writing in a time when it was disgraceful not to write a grammatical letter, with something positive in it. They did not scratch down a little careless slang, but felt it due to the recipient, who bore the expense of postage, to say something worth having. Thus they learnt the habit of thinking and writing good English, and it occurred to them without effort. Questions are sometimes asked about style. Good grammar and attention to punctuation, with a little common sense and avoiding of repetitions, ambiguities, or abrupt turns, are the secret of style. To read aloud and mark what jars on the ear, or is liable to be misunderstood, is a great help. A real kind, critical listener is the chief benefit, really the chief of all, but even Molière's old woman is better than nothing. One's own ear may be awake to blunders, even if the critic be perilously admiring.

And of all things to be avoided is any kind of ready-made facetiousness. Allusions to Scripture, such as 'fearfully and wonderfully made,' or 'the last state of that man is worse than the first,' are absolutely profane, and can only be excused by supposing the writers ignorant or thoughtless; but there are many others adopted as a sort of cheap liveliness; for instance, 'slept the sleep of the just,' was, we believe, once a clever turn in a French book, but it has come to be used merely for slept soundly, and amuses no one, any more than does, 'the light fantastic toe' in a county paper's account of wedding festivities.

Mr. Besant recommends writing poetry (not always for publication) as a training in rhythmical expression. He is right; it is a help to good prose, and the masters of the art wrote prose that may be actually read as poetry; witness 'The Rose and the Ring,' and Dickens's higher descriptive pages. But let no one try to publish poetry, even in a parish magazine, without trying it by the rules of measure and metre. 'Native wood-notes wild,' may, by the help of a tolerable ear, and likewise imitation, sound well for some time, especially when they are an unconscious parody of a familiar hymn; but by-and-by comes an unmanageable word or thought, which is crammed by the head and shoulders into the unfortunate stanza which has to swallow it. Half our aspirant poets do not know that verses ought to be capable of being scanned, and as to their blank verse, it is prose measured off in lengths. To put down verses as they rise in the mind or fancy, by the ear, is a very pleasant occupation, and even more, it often relieves the mind of strong feeling, whether high, meditative, or sorrowful. If so, it has the soul of poetry, but it cannot have the body without conforming to rule, any more than a sweet voice and good ear will make a real singer without knowledge of music. Whoever wants to make any real use of poetic talent, should try the compositions by rules, such as are to be found under the head of 'Prosody' in an Encyclopædia, and in one of the National Society's manuals, 'On the Art of Teaching English Literature, No. 1; by Canon Warburton.' The cost is eightpence. It would be no small benefit to editors if all would-be poets would try their verses by the rules here given.

There are books, generally the first works of some really powerful person, written in *gaieté de cœur* or with real meaning. Such are many books now classics; and later, 'Peter Simple.' 'Harry Lorrequer,' Southey's 'Doctor,' 'Pickwick,' which carry one along by their swing, without much plot. 'John Inglesant' may be numbered among these, perhaps, but as a rule a plot is needful, a central aim, to which the characters must work, and which has to produce its fruits. Even a child's books, in spite of the beloved examples of Frank and Rosamond, needs to drive at something definite, and indeed, in Rosamond, each chapter is a little, well-pointed tale in itself, only all strung on the same heroine.

Another thing required of an author is summed up in a verse of Ecclesiasticus: 'Be not ignorant of anything in a great matter or a small.' Verify whatever you may have set down. Then we should not have full moons twice in a month; Orion shining on summer evenings; birdsnesting in September; primroses and poppies in the same nosegay; rattlesnakes in India; tomatoes in Italy before the discovery of America; cygnets shaming the whiteness of their parents; ladies smelling lovely bouquets of sea anemones, or a philanthropic glow-worm, anxious to be of use, lighting the epitaph on a headstone in a consolatory manner; and lucifer matches in the days of John Wesley.

Methods and ways of working vary, and no rule can be laid down. Some can write best by dashing on, and correcting afterwards; others go step by step; some plan out the contents of every chapter, as did Harriet Martineau; some go on as the characters lead them; some can only write when in the vein, others can perform their daily tasks, like Trollope, without dependence on mood. The point is really the pains, the polish, and the conscience of the work; and by conscience there is much implied. There is the resolution to let no need of gain lead to pandering to the popular taste when it is for evil; the determination to deal with nothing but what is purifying, truthful, and elevating; the further withstanding of temptations to irreverence, and the honesty of giving thoroughly good, sound, unscamped work, such as may not swell the flood of worldliness and evil.

Woman can often speak with great effect to her own generation, even if her achievements do not obtain lasting fame, and this should be her aim. I have written hitherto only of her work in fiction; where she can deal with more solid subjects, her pen can be most valuable. Essays like Anne Mozley's, histories, memoirs, science teachings made comprehensible to the popular or the childish mind, all these are subjects in which women can worthily excel. A good school book is a very profitable article till it is superseded, as it is sure to be in these days of progress.

For now we come to the business side of the matter. Mr. Besant has written excellent advice to authors, and experience for self and friends fully confirms what he says: the first start is a difficulty, but real merit will in time find its level.

Magazines seem, at first sight, the safe region for trying the wings, but they are so overcrowded that rejection often only means that there is no suitable opening. A paper of any superiority is, however, sure to find entrance somewhere, but there is a profusion of writing 'ower bad for blessing, and ower good for banning', and a good many refusals generally (though not always) show the MS. to be of this quality at least. The same may be said of offers to publishers. Some decline because their hands are full of other matter of the same kind, or because the subject is not in their own line, so that it is better to try, try again and again.

But on no account let eagerness to gain a hearing induce a novice to undertake to advance a sum for the printing or publishing. Such a plan does not, as a rule, come from the superior and trustworthy houses. They take a book on their own risk or not at all, and there are, unhappily, many cases on record where the aspirant has not only never had any return for the money laid down, but has never seen any more of the production itself.

A person who has no veteran *littérateur* to advise and direct the first venture, will do best to consult the Authors' Society. The address is 4, Portugal Street, Lincoln's Inn Fields, the subscription a guinea a year, and there a candid opinion may be obtained as to whether a MS. is worthless or marketable, and likewise, where it may be best and most safely disposed of.

There is a fee for having a MS. read, but this is well worth paying to spare hope deferred in the case of a mediocre one, or to assist a worthy one.

When a paper is accepted by a magazine, it is desirable always to be clear whether the payment is for first appearance or copyright. This differs in many cases, and it is wiser, except in special instances, to retain the copyright, though at some sacrifice of present gain. If the author arrives at the honour of 'collected works' it is very troublesome to have to deal with varied claims of passing publications, and worse still to see their reappearance with no control over them.

Literature, like other avocations open to women, is all the worse for those really dependent on it, because they are undersold by those to whom remuneration is unimportant, and this out of ignorance and desire to gain a hearing. Therefore, it is right to insist on a fair price, and not to close in haste with any offer for less. Magazines have stated tariffs for the writing in their pages, and this will enable one to estimate the value of his works; but name, fame, and success go for so much that first undistinguished efforts can only bring moderate profits, unless they make a *hit*.

It is wiser to have agreements looked over before signature by an experienced eye. Such, the Authors' Society offers, and it is invaluable in preventing errors, and—where the house is not one of the great ones, free from all suspicion—in keeping a check on the publishers. Coleridge and Southey spoke of the 'thriving bookseller' as like him

'who sate like a Cormorant
Perched on the tree of knowledge.'

And the unguarded now and then receive circulars sent forth from varieties of cormorants' crags, which they would do wisely to consign immediately to the waste-paper basket.

The accredited means of publishing are either selling the copyright at a fair price, which of course is all that the author can ever expect, or—which is the method most in favour for a young untried writer—for the publisher to take the whole risk and half the profits, giving the other half to the author. This involves no loss to the author, and often is very satisfactory in the hands of any one of the higher and more honourable men of the trade. But there is a possibility with others of heavy percentages on sales, and charges for advertisements which mulct the author heavily. Sometimes the publisher offers a royalty—a round sum on a specified number of copies—and after they are sold, a fixed amount for each copy in proportion to the price; but this is not often done unless the author's name is a guarantee, or the subject is one certain to command popularity.

Again, the author can publish at his own expense, allowing a percentage to the publisher, and inspecting the accounts, but this is unsafe except where the author's position is established, or—as sometimes happens in the case of books intended for distribution—where it is to be sold at a price below the ordinary rate.

If none of these methods are open, there is nothing for it but either to decide that literature is not the vocation of the aspirant, or else to persevere till something is accepted, and the horsehair thus let down by which the beetle is to ascend!

Then come the proofs. How delightful are the first, how well they are revised—probably with a pepperbox of commas ready to drop on them, and sheer delight and diversion in printer's errors! By the bye, printers evidently do not love either colons or semicolons, and many a sentence which ought euphoniously to be divided by the latter, is either made to drag on with an ineffective comma, or cut short off with a full-stop before the sense is concluded. Also, whether by their fault or the writer's is uncertain, the nominative absolute prevails. 'A fair evening, the trees all lovely green,' is no sentence, nor is, 'A fine lad with a roguish mouth and pug nose.' Every sentence must have a verb, or it is no sentence at all—a mere absurd interjection.

The book is out! Notices probably come in. They are not apt to be such as once they were—the fuller ones often valuable and instructive in the way of criticism, favourable or adverse. There is little time or space for such work now. One thing I would say: that it seems to me an unworthy thing to solicit a favourable notice. Surely one's book goes out to stand on its own merits, not to be pushed and puffed. The point is, to learn whether it is good for anything, and what mannerisms are to be avoided. Praise in a review is very delightful, but it must be unsolicited to be worth having. Sometimes people actually sent round in type their favourite sentences for the reviewers to insert! This is a really absurd puff, pretty certain to prejudice the critics.

On one side, it is better not to be too eager for reviews, or to pin one's feeling on them as Charlotte Brontë did when she cried all night over what was said of *Jane Eyre*. On the other, it is not wholesome entirely to avoid the sight. George Eliot was not allowed to see unfavourable criticisms, and thus the chances of improvement were missed. Keats' death, through the 'Quarterly'—savage and tartarly—was a myth; and when Mrs. Wood made a malevolent critic slay a book and its author by writing in all the reviews and papers, she forgot how unlike they all are, and how impossible the feat would be. Depend upon it, a good book will raise its head above censure, or, still worse, neglect, at the first. And when the name is made, come the trials of overmuch work, leading to careless- ness and to requests for performances, more with a view to the space in the periodical than to the scope of the tale, often leading to conclusions spoilt by crowding of incidents and want of giving scenes their due development.

One thing more it may be well to say. There is at present a taste for sensation, and a certain conventional distaste for a moral, pure, and religious tone. It is a fatal thing to be led away by it. If for every idle word we speak we are to give account, how much more for every word we write? And setting aside this awful aspect: what is written without the salt of life does not live, or acquire fame. Even remuneration is only ephemeral. Evil is a dead weight, sinking the performance.

It is true that women's good heroes are apt to be called prigs. But be content to have them so. If you sacrifice your womanly nature in the attempt at the world's notion of manly dash, you only sacrifice yourself, and mar the performance, unless it is only a very slight sketch from the outside. A woman cannot do a man truthfully from within, any more than one nation- ality can represent another from within. And if the ideal given is often called a prig, it is because she is incapable of the '*Carle-hemp*' in part, and also in part, because a certain depth of self-respect and of self-assertion, often bordering on self- conceit, is really a needful weapon of defence in the midst of scenes of temptation. Boys and good poor people find it so. There is much to be said for the so-called prig; but if you find your hero growing into one, frankly own it, or else give him some loveable weakness.

PART IV

Tables and Bibliography

Note on the Genealogical Tables for the Linked Novels of Charlotte Yonge

By Violet Powell

Discrepancies in dates are indicated by an alternative date or a question mark. A question mark is also used to indicate a major anomaly such as Kate Somerville (*Beechcroft at Rockstone*) appearing as a contemporary of Gillian Merrifield, then aged about seventeen, when Lord Somerville, Kate's father, could not have been born before 1852 (*Castle Builders* and *Pillars of the House*). The compilation of these tables owes much to the generous kindness of Miss Marghanita Laski, who placed the results of her comprehensive genealogical researches at my disposal. I must also thank my neighbour, Miss Barbara Creswick, and my sister, Lady Pansy Lamb, for the indefinite loan of those of Miss Yonge's works which I do not myself possess. I can only apologize for errors and omissions in the words of Lady Merrifield when writing of the engagements of her two eldest daughters: 'There is some connection with the Underwoods though I have not quite fathomed it.'

Genealogical Tables
- I. Mohun, White, Prescott, Grey Rotherwood.
- II. Charlecote, Sandbrook, Fulmort, Raymond.
- III. May, Ernescliffe, Rivers, Ward.
- IV. Underwood, Harwood, Vanderkist.
- V. Liddesdale, Audley, Berners, Willoughby.
- VI. Ormersfield, Frost, Dynevor, Conway, Ponsonby.
- VII. Caergwent, de la Poer, Wardour.
- VIII. Merrifield

TABLE I

SCENES AND CHARACTERS *begins 1845*
TWO SIDES OF THE SHIELD *begins 1878-80*
BEECHCROFT AT ROCKSTONE *begins 1879-81*
LONG VACATION *begins 1888*
MODERN BROODS *begins 1889*

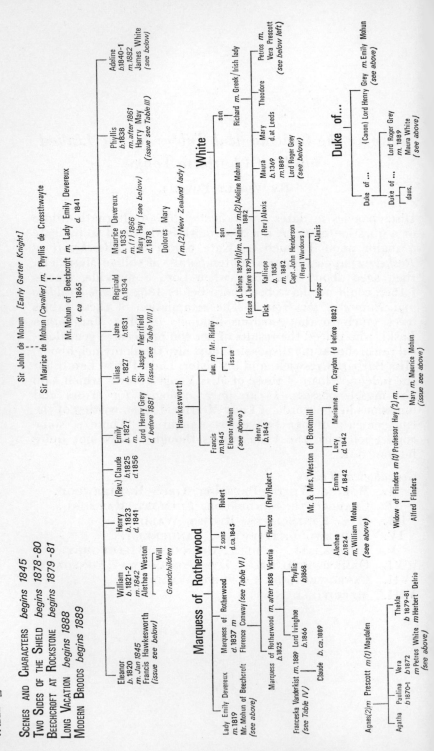

TABLE II

HOPES AND FEARS *begins circa 1830*

see also

PILLARS OF THE HOUSE

Mervyn

son [*Great-Uncle Mervyn*]

son

son

Fulmort *m.* Augusta
d. 1855 — *d.* 1856

Charlecote

Sandbrook

Gen. Sir Christopher Charteris *m.* Horatia

Raymond

Augusta
b. 1824
m. 1854
Admiral Sir Nicholas Bannerman
[*3rd wife*]

Juliana
b. 1827 *d.* 1860
m. 1855
Sir Bevil Acton Bart.

Juliana

John Mervyn
b. 1829
m. 1861
Cicely Raymond
(*see below*)

Robert Mervyn
b. 1832

Bertha
d. in infancy

Phoebe
b. 1838
m. 1862
Humfrey Charlecote Randolf
(*see below*)

Maria
b. 1840
d. before 1860

Bertha
b. 1842

Charles Charteris M.P.
d. before 1852

Christopher Capt. R.N.
d. 1858
m. Canadian lady

Lucilla Horatia
b. 1808
d. 1837
m. Owen Sandbrook
(*see left*)

Charles
b. 1821
m. 1854 Eloisa

Caroline
b. 1823
m. before 1854

Horatia
b. 1824

Humfrey (*disinherited*)

Humfrey

(Rev) son
d. ca. 1830

son

son

dau. *m.* Major Randolf (2) *m.* (1) American lady (2) *m.* American gentleman

Humfrey Charlecote *m.* 1862 Phoebe Fulmort (*see above*)
b. ca 1837

Humfrey
b. 1800
d. 1839

George

son

son

dau.
d. 1838

Honora
b. 1807
(Rev) Peter Prendergast *m.* 1861 Lucilla
b. 1832

dau. *m.* Mr. Sandbrook

Owen *m.* 1830 Lucilla Horatia Charteris
b. 1804 (*see right*)
d. 1839

son

Edna Murrell *m.* 1854 Owen Charteris
d. 1855 *b.* 1834

Owen Charteris
b. 1855

Mary
b. 1837
d. 1838

Sir John Raymond Bart.

(Rev) George *m.* dau.

(Rev) Charlecote
b. 1829

John

Susan

Harriet

other issue

Cecily *m.* 1861 John Mervyn Fulmort
b. 1832 (*see above*)

dau. *m.* Holmby

dau. *m.* soldier

2 children

TABLE III

THE DAISY CHAIN *begins* 1847

THE TRIAL *begins* 1859

Doctor Thomas May D.D. *fl.* 1650

Doctor Richard May *m.* 1825 Margaret Mackensie
b. 1802   *d.* Oct. 1847

(Rev) Richard
b. 1828

Margaret
b. Aug. 1829
d. Dec. 21 1854 *m.* 1854
George Rivers
(*see below*)

Flora
b. Feb. 1831 *m.* 1850
George Rivers
(*see below*)

(Rev) Norman Walter
b. Dec. 1831 *m.* 1854
Margaret (Meta) Rivers

Richard Rivers
b. 1855 *m. before* 1884

Harry

Ethel

Ethelred
b. Oct. 1832

Harry
b. May 5 1832 *m. after* 1861
Phyllis Mohun
(*see Table I*)

Mary   Lily   Maggie

Mary
b. 1836 *m.* 1861
Charles Cheviot

Charlie
b. 1862

Thomas
b. 1839 *m.* 1864
Averil Ward
(*see below*)

Blanche
b. 1842 *m.* 1859
Hector Ernescliffe

son
b. 1861

Aubrey Spencer
b. 1844

Gertrude Margaret
b. Aug. 1847 *m.* 1873
Lancelot Oswald Underwood
(*see Table IV*)

Mackenzie

Professor Norman Mackenzie *m.* dau
d. 1835

issue

Margaret
m. Dr. May
(*see above*)

Norman
d. before 1847

issue

Flora
m. 1835
Harry Arnott

Lord Glenbracken

Lord Glenbracken

Norman Ogilvie (*Master of Glenbracken*) *m.* 1854 Miss Dunbar

Marjorie

Axworthy

son

Sam
b. ca. 1830
d. 1863

Francis
d. July 1860

son (*apothecary*)

dau.
(*lived in China*)

dau. *m.* 1834 Mr. Ward (*surgeon*)
d. 1859   *d.* 1859

Ward

Henry (*surgeon*)
b. 1835 *m.* 1865
widow of a Virginian doctor

Averil
b. 1840-1 *m.* 1864
Thomas May (*see above*)

(Rev) Leonard
b. July 20 1842

Minna
b. 1851
d. 1863

Ella
b. 1852

Averil
d. before 1859

Lord Cosham [Earl]

Lord Cosham

dau.
d. before 1847

Margaret Agatha
b. 1331
m. Norman May
(issue see above)

Rivers

Dorothy
living 1851 *m.* [2] Mr. Rivers *m.* [1]

issue

George *m.* Flora May
b. 1820
d. before 1884

Leonora
b. 1851
d. 1852

Margaret
b. 1854
d. 1872

Leonora *m.* Langdale

Leonora   Agatha

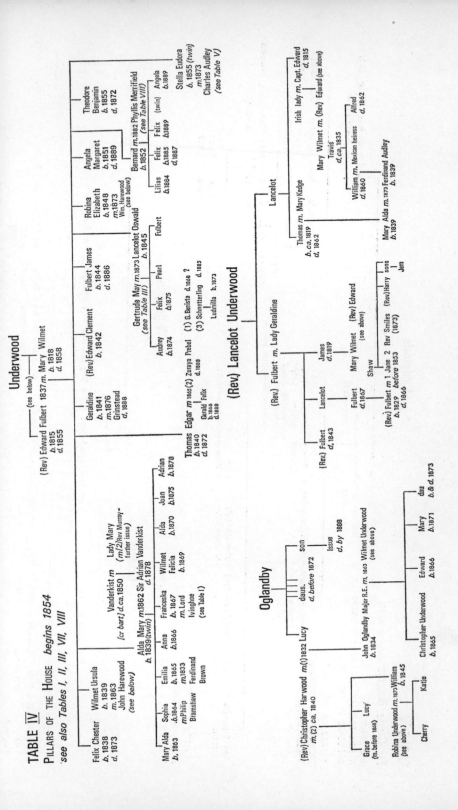

TABLE IV

PILLARS OF THE HOUSE *begins 1854*

see also Tables I, II, III, VII, VIII

Underwood

(Rev) Edward Fulbert 1837 m. Mary Wilmet
b.1818
d.1858

(Rev) Edward Fulbert
b.1815
d.1855

Felix Chester b.1838 d.1873

Wilmet Ursula b.1839 m.1863 John Harewood *(see below)*

Vanderkist m. Lady Mary *(cr bart) d.ca.1850 (m1/2)Rev Murray — further issue* d.1878

Alda Mary m.1862 Sir Adrian Vanderkist b.1839(twin)

Mary Alda b.1863

Sophia b.1864 m.Philip Bramshaw

Emilia b.1865 m.1833 Ferdinand Brown

Anna b.1866

Franceska b.1867 m. Lord Ivinghoe *(see Table I)*

Wilmet Felicia b.1869

Alda b.1870

Joan b.1875

Adrian b.1878

Geraldine b.1841 m.1876 Grinstead d.1886

(Rev) Edward Clement b.1842

Thomas b.1840 d.1872

Edgar m.1865(2) Zoraya Prebal d.1888

Gerald Felix b.1865 d.1888

Audrey b.1874

Felix b.1875

Pearl b.1875

(1) G.Benista d.1868 ?
(3) Schnetterling d.1865

Ludmilla b.1873

Fulbert James b.1844 d.1886

Gertrude May m.1873 Lancelot Oswald b.1845 *(see Table III)*

Fulbert

Robina Elizabeth b.1848 m.1873 Wm. Harewood *(see below)*

Angela Margaret b.1851 d.1889

Bernard m.1882 Phyllis Merrifield b.1852 *(see Table VIII)*

Lilias b.1884

Felix b.1885 d.1887

Theodore Benjamin b.1855 d.1872

Stella Eudora b.1855 (twin) m.1873 Charles Audley *(see Table V)*

Felix b.1889

Angela b.1889

(Rev) Lancelot Underwood

(Rev) Fulbert m. Lady Geraldine

Lancelot

Thomas m. Mary Kedge
b.ca.1819
d.1862

Irish lady m. Capt. Edward d.1815

Mary Wilmet m. (Rev) Edward *(see above)*

Travis d.ca.1835

William m. Mexican heiress d.1860

Alfred d.1862

Mary Alda m.1873 Ferdinand Audley b.1839

(Rev) Fulbert

(Rev) Fulbert d.1843

Lancelot

James d.1819

Mary Wilmet *(see above)*

(Rev) Edward

Shaw

Fulbert d.1867

(Rev) Fulbert m 1 Jane 2 Rev Smiles (1873)
b.1829 before 1853
d.1866

(Rev) Harry sons

Jem

Oglandby

(Rev) Christopher Harwood m.(1)1832 Lucy

m.(2) ca.1840

John Oglandby Major R.E. m. 1863 Wilmet Underwood b.1834 *(see above)*

son

daus. d. before 1872

Issue d. by 1888

Christopher Underwood b.1865

Edward b.1866

Mary b.1871

dau b.& d.1873

Grace (m.before 1868)

Lucy

Robina Underwood m.1873 William b.1845 *(see above)*

Cherry

Katie

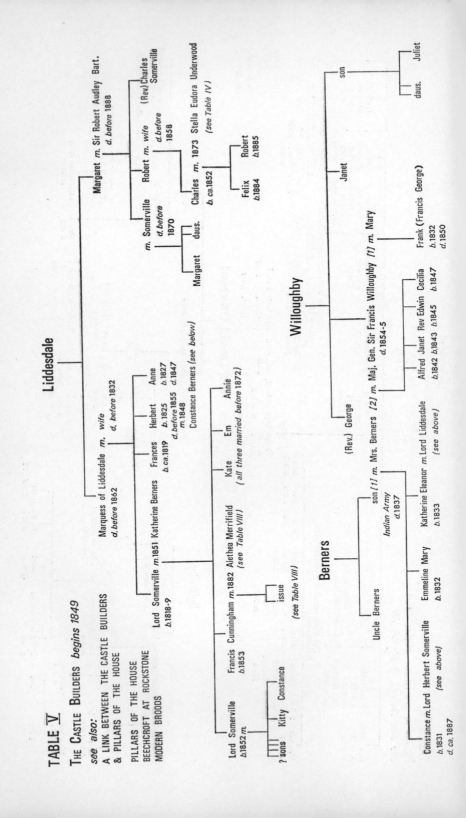

TABLE V

The Castle Builders *begins 1849*

see also:

A LINK BETWEEN THE CASTLE BUILDERS
& PILLARS OF THE HOUSE

PILLARS OF THE HOUSE
BEECHCROFT AT ROCKSTONE
MODERN BROODS

Liddesdale

Margaret *m.* Sir Robert Audley Bart.
d. before 1888

Marquess of Liddesdale *m.,* wife
d. before 1862 · *d. before 1832*

Robert *m.* wife · (Rev) Charles Somerville
d. before 1858
Charles *m.* 1873 Stella Eudora Underwood
b. ca. 1852 · *(see Table IV)*

Felix · Robert
b. 1884 · *b. 1885*

m. Somerville
d. before 1870

Margaret · daus.

Frances · Herbert · Anne
b. ca. 1819 · *b. 1825* · *b. 1827*
· *d. before 1855* · *d. 1847*
· *m. 1848*
· Constance Berners *(see below)*

Lord Somerville *m.* 1851 Katherine Berners
b. 1818-9

Kate · Em · Annie
(all three married before 1872)

Francis Cunningham *m.* 1882 Aiethea Merrifield
b. 1853 · *(see Table VIII)*

issue
(see Table VIII)

Lord Somerville
b. 1852 m.

? sons

Kitty · Constance

Willoughby

son *[1] m.* Mrs. Berners *[2] m.* Maj. Gen. Sir Francis Willoughby *[1] m.* Mary
d. 1854-5

Janet · son

daus. · Juliet

(Rev.) George

Alfred · Janet · Rev Edwin · Cecilia · Frank (Francis George)
b. 1842 · *b. 1843* · *b. 1845* · *b. 1847* · *b. 1832*
· · · · *d. 1850*

Berners

Uncle Berners

son *[1] m.* Mrs. Berners *[2] m.*
Indian Army
d. 1837

Katherine Eleanor *m.* Lord Liddesdale
b. 1833 · *(see above)*

Emmeline Mary
b. 1832

Constance *m.* Lord Herbert Somerville
b. 1831 · *(see above)*
d. ca. 1887

TABLE VI

DYNEVOR TERRACE *begins 1847*

see also:
TWO SIDES OF THE SHIELD
BEECHCROFT AT ROCKSTONE

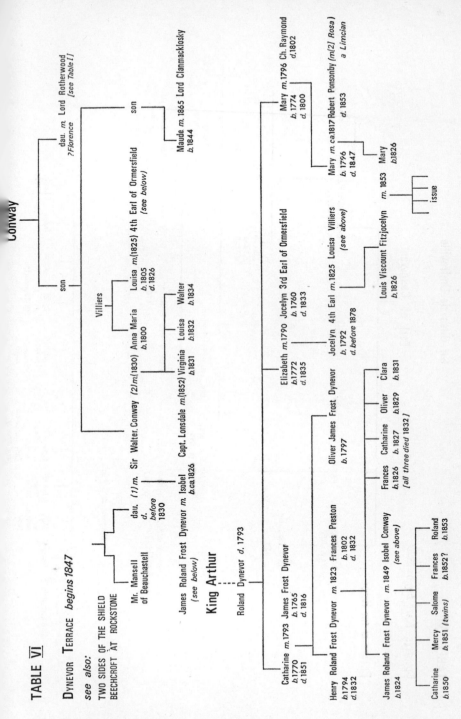

Conway

dau. m. Lord Rotherwood [see Table I]

?Florence

son

son

Villiers

Mr. Mansell of Beauchastell

dau. (1) m. Sir Walter Conway (2) m.(1830) Anna Maria b.1800

Louisa m.(1825) 4th Earl of Ormersfield (see below) b.1805 d.1826

Maude m. 1865 Lord Clanmacklosky b.1844

d. before 1830

Capt. Lonsdale m.(1852) Virginia b.1831

Louisa b.1832

Walter b.1834

James Roland Frost Dynevor m. Isobel b.ca.1826
(see below)

King Arthur

Roland Dynevor d.1793

Elizabeth m.1790 Jocelyn 3rd Earl of Ormersfield b.1772 b.1760 d.1835 d.1833

Mary m.1796 Ch. Raymond b.1774 d.1802 d.1800

Jocelyn 4th Earl b.1792 d. before 1878

Mary m. ca.1817 Robert Ponsonby (m/2) Rosa) b.1796 d.1853 a Limcian d.1847

4th Earl m.1825 Louisa Villiers (see above)

Mary b.1826

Louis Viscount Fitzjocelyn b.1826

m.1853

issue

Catharine m.1793 James Frost Dynevor b.1770 b.1765 d.1851 d.1816

Oliver James Frost Dynevor b.1797

Frances b.1826

Catharine b.1827

Oliver b.1829

Clara b.1831

[all three died 1832]

Henry Roland Frost Dynevor m. 1823 Frances Preston b.1794 b.1802 d.1832 d.1832

James Roland Frost Dynevor m.1849 Isobel Conway b.1824 (see above)

Catharine b.1850

Mercy b.1851

Salome (twins)

Frances b.1852?

Roland b.1853

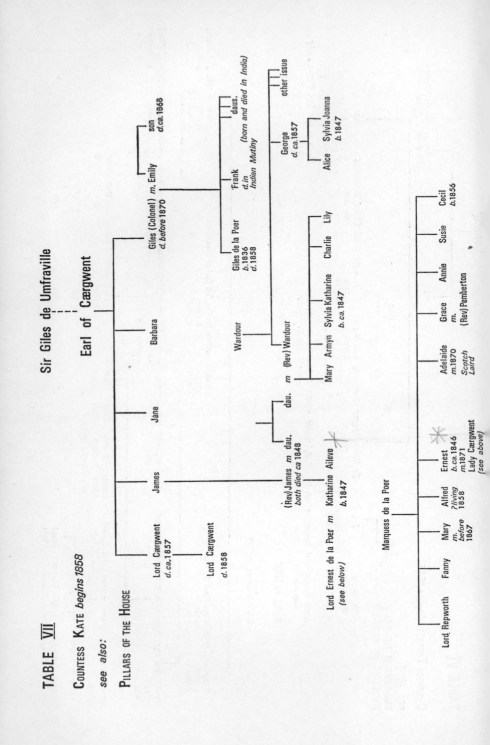

TABLE VIII

Stokesley Secret *begins* 1857
Two Sides of the Shield
Beechcroft at Rockstone
Long Vacation
Modern Broods

Merrifield of Stokesley

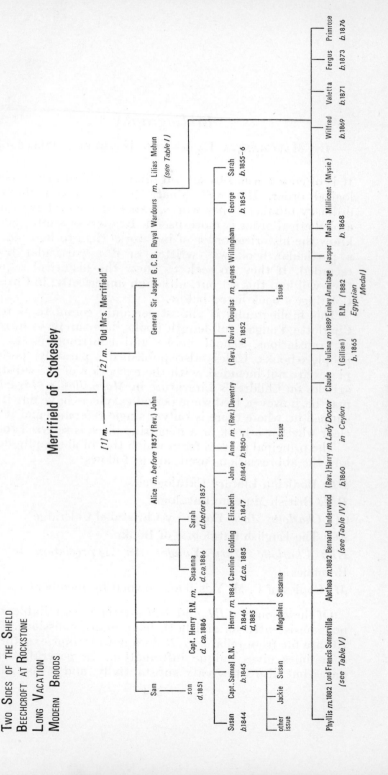

Bibliography

By Marghanita Laski and Kathleen Tillotson

It is of course usual to set out bibliographical lists in chronological order. But with Charlotte Yonge and the extraordinary number of her works, experience has shown that an alphabetical order is more useful. Readers less often want to know the historical order of her works than to find out when a particular book was written or if a particular book is recorded. If they do seek to know the historical sequence, they will find this set out, although imperfectly, in Christabel Coleridge's book listed below.

This bibliography is almost certainly complete as regards Charlotte Yonge's full-length books, less surely so in respect of translations, school books and contributions to other people's books. Unless also published separately, periodical pieces are not included, with the exception of the substantial articles on Children's Literature in *Macmillan's Magazine*. It may be, however, that some periodical pieces have unwittingly slipped in, where there is only a single reference and it is not clear whether a book or a magazine piece is referred to.

The principal sources from which this bibliography derives, and the abbreviations used, are as follows:

BL: Bodleian Library Catalogue
BM: British Museum Catalogue
CC: Charlotte Mary Yonge by Christabel Coleridge
EC: The English Catalogue of Books
ER: Charlotte Mary Yonge: An Appreciation by Ethel Romanes
M: Copies of C. M. Y.'s books owned by members

Of these sources, *BL* and *BM* are the most reliable, though not consistently so, and both have many omissions. *CC* and *EC* are far from reliable. *ER* does not attempt exactness but sometimes gives unique information. In general, not only dates but also titles vary substantially, and it may often be that an apparently independent work is in fact already listed under another name; for example, *The Instructive Picture Book* appears in many lists under its sub-title *Lessons from the Vegetable World*, and there exists an edition of *The Cunning Woman's Grandson* called simply by the sub-title, *A Tale of Cheddar, a Hundred Years Ago.*

Where two or more sources agree on a date, this is the one given; where there is equal disagreement, this is indicated. Where the existence of a title is known from only one source, this is given.

Earlier appearances in magazines are indicated where known. Abbreviations used are:

ChC: The Churchman's Companion
MP: The Monthly Packet
MY: [Mozley's] *Magazine for the Young*

1844 *Abbey Church, or, Self-Control and Self-Conceit*
1864 *The Apple of Discord, a Play*
1884 *The Armourer's 'Prentices*
1886 *Astray: A Tale of a Country Town*, with M. Bramston, C. Coleridge, E. Stuart (serialized in *MP*, July 1885 to February 1886)
1881 *Aunt Charlotte's Evenings at Home with the Poets: A collection of poems for the Young, with conversations, arranged in twenty-five evenings*
a 1876 *Aunt Charlotte's Scripture Readings* (see *MP* January 1876, Notes)
1883 *Aunt Charlotte's Stories of American History*, with J. H. Hastings Weld
1875 *Aunt Charlotte's Stories of Bible History for the little ones* (According to *EC*, this book, of 12mo size and costing 2*s.*, was published in 1876; for 1874 it lists *Aunt Charlotte's Bible History*, a 16mo volume costing 6*s.*)
1873 *Aunt Charlotte's Stories of English History for the little ones*
1874 *Aunt Charlotte's Stories of French History for the little ones*
1877 [*CC* and *EC*] 1878 [*BL* and *BM*] *Aunt Charlotte's Stories of German History for the little ones*
1876 *Aunt Charlotte's Stories of Greek History for the little ones*

A Chaplet for Charlotte Yonge

1877   *Aunt Charlotte's Stories of Roman History for the little ones*

1893   'Authorship' in *Ladies at Work*, with an Introduction by Lady Jeune. (Also in *MP*, September 1892)

1888   *Beechcroft at Rockstone* (serialized in *MP*, January 1887 to December 1888)

1882   *Behind the Hedges, or, War in the Vendée*, by H. de Witt. Translated from the French

1881   Edited *Beneath the Cross: Readings for Children in Our Lord's Seven Sayings*, by Florence Wilford

1856   *Ben Sylvester's Word*

1884   Prefaces to *Charity: Scripture Texts and Sacred Songs; Faith: Scripture Texts*, etc.; *Hope: Scripture Texts*, etc.; *Mercy and Peace: Scripture Texts*, etc.

1862, 1865   *Biographies of Good Women* (First and second series)

1864   *A Book of Golden Deeds of all Times and all Lands*

1869   *A Book of Worthies, gathered from the Old Histories and now written out anew*

1879   *Burnt Out: A Story for Mothers' Meetings*

1880   *Bye-Words: A Collection of Tales new and old*

1870   *The Caged Lion* (serialized in *MP*, July 1868 to December 1869)

Cameos from English History:
1868   I. From Rollo to Edward
1871   II. The Wars in France
1877   III. The Wars of the Roses
1879   IV. Reformation Times
1883   V. England and Spain
1887   VI. Forty Years of Stewart Rule
1890   VII. The Rebellion and Restoration
1896   VIII. The End of the Stewarts
1899   IX. The Eighteenth Century
(originally in *MP*, irregularly from 1856 to 1889)

1895   *The Carbonels*

1854   *The Castle Builders, or, The Deferred Confirmation* (serialized in *MP*, April 1851 to May 1853)

1881   *Catherine of Aragon, and the Sources of the English Reformation*, by A. du Boys. Edited and translated from the French

1886   *Chantry House*

1868   *The Chaplet of Pearls, or, The White and Black Ribaumont*

1838 *Le Château de Melville, ou, Recréations du Cabinet d'Etude* (This, Charlotte Yonge's first published work, is dated 1839 by both *EC* and by G. Battiscombe in her *Charlotte Mary Yonge*; but CMY's own reference to the work in *John Keble's Parishes*, p. 103, suggests that 1838 is correct.)

1881 *Cheap Jack*

1869 'Children's Literature' (three articles in *Macmillan's Magazine*)

1893 *Chimes for the Mothers: A Reading for Each Week in the Year*

1887 Edited *Chips from the Royal Image: Being Fragments of the Eikon Basilike of Charles I*, by A. E. M. Anderson Morshead

1862 *The Chosen People: A Compendium of Sacred and Church History for School Children*

1858 *The Christmas Mummers* (serialized in *MY*, May 1857 to March 1858)

1865 *The Clever Woman of the Family*

1891 *The Constable's Tower, or, The Times of Magna Charta*

Conversations on the Catechism (originally in *MP*, 1851 to 1857):
1859 The Commandments; To the end of the Creed
1863 Means of Grace

1888 (*ER*) *Conversations on the Prayer Book* (perhaps the same as *Preparation of Prayer Book Lessons, q.v.*)

1894 *The Cook and the Captive, or, Attalus the Hostage*

1862 *Countess Kate* (serialized in *MY*, October 1861 to December 1862)

1892 *The Cross Roads, or, A Choice in Life*

1889 *The Cunning Woman's Grandson: A Tale of Cheddar a Hundred Years Ago*

1856 *The Daisy Chain* (Part I serialized in *MP*, July 1853 to December 1855)

1885 *The Daisy Chain Birthday Book*, gathered by Eadgyth

1872 *Dames of High Estate*, by H. de Witt. Edited and translated from the French

1867 *The Danvers Papers: An Invention*

1888 *Deacon's Book of Dates: A manual of the world's chief historical landmarks, and an outline of universal history*

1878 *The Disturbing Element, or, Chronicles of the Blue-bell Society* (One of several stories in the Blue-bell series: *ER*)

1866 *The Dove in the Eagle's Nest*

1857 *Dynevor Terrace, or, The Clue of Life*

1876 *Eighteen Centuries of Beginnings of Church History*

1883 *English Church History, adapted for Use in Day and Sunday Schools* (second series in *MP*, January to August 1890)

1881–3 *English History Reading Books, adapted to the requirements of the New Code: Standards II-VI, and Supplemental Reading Book*

1898 *Founded on Paper, or, Uphill and Downhill between the Two Jubilees* (a sequel to *The Carbonels*)

1860 *Friarswood Post Office* (serialized in *MY*, August 1858 to August 1859)

1893 *The Girl's Little Book*

1882 *Given to Hospitality* (in *MP*, May 1882)

1880 Preface to *Gold Dust: A Collection of Golden Counsels for the Sanctification of Daily Life*, translated from the French by E. L. E. B.

1893 *Grisly Grisell, or, The Laidly Lady of Whitburn: A Tale of the Wars of the Roses*

1888 *Hannah More* ('Eminent Women' series)

1892 *(BL) The Hanoverian Period, with Biographies of Leading Persons*

?1856 *Harriet and her Sister* (*EC* lists together, undated, *Harriet and her Sister, Leonard the Lion-Heart, London Guide, Midsummer Day* [*qq.v.*], and *The Railway Children* by CMY; it also gives, for 1858, *Harriet and her Cousin* by CMY. An anonymous book, *Harriet and her Cousin*, was published in 1823. The *BM* has also an anonymous book *Harriet and her Sister* [3rd edn. 1856], published by Mozley and from internal evidence almost certainly by CMY)

1854 *Heartsease, or, The Brother's Wife*

1853 *The Heir of Redclyffe*

1850 *Henrietta's Wish, or, Domineering: A Tale* (serialized in *ChC*, January 1849 to May 1850)

1853 *The Herb of the Field* (revised and corrected from 'Chapters on Flowers' in *MY*, February 1850 to December 1852)

1900 *The Herd Boy and his Hermit*

1885 *Higher Reading-Book for Schools, Colleges and General Use*

n.d. *(M) Hints on the Religious Education of Children of the Wealthier Classes*

1882 *Historical Ballads: Arranged to meet the New Code of 1882, Schedule II, English* (in three parts)

1864 *Historical Dramas*

1868–70 *Historical Selections: A Series of Readings in English and European History*, with E. Sewell

1863, revised 1884 *A History of Christian Names* (part appeared in *MP* as 'Name-Fancying', May 1852 to August 1862)
1872 *A History of France*, in *Historical Course for Schools*, edited E. A. Freeman (250 pp. in 1887 edn.)
1878 *A History of France*, in *History Primers*, edited J. R. Green (126 pp. in 1898 edn.)
1855 *The History of the Life and Death of the Good Knight Sir Thomas Thumb*
1897 Preface to *The History of the Universities Mission to Central Africa*, by A. E. M. Anderson Morshead
1860 *Hopes and Fears, or, Scenes from the Life of a Spinster*
1881 *How to Teach the New Testament*
1872 *In Memoriam Bishop Patterson: Being with additions the substance of a memoir published in the 'Literary Churchman'*
1857 *The Instructive Picture Book, or, Lessons from the Vegetable World*
1871 Preface to *Journal of the Lady Beatrix Graham*, by J. M. F. Smith
1898 *John Keble's Parishes: A History of Hursley and Otterbourne*
1886 *Just One Tale More*, with other authors
a 1885 *Kaspar's Summer Dream* (quoted in *The Daisy Chain Birthday Book, q.v.*)
1850 *Kenneth, or, The Rear Guard of the Grand Army*
1869 *Keynotes of the First Lessons for every Day in the Year*
1848 *Kings of England: A History for Young Children* (*BL* and *BM* date this book 1848, *CC* and *EC* date it 1852; but the first edition of *Langley School*, 1850, is by the author of *The Kings of England*)
1881 *Lads and Lasses of Langley*
1874 *Lady Hester, or, Ursula's Narrative*
1855 *The Lances of Lynwood* (serialized in *MP*, January 1853 to December 1854)

Landmarks of History:
1852 I. Ancient History from the Earliest Times to the Mahometan Conquest
1853 II. Middle Ages: from the Reign of Charlemagne to that of Charles V
1857 III. Modern History: from the Reformation to the Fall of Napoleon
1883 *Landmarks of Recent History, 1770–1883*

1883 *Langley Adventures*

1882 *Langley Little Ones: Six Stories*

1850 *Langley School* (the first fifteen of its twenty-seven chapters were serialized in *MY*, September 1846 to December 1848)

n.d. (*ER*) *A Langley Story*

between 1854 and 1862 *Last Heartsease Leaves*
(*Heartsease* was published in 1854. The first known reference to *Last Heartsease Leaves* is in *MP*, February 1862, when a correspondent is told that 'the continuation of *Heartsease* was printed for sale at a bazaar', and apparently copies are still available, for in December 1863 a correspondent is told that a copy will be sent her for 1*s*. in stamps. In 1864 it is unavailable, but in May 1865 we learn that 'The concluding chapter of *Heartsease* is in the 13th Number of Events of the Month'. *Events of the Month* was a small periodical published by Mozley, and *Lost* [sic] *Heartsease Leaves* appeared in it in January 1865. Thereafter it was again unobtainable until, in response to constant demand, it was reprinted in *MP*, June 1876. In 1900 it was reprinted separately at Bournemouth, in aid of a church restoration fund.)

1856 *Leonard the Lion-Heart* (serialized in *MY*, March to June 1856

1871 *Life and Adventures of Count Beugnot, Minister of State under Napoleon I*, by Count H. d'Ideville. Edited and translated from the French

1873 *Life of John Coleridge Patteson, Missionary Bishop to the Melanesian Islands*

1890 *Life of H.R.H. the Prince Consort*

1854 *The Little Duke, or, Richard the Fearless* (serialized from the 1st number of *MP*, January to October 1851)

1871 *Little Lucy's Wonderful Globe*

1886 *The Little Rick-Burners*

n.d. (*EC*) *London Guide* (see *Harriet and her Sister*; this title is almost certainly confused with *London Pride*, below)

n.d. (*BL*) *London Pride*

1895 *The Long Vacation*

1880 *Love and Life: An Old Story in Eighteenth-Century Costume*

1879 *Magnum Bonum, or, Mother Carey's Brood* (serialized in *MP*, January 1877 to December 1879)

1900 *The Making of a Missionary, or, Day Dreams in Earnest*

1877   *A Man of Other Days: Recollections of the Marquis Henry Joseph Costa de Beauregard, selected from his papers by his great-grandson.* Edited and translated from the French

1858   *Marie Thérèse de Lamourous, Foundress of the House of La Misericorde at Bordeaux,* by the Abbé Pouget. Abridged and translated from the French

?1880 (*BM*)   *Mary and Norah, or, Queen Katherine's School* (This, and *Nelly and Margaret* [*q.v.*] with which it is bound up, are said on the titlepage to have been 'edited' by CMY, but there is nothing in the stories to suggest they have an external source.)

1860   *The Mice at Play* (No. 7 of the *Magnet Stories for Summer Days and Winter Nights*; 8 vols., 1860–5)

Before 1844 (n.d. *EC*)   *Midsummer Day* (see *Harriet and her Sister* and p. 183)

1883   *The Miz Maze, or, The Winkworth Puzzle: A Story in Letters by Nine Authors.* With F. Awdry, M. Bramston, C. R. Coleridge, F. M. Peard, etc.

1900   *Modern Broods, or, Developments Unlooked For*

1886   *A Modern Telemachus* (serialized in *MP*, January to December 1886 under the title *A Modern Quest of Ulysses*)

1890   *More Bywords* (this volume contains one of the 'link' stories, 'Come to her Kingdom', originally in the Christmas number of *MP*, 1889)

1871   *Musings over 'The Christian Year' and 'Lyra Innocentium' together with a few gleanings of Recollections of the Rev. J. Keble, gathered by Several Friends* (originally in *MP*, November 1868 to November 1870)

1875   *My Young Alcides: A Faded Photograph*

n.d. (*M*)   *Mystery of the Cavern* (serialized in *MP*, January to December 1867; was issued with 2nd edn. of *Abbey Church* in 1872)

1889   *Neighbour's Fare* (in Skeffington and Sons' series of *New and original tales for Boys and Girls from six to fourteen*)

?1880 (*BM*)   *Nelly and Margaret, or, Good for Evil* (see *Mary and Norah*)

1868   *New Ground: Kaffirland* (serialized in *MY*, January 1863 to November 1866)

1888   *Nurse's Memories*

1885   *Nuttie's Father*

1891   *Old Times at Otterbourne*

1892   *An Old Woman's Outlook in a Hampshire Village* (in *MP*, January to December 1892) n.d. (*ER*) *One Story by Two Authors*, with Jean Ingelow (serialized in *MP*, February 1860 to October 1861)

1888 *Our New Mistress, or, Changes at Brookfield Earl*

1872 *P's and Q's, or, The Question of Putting Upon*

1871 *A Parallel History of France and England, consisting of Outlines and Dates*

1889 *The Parent's Power: Address to the Conference of the Mother's Union*

1898 (*CC*) 1899 (*BM*) *The Patriots of Palestine: A Story of the Maccabees* (the book itself is undated)

1882 *Pickle and his Page Boy, or, Unlooked For: A Story*

1860 *Pigeon Pie* (serialized in *MP*, November 1851 to October 1852)

1897 *The Pilgrimage of the Ben Beriah*

1873 *The Pillars of the House, or, Under Wode, Under Rode* (serialized in *MP*, January 1870 to December 1873)

1871 *Pioneers and Founders, or, Recent Works in the Mission Field*

1885 *Pixie Lawn* (in *Please Tell Me a Tale: Short Original Stories for Children*)

1870 (*BM*) 1871 (*CC*) *The Population of an Old Pear Tree, or, Stories of Insect Life*, by E. van Bruyssel. Edited and translated from the French

1881 *Practical Work in Sunday Schools*

1888 *Preparation of Prayer-Book Lessons* (in *MP*, January 1884 to October 1888; perhaps the same as *Conversations on the Prayer-Book, q.v.*)

1866 *The Prince and the Page: A Story of the Last Crusade* (serialized in *MP*, January to December 1865)

1868 *The Pupils of St. John the Divine*

n.d. (*M*) *Questions on the Catechism*

1874 *Questions on the Collects*

1874 *Questions on the Epistles*

1874 (*BL* and *BM*) 1875 (*CC* and *EC*) *Questions on the Gospels*

1872 *Questions on the Prayer-Book*

1881 *Questions on the Psalms*

1855 *The Railroad Children* (in *MY* in 1849)

1864 *Readings from Standard Authors*

1901 *Reasons why I am a Catholic and not a Roman Catholic*

1875 *Recollections of Colonel de Gonville*, published by his daughter, the Countess de Mirabeau. Edited and translated from the French

1873 *Recollections of a Page at the Court of Louis XVI*, by

Felix Count de France d'Hézecques. Edited and translated from the French
1896 *The Release, or, Caroline's French Kindred* (Part I appeared in *MP*, Christmas number, 1894, under the title 'Caroline's Defiance')
1889 *A Reputed Changeling, or, Three Seventh Years Two Centuries Ago*
1894 *The Rubies of St. Lô* (originally in *MP*, Christmas number, 1890)
1847 *Scenes and Characters, or, Eighteen Months at Beechcroft*
1899 *Scenes from 'Kenneth', etc.*

Scripture Readings for schools, with comments:
1871   I. Genesis to Deuteronomy
1872   II. From Joshua to Solomon
1874   III. The Kings and the Prophets
1876   IV. Gospel Times
1879   V. Apostolic Times

1862   *Sea Spleenwort and Other Stories*
1869   *The Seal, or, The Inward Spiritual Grace of Confirmation*
1875   Memoir in *Sermons* by G. C. Harris
1891 (*EC*)   *Seven Heroines of Christendom* [6th edn.]
1883   *Shakespeare's Plays for Schools*, abridged and annotated
1867   *A Shilling Book of Golden Deeds* (selected from *A Book of Golden Deeds*)
1879 (*EC*)   *Short English Grammar for Use in Schools*
1896   Introduction to *Sintram and his Companions*, by De la Motte Fouqué
1891 (*BL*)   *Simple Stories relating to English History*
1867   *The Six Cushions* (serialized in *MP*, January to December 1866)
1868   Introduction to *Sketches of the Rites and Customs of the Greco-Russian Church*, by H. C. Romanoff
1890   *The Slaves of Sabinus: Jew and Gentile*
1882   *Sowing and Sewing: A Sexagesima Story*
1882   *Sparks of Light*, by H. de Witt. Edited and translated from the French
1892   *The Stewart Period, with Biographies of Leading Persons*
1861   *The Stokesley Secret* (serialized in *MY*, January 1860 to April 1861)
1870 and 1872   *A Storehouse of Stories*, 1st and 2nd series. Edited with Introductions

213

1878 *The Story of the Christians and Moors of Spain*

1894 *The Story of Easter*

1883 *Stray Pearls: Memoirs of Margaret de Ribaumont, Viscountess of Bellaise* (serialized in *MP*, January 1881 to May 1883)

1860 *The Strayed Falcon* (No. 21 of the *Magnet Stories*; see *The Mice at Play*)

1893 *The Strolling Players: A Harmony of Contrasts*, with C. Coleridge (serialized in *MP*, January 1892 to March 1893)

1882 *Talks about the Laws we live under, or, At Langley Night-School*

1886 *Teachings on the Catechism: For the Little Ones*

1892 *That Stick* (serialized in *MP*, January to December 1891)

n.d. (*ER*) *The Third Standard* (said to be a Langley story)

1876 *The Three Brides* (serialized in *MP*, January 1874 to June 1876)

1893 *The Treasure in the Marches*

1864 *The Trial: More Links of the Daisy Chain* (serialized in *MP*, January 1862 to April 1864)

1892 *The Tudor Period, with Biographies of Leading Persons*

1891 (*BL*) 1892 (*EC*) *Twelve Stories from Early English History*

1891 (*BL*) *Twenty Stories and Biographies from 1066 to 1485*

1852 *The Two Guardians, or, Home in this World* (serialized in *ChC*, July 1850 to February 1852)

1891 *Two Penniless Princesses* (serialized in *MP*, January to December 1890)

1885 *The Two Sides of the Shield* (serialized in *MP*, January 1884 to June 1885)

1869 *Two Years of School Life*, by Elise de Pressensé. Edited and translated from the French

1887 *Under the Storm, or, Steadfast's Charge*

1882 *Unknown to History: A Story of the Captivity of Mary of Scotland* ('freely adapted' as 'A play for women in three acts' in 1953 by Joan Brampton, under the title *Bride Unknown*)

1880 *Verses on the Gospel for Sundays and Holydays*

1886 (*BL* and *BM*) 1887 (*CC* and *EC*) *Victorian Half-Century: A Jubilee Book*

1896 *The Wardship of Steepcombe*

1864 *The Wars of Wapsburgh*

1891 and 1892 *Westminster Historical Reading-Books*

1887 *What Books to Lend and What to Give*
1882 Preface to *Whispers of Love and Wisdom*, by A. Cazanove
1881 *Wolf*
1887 *Womankind* (serialized in *MP* January 1874 to June 1877)
1897 In *Women Novelists of Queen Victoria's Reign:* an essay on Lady Georgiana Fullerton, Mrs. Stretton and Anne Manning
a 1876 *Worthies of English History* (see *MP*, January 1876, Notes)
a 1876 *Worthies of Ancient History* (see *MP*, as above)
1861 *The Young Stepmother, or, A Chronicle of Mistakes* (serialized in *MP*, April 1856 to December 1860)
1879 *The Youth of Queen Elizabeth*, by L. Wiesener. Edited and translated from the French

MAGAZINES EDITED BY C. M. YONGE

c. 1859 *The Barnacle*. A manuscript magazine of the Goslings, later merged in 'Arachne and her Spiders', in *MP* (*ER*)
1890 to 1900 *Mothers in Council*
1851 to 1894 *The Monthly Packet of Evening Readings for Younger Members of the English Church* (with C. Coleridge, 1891 to 1894)
1860 to 1875 *The Monthly Paper of Sunday Teaching*

BOOKS AND ESSAYS ABOUT C. M. YONGE

1861 *National Review*, 'Ethical and Dogmatic Fiction: Miss Yonge'
1901 Edith Sichel in *Monthly Review*, 'Charlotte Yonge as a Chronicler'
1903 Christabel Coleridge: *Charlotte Mary Yonge, Her Life and Letters*
1904 *Church Quarterly* (January) 'Charlotte Mary Yonge'
1908 Ethel Romanes: *Charlotte Mary Yonge, an Appreciation*
1908 Eleanor Hall: Introduction to *The Dove in the Eagle's Nest* (Everyman library)
1909 Alice Meynell: Introduction to *The Heir of Redclyffe* (Everyman library)
1910 Eugene Mason: Introduction to *The Little Duke* (Everyman library)

1911   Lucy M. Crump: Introduction to *The Lances of Lynwood* (Everyman library)

1943   Georgina Battiscombe: *Charlotte Mary Yonge*, with an Introduction by E. M. Delafield

1947   Margaret Mare and Alicia C. Percival: *Victorian Best-Seller: The World of Charlotte M. Yonge*

1958   George Every: 'Dolores Mohun' in *S.S.M.* [Society of the Sacred Mission] *Journal*, Vol. 59, Michaelmas.

1965   Charlotte Haldane: Introduction to *The Heir of Redclyffe* (Duckworth)

1965   Gilian Avery: 'Charlotte Mary Yonge' in *Nineteenth-Century Children*

1965   Kathleen Tillotson: 'The Heir of Redclyffe' (broadcast, January, 1953) in *Mid-Victorian Studies*

A CURIOSITY

1944   Mrs. Hicks Beach: *Amabel and Mary Verena* (a continuation of *The Heir of Redclyffe*)